w/o

Insights

General Editor: Clive Bloom, Principal Lecturer in English, Middlesex University

Editorial Board: Clive Bloom, Brian Docherty, Gary Day, Lesley Bloom and Hazel Day

Insights brings to academics, students and general readers the very best contemporary criticism on neglected literary and cultural areas. It consists of anthologies, each containing original contributions by advanced scholars and experts. Each contribution concentrates on a study of a particular work, author or genre in its artistic, historical and cultural context.

Published titles

Clive Bloom (*editor*)
JACOBEAN POETRY AND PROSE: Rhetoric, Representation and the Popular Imagination
TWENTIETH-CENTURY SUSPENSE: The Thriller Comes of Age
SPY THRILLERS: From Buchan to le Carré

Clive Bloom, Brian Docherty, Jane Gibb and Keith Shand (*editors*)
NINETEENTH-CENTURY SUSPENSE: From Poe to Conan Doyle

Dennis Butts (*editor*)
STORIES AND SOCIETY: Children's Literature in a Social Context

Gary Day (*editor*)
READINGS IN POPULAR CULTURE: Trivial Pursuits?
THE BRITISH CRITICAL TRADITION: A Re-evaluation

Gary Day and Clive Bloom (*editors*)
PERSPECTIVES ON PORNOGRAPHY: Sexuality in Film and Literature

List continued on next page

The Death of the Playwright?

Modern British Drama and
Literary Theory

Edited by Adrian Page
Principal Lecturer in English and
Communication Studies
Luton College of Higher Education

MACMILLAN

First published 1992 by
THE MACMILLAN PRESS LTD
Houndmills, Basingstoke, Hampshire RG21 2XS
and London
Companies and representatives
throughout the world

ISBN 0–333–51315–0 hardcover
ISBN 0–333–51316–9 paperback

A catalogue record for this book is available
from the British Library.

Reprinted 1994

Printed in Great Britain by
Antony Rowe Ltd
Chippenham, Wiltshire

Contents

Contents

Preface

This volume contains nine essays which debate issues arising from contemporary literary theory in relation to drama of the modern period. The authors propose new theoretical approaches to recent drama which derive from post-structuralism, semiotics, feminism, Bakhtinian theory and psychoanalysis. The essays range over much of the 'canonical' drama which has been subjected to literary approaches and suggest ways of re-reading well-known texts. The introduction addresses the theoretical issues raised by Barthes' essay 'The Death of the Author' and surveys the writing which explores the relationship between theory and drama in the light of them. The collection as a whole both continues current debates and seeks to demonstrate where literary theory can draw attention to the particular qualities of modern drama. The collection covers aspects of the work of Ann Jellicoe, Alan Bleasdale, Jill Hyem and Anne Valery, Shelagh Delaney, Samuel Beckett, Harold Pinter, Howard Brenton, Howard Barker, John McGrath, Joe Orton, Caryl Churchill, Trevor Griffiths and David Hare.

Acknowledgements

Trevor Griffiths and Wendy Wheeler would like to acknowledge the support of the Polytechnic of North London, Faculty of Humanities Research Committee, and wish to thank Claire Buck, David Oswell, and Kathy Rooney for their helpful comments on drafts of their essay.

Thanks are due to Faber and Faber Limited for their permission to reproduce extracts from *Waiting for Godot* by Samuel Beckett, and *The Sport of My Mad Mother* by Anne Jellicoe.

Notes on the Contributors

Edward J. Esche is a lecturer at Anglia Higher Education College where he specialises mainly in Renaissance and twentieth-century writing, and critical theory. He is the author with Nigel Wheale of *Writing and Society 1570–1660* which aims to apply the recent developments of New Historicism to the writing of the period.

Peter Griffith studied English at King's College Cambridge, and Education at London University Institute of Education, before teaching in a wide variety of schools for ten years. He also worked for a while in the extra-mural department of Stockholm University. Since 1976 he has been employed by the Open University where he is currently Director of Professional Development in Education. He is the author of *Literary Theory and English Teaching*.

Trevor R. Griffiths lectures in the School of Literary and Media Studies and is currently Humanities Faculty Research Director at the Polytechnic of North London. He has research interests in contemporary theatre and performance analysis. His most recent book (with Carol Woddis) is *The Bloomsbury Theatre Guide*.

Audrey McMullan is the Beckett Research Fellow at the University of Reading, Department of French. She has published articles on Beckett in *Modern Drama, Journal of Beckett Studies* and *French Studies*.

Adrian Page is a Principal Lecturer in English at Luton College of Higher Education. He has also taught at the Bowen-West Community Theatre in Bedford. He has research interests in postmodernism and contemporary fiction, cultural theory and contemporary drama. He is co-editor of *Teaching the Text* with colleagues from Bedford.

Chris Pawling is Principal Lecturer in Communications at Sheffield City Polytechnic and course leader for the MA in Communication Studies. He has written articles on literary theory and the sociology of culture for a number of journals and has edited a collection of essays entitled *Popular Fiction and Social Change*. His most recent publication is *Christopher Caudwell: Towards a Dialectical Theory of Literature*.

Tessa Perkins has taught and researched Sociology, Women's Studies and Media Studies at various institutions. She is currently Senior Lecturer in Communication Studies at Sheffield City Polytechnic. She is co-author (with Veronica Beechey) of *A Matter of Hours*, a book about women's part-time employment and has also written articles on cultural theory. Her most recent article is 'The Politics of "Jane Fonda"' in a forthcoming publication edited by Christine Gledhill.

Rick Rylance is Senior Lecturer in English at Anglia Higher Education College. He is an editor of the journal *Ideas and Production* and has published *Debating Texts: a Reader in Twentieth-Century Literary Theory and Method* and articles on nineteenth- and twentieth-century literature and culture. He is presently writing a book on Roland Barthes.

Jane Thomas worked as Community Theatre and Education Officer for Hull Truck Theatre Company while completing a PhD on women in the novels of Thomas Hardy. Since then she has published a number of articles on contemporary women writers and has written entries on British, American and Russian novelists, poets and dramatists for the forthcoming *Yale Feminist Companion to Women Writers*. She is now employed as a part-time Lecturer in English at Hull University.

Judith Thompson is a Senior Lecturer in English Literature at Hatfield Polytechnic. She has for a number of years been involved in devising and teaching courses on theatre, and on women's writing, and is currently writing a book on 'Women and Theatre'.

Wendy J. Wheeler lectures in the School of Literary and Media Studies at the Polytechnic of North London. She has research interests in psychoanalytic criticism, post-modernism, drama, and the novel.

1

Introduction

ADRIAN PAGE

THE DEATH OF THE PLAYWRIGHT?

Despite the proliferation of literary theory in recent years, little attention has been paid to modern drama. One reason why this is so may be that modern drama has not been prone to the fallacies that modern theory has set out to expose. When Barthes declared the 'death of the author', he announced that 'We know now that the text is not a line of words releasing a single "theological" meaning (the "message" of the Author-God) but a multi-dimensional space in which a variety of writings, none of them original, blend and clash.'[1] The practice of theatre directors takes full account of this: productions of plays are not constrained by the need to reveal a playwright's intentions as only he or she wishes. Playwrights such as Beckett and Pinter have freely admitted that they are unable as well as unwilling to state exactly what their own works mean. Few practitioners of modern theatre are likely to subscribe to the opinion, which Barthes attacks so vigorously, that 'To give the text an Author is to impose a limit on that text, to furnish it with a final signified, to close the writing.'[2] The need to declare the death of the author, the denial of the author as the ultimate source of the text's meaning, seems more pertinent to literary criticism than the theatre. In the sense in which Barthes intends the expression, the playwright has been 'dead' for some time. Theatrical productions illustrate vividly the freedom which those who work in the theatre assume with regard to dramatic texts.

Literary theory has to some extent, therefore, taken on characteristics of drama: as Terry Eagleton writes, 'Most literary theories, in fact, unconsciously "foreground" a particular literary genre and derive their general pronouncements from this.'[3] One example of the way that theory has assimilated dramatic concepts is the popularity of the analogy between the reader of literature and the producer of drama. Both reader and theatrical producer are responsible for real-

1

ising their respective texts in their ultimately meaningful form: as a literary interpretation or a play. Without these operations, neither text could really be said to exist in the fullest sense. The analogy serves for Barthes to distinguish between the reader who approaches a text creatively and the passive consumer who absorbs the apparent meaning uncritically.

The recognition that there can be a creative reading of dramatic texts, however, problematises the relationship between text and performance. Eagleton insists that 'a dramatic production does not "express", "reflect" or "reproduce" the dramatic text on which it is based; it "produces" the text, transforming it into a unique and irreducible entity'.[4] If the producer's work is truly creative it must differ in some way from the dramatic text rather than providing a pale imitation of it. In drama the text and the performance belong to different signifying systems, whereas in literature it is sometimes argued that the person who produces a reading of a text is the only avenue by which meaning comes to light. The dramatic production is generally assumed to be, as Erika Fischer-Lichte has argued, 'both a work of its own *and*, at the same time, a transformation of the script.'[5] The performance text cannot, therefore, be entirely foreshadowed in a written version or the work of the producer would amount to no more than exposition and recreation. On the other hand, where a written text exists, there must be some relation between this and performance if the stage spectacle is to be regarded as a performance of the same play. The analogy between the two types of 'producers' wears thin when it is realised that the theatrical producer does not enjoy quite the same degree of freedom as Barthes' reader.

Martin Esslin's *The Field of Drama* incorporates a great deal of recent theoretical approaches to textual study into drama criticism, including the view that 'drama can hardly ever be reduced to a clear-cut personal statement by an individual creator, fully in control of the exact meaning of every element and sign contained in the message emitted'.[6] Esslin acknowledges the 'death' of absolute authorial control, in other words, and in the absence of a playwright who can dictate exactly how the text should be treated, he asserts that drama is a 'blueprint for mimetic action' which presents us with a 'simulacrum' of reality. The audience are therefore free to interpret theatrical signs as they choose because they are presented with a spectacle which is as open to interpretation as the world around us. Whilst this preserves the freedom of the audience, it raises the question of whether the playwright has any degree of control over the reception of the text at all. Esslin sees his theories echoed in the title of Artaud's famous work, *The Theatre and Its Double* in that the theatre is a representation of reality which is identical to it.

Derrida's reading of Artaud, however, is radically different from Esslin's: for him 'Artaud wants to have done with the *imitative* concept of art.'[7] Derrida reads Artaud as denying that theatre is the re-presentation of something that already exists. The Theatre of Cruelty is intended to be a compelling spectacle which arouses profound emotions in an audience. As such it must be a creation of a new, uniquely moving event which is disturbing in itself, not because it refers to disturbing realities. Artaud's theatre, on this account, is not the double of real life because it corresponds exactly to it, but because 'It is life itself in the extent to which it is unrepresentable.'[8]

Artaud's theatre rejects the domination of the text and the Author-God, proposing instead 'a theater of *deviation* [my italics] from the groundwork of a preestablished text, a table written by a God-Author who is the sole wielder of the primal word'.[9] To attribute this power to the writer is to compromise the creative freedom of performers to give us a new 'believable reality' as Artaud calls it.

Derrida sees Artaud as an ally of poststructuralism, therefore, since his theory speaks against the view that the theatre is a simple vehicle of communication between playwright and audience. To assume that the dramatic text 'contains' the performance is an example of what Derrida calls 'the metaphysics of presence' and subscribes to the doctrine of logocentrism whereby writing is seen as an accurate transcription of speech. Artaud's appeal for Derrida seems to lie in his description of performance as an example of 'free play' with the undecidable elements of a written text.

A complete severance of performance from text, however, implies that playwrights can never hope to reflect reality and address issues which are of social importance. Whereas literary theory has often seemed to isolate the text from any relationships with reality, in modern drama there is a demand for writing which will call attention to social issues. The challenge which drama poses for literary theory, therefore, is to produce a theory of theatre which allows some didactic intention without resorting to a moribund concept of a single meaning authorised by the playwright. One of the central problems which this collection focuses on is the extent to which the playwright can be resurrected as a wielder of meaning without suppressing the creative responses to his or her written text.

Artaud's theories represent the most emphatic denial of the play-wright's authority but only insofar as the dramatic text *legislates* on the nature of the performance. Even he was obliged, as Derrida notes, to resort to writing down what was to be performed although he vehemently denounces the 'dictatorship' of the writer. Artaud's impetus takes the theatre away from its literary origins where its power resides in what is said. This does not prevent drama from dealing with issues such as oppression, however. As Artaud expressed it in a deliberately paradoxical vein, 'I am writing for illiterates.'[10] Christopher Bigsby has described in some detail how recent drama which is committed to the presentation of social issues has begun to distrust the written word.[11] This is perhaps in part a result of the influence of Saussure's linguistics which has popularised the view that language is not so much a structure which corresponds to the structure of reality as a superimposition of structures derived from ideology. Saussurean linguistics therefore lends support to the view that language is not simply mimetic and a means of representing reality in a manner which is acceptable to everyone, and it also implies that any representation is inevitably coloured by the ideology of the writer. Furthermore if language is not a 'neutral' means of representation, a theatre audience can be expected to interpret any play in a diversity of ways.

Derrida notes that there is the suggestion of a 'solution' to the problem of the playwright's authority in Artaud's writings; as he observes, 'For the theatre to be neither subjected to this structure of language, nor abandoned to the spontaneity of furtive inspiration, it will have to be governed according to the requirements of another language and another form of writing.'[12] A further challenge to drama which playwrights such as Caryl Churchill have begun to take up, is to develop a new notation which is directive without prescribing exactly how it is to be treated in performance and which treats socially relevant issues.

Judith Thompson's chapter, '"The World Made Flesh": Women and Theatre', reveals how Artaudian doctrines can be exploited to represent the lives of women who suffer various forms of oppression by *showing* realities rather than talking directly about them. Feminist literary theory has attacked the 'essentialist' theories which imply that there is a feminine nature to be represented and has also demonstrated that our language is not adequate to express the full reality of women's lives. By drawing on examples of modern drama which exploit Artaudian and Brechtian techniques, Judith Thompson argues that the break with mimetic and literary traditions in the theatre enables women to create the world of those who do not always have the linguistic power to articulate their own distress.

DRAMA AND THE CLASSIC REALIST TEXT

It is sometimes assumed that drama which consists entirely of dialogue with no conspicuous intervention by the playwright is therefore a pure 'slice of life'. Szondi's concept of 'absolute drama' takes the 'death of the playwright' to this extreme: 'The Dramatist is absent from the Drama. He [sic] does not speak; he institutes discussion. The Drama belongs to the Author only as a whole, and this connection is just an incidental aspect of its reality as a work.'[13] As Jochen Schulte-Sasse comments in his introduction to Szondi's work, 'his belief in the mimetic nature of art neutralises his critical methodology.'[14] The Saussurean emphasis is not on what language refers to but on the interrelationships within the system of signs which reveal the manner in which reality is structured by language. The theory of the classic realist text, however, has opened up the issue of how a writer can direct and dominate our perception of what purports to be an unadulterated representation of reality.

Colin MacCabe defines a classic realist text as 'one in which there is a hierarchy among the discourses which compose the text and this is defined in terms of an empirical notion of truth'.[15] MacCabe's work on the nineteenth-century novel in *James Joyce and the Revolution of the Word* demonstrates how this can be achieved by an authorial meta-language which comments on narrative discourse and provides the reader with an authoritative interpretation of how direct speech should be understood. In the media, where the writer's presence is not so clearly evident, however, technology can nonetheless be employed to organise a hierarchy of readings. The political television broadcast, for example, often features a politician in homely surroundings who occupies a large part of the screen. The effect created is that we are confronted with someone who has entered our homes for a comfortable chat on an inter-personal level and is offering us helpful advice. Television in particular is an ideal medium to achieve this effect, as the means of enunciation, the vast array of expensive technology which makes the broadcast possible, are suppressed, so that we concentrate instead on the enounced, what is said. The media which assist this process easily make us forget that what we are watching is a construction of reality rather than reality itself.

In the theatre there are also ways of establishing the direct influence of the playwright on the text from which he or she is absent. In the case of the performance text, Derrida reminds us that the prompter can bring the writer's authority to bear on the performers. With the dramatic text there are also ways for a playwright to prescribe how particular scenes should be played despite their absence. In what Martin Esslin calls the Nebentext, or the stage directions, a playwright can ordain exactly how the dialogue is to be played and what effects should derive from it. John Osborne's *Look Back in Anger* contains lines such as, 'Jimmy has recovered slightly, and manages to sound almost detached.' (p. 59) in the Nebentext which perform a very similar function to the metalanguage of the nineteenth-century novelist.

Colin MacCabe also cites the example of the film *Klute* which, although it was presented and praised as realism, allows Klute the detective the subject-position in which he can speak with authority about the woman Bree, thereby making him the source of knowledge about her. It is through him that we presume to learn the 'truth' about Bree's life and not simply the narrative structure of the film. Klute is given the role of summing up her existence and is not otherwise contradicted. In stage drama the same technique can be used. Jimmy Porter makes the kind of metadramatic remarks at the end of Osborne's play which can be seen as directing criticism to the play's meaning. One such example is his assessment, 'They all want to escape from the pain of being alive. And most of all from love.' (p.93) This remark, by virtue of its generality and its apparent analytic insight, could easily be adopted by the audience as a final commentary on the play. It takes critical detachment to see that it could equally well be applied to Jimmy himself and that he is not able to offer comments as an external observer who is entirely removed from the situation on which he pronounces. What MacCabe calls 'the position of dominant specularity' in which an audience can see the 'truth' of events unfolding from a particular point of view, is not, according to MacCabe, able to deal with the contradictions of reality such as this. Seeing things through Jimmy Porter's eyes is not likely to make the audience critical spectators.

Chris Pawling and Tessa Perkins, in 'Popular Drama and Realism: the Case of Television', take issue with MacCabe's view that the closed text of realism is not a 'progressive' form of art because it 'fixes the subject in a position from which everything becomes obvious', thereby depriving the audience of the opportunity to adopt the critical stance. Writers on the left have warned of the effects of television naturalism because it fails to exploit the medium's potential for objective presentation. John McGrath, for example, attacks the genre on the grounds that 'Naturalism contains everything within a closed system of relationships. Every statement is mediated through the situation of the character speaking. . . . In terms of presenting a picture of society, it can only reveal a small cluster of subjective consciousnesses, rarely anything more.'[16] McGrath's objection to television naturalism is very similar to the criticisms made of the classic realist text; where we should expect to find an unadulterated portrayal of things as they are, there is only the commentary of individual characters to make sense of the narrative.

Pawling and Perkins demonstrate that television drama which adopts MacCabe's progressive formal characteristics can nonetheless fix the subject in a position of dominant specularity despite confronting the viewer with the writer's frame of representation and making the act of enunciation clear. They also discuss drama which does not employ these characteristics and where, as Esslin comments, 'the "Haupttext" and "Nebentext" (words and stage directions) are indissolubly wedded together.'[17] Despite this aspect of certain productions, the viewer can still be offered a number of subject positions which need to be thoughtfully discriminated. The example of *Tenko* is used to defend the view that a playwright can address an issue in a realist style without sacrificing the freedom of the viewer to be critical.

THE LANGUAGE(S) OF DRAMA

Whereas in some literary texts there may be clear diegetic remarks which orient the reader towards the author's position of dominant specularity, in dramatic texts where the playwright is absent, this cannot occur so blatantly. It is often the director's function to make use of diegetic resources such as lighting on stage or the camera angle on television in order to foreground a privileged reading of the dramatic work.

This does not leave the dramatic text entirely open to readings of all kinds, however, since the language of drama need not be purely verbal. Other systems of signification can coexist within the dramatic text to provide a number of possible readings without necessarily foregrounding one as the dominant position with a monopoly of the truth. The semiotics of drama is still a relatively new discipline, yet it does promise to show how the playwright can encode meanings which are not organised into hierarchical structures of the kind that MacCabe describes. The literary notion of the classic realist text depends heavily on the relations between the verbal exchanges which compose the text, but semiotics has begun to reveal the more complex nature of dramatic discourse.

The development of a 'science of signs' has stressed the social origins of signifying practices and their basis in ideology in a manner which has at times overlooked the role of the writer. Colin MacCabe has identified the theoretical problem which this gives rise to as follows: 'The question is: how are we to understand these determinations without producing on the one hand an author autonomously producing meanings in a sphere anterior to their articulation and on the other an audience imposing whatever meaning it chooses on a text?'[18] The problem is similar to that which Derrida has detected: how can the playwright work within semiotic conventions which do not compel the audience to decode the text precisely as he or she stipulates yet at the same time direct them to the play's ideology and limit their freedom of interpretation? Brecht's concept of the gestus is a reminder of how stage signs can be ideological.

Martin Esslin's approach to the semiotics of dramatic texts begins with the linguistic theory of speech-acts. The verbal components of drama are considered not for their content but as actions of various kinds. When, for example, Jimmy Porter says, 'Darling I'm sorry' after causing Alison to burn her arm on the iron his words constitute the act of apologising. Once the text is understood at the level of these performative utterances, the semiotic codes which performers employ can be used to reinforce the nature of the speech-act by, for example, using a contrite tone of voice.

It is not possible to treat the entire text as a collection of separate speech-acts, however, since it is the manner in which they are combined which composes the actual dramatic discourse. As Keir Elam describes it, the text is a combination of illocutionary acts (acts which are performed *in* saying something) and perlocutionary acts (acts performed *by* saying something) which together 'account for the central events in the play'.[19] Thus the perlocutionary speech-act of persuading someone might be accomplished by several illocutionary acts of stating facts. Perlocutionary acts are higher-order descriptions of the dynamics of verbal action which must be considered in order to read each utterance appropriately. Derrida's debate with the speech-act philosopher John Searle revolved around the question of whether speech-acts could be seen as the basis of language. Derrida's argument, insofar as it can be detected, appears to have been that speech-acts are not the fundamental building-blocks of language since without presuming some wider context they can be interpreted in any number of ways. The concept of a combination of illocutionary and perlocutionary acts avoids this pitfall by not assigning a value to individual acts until the actual context is considered.

In *Look Back in Anger*, Helena attempts to persuade Alison to go to church with her – an action which will signify that she can escape the mental domination of Jimmy. Towards the end of the first scene of the second act the action of the play focuses on whether Alison will succeed in demonstrating her independence from Jimmy. Earlier on, Helena has brought two prayer-books on stage in preparation for their visit to the church, and Alison's acceptance of Helena's argument, 'You can't go on living like this any longer' (p. 46) is signed by picking up the prayer-book as she leaves. The accomplishment of the perlocutionary act of persuading Alison to rebel against Jimmy is signified by an action rather than another speech-act.

The philosopher J. L. Austin points out in his study of speech-acts that perlocutionary acts are not conventional.[20] This is to say that there are no clear conventions as to how perlocutionary acts are achieved. A performer can show that they have been persuaded in a number of ways, none of which need be implied in the written text. It is also possible that a performer can substitute his or her own signs for those in the script and still achieve the same overall effect. In this example it is possible to see how the performers of drama have freedom to adopt a range of sign systems which are chosen without reference to an explicit intention on the part of the playwright, yet which are nonetheless governed to some extent by the nature of the text.

Esslin refers to the fundamental 'situations' which make up the text, and it may be the perlocutionary acts which he has in mind: to transform certain illocutionary acts may not recognisably alter the play, but to deviate from the pattern of perlocutionary acts constitutes a radical revision of the narrative structure. If Alison was not persuaded to go to church, we could argue that we were encountering a new play, not a new production of *Look Back in Anger*.

The 'grammar' of dramatic discourse is therefore a complex interaction of verbal utterances which sometimes requires non-verbal signs to become coherent. Ed Esche's chapter, 'Shelagh Delaney's *A Taste of Honey* as Serious Text: A Semiotic Reading', reveals the literary bias of many reading of Delaney's play which have not addressed the function of signs in the text. He shows how the classical literary concept of tragedy can, however, be applied to *A Taste of Honey* by a consideration of sign systems which emerge when Esslin's fundamental semiotic concepts are applied. This reading of the play demonstrates the existence of ideological meanings which, although they can be discriminated, are not necessarily 'preferred' and can coexist with the joyful elements of the play to manifest important contradictions.

BEYOND REPRESENTATION

Commenting on the difficulties of analysing theatrical performance into discrete signifying units, Keir Elam writes, 'It is only if one considers the performance in Saussurean terms, as an act of *parole* governed by a theatrical *langue* which stipulates the units involved and establishes rules for their selection and combination that one can hope to "slice up" the discourse.'[21] The structuralist assumption that there are general laws of semiotics from which particular uses of signs can be inferred, however, neglects the potential for drama to create new signs and establish new conventions. Julia Kristeva's critique of semiotics attacks its reliance on a scientific model whereby a theory enables us to predict how signs will be used. Rather than producing a global theory which characterises all potential uses of signs, semiotics is, for Kristeva, a theory which is constantly modified by its discovery of new sign-systems. As Toril Moi remarks, 'Language then, for her is a complex *process* rather than a monolothic system.'[22]

This is not to say, however, that semiotics is a futile pursuit of principles of signification. As Kristeva maintains, semiotics is not circular, it is progressive: it is a continual attempt to chart the patterns of production which give rise to new sign-systems rather than the search for a comprehensive theory of all possible signs. Thus, in Kristeva's words, semiotics 'can never be separated from the theory constituting it'.[23]

One such attempt to produce a separate theory is that of Alessandro Serpieri who proposes that 'The speeches of the *dramatis personae* should be segmented on the basis of units of deictic orientation

which change every time the axis of reference (of the speaker towards himself, towards another character, or towards an absent
addressee) changes within discourse.'[24] Applying this theory to the
text of *Look Back in Anger*, however, illustrates Kristeva's point. The
following lines are spoken by Jimmy Porter on discovering that
Hugh's mum, a woman he was very close to, has had a stroke. He is
seeking Alison's support.

> She got a kick out of you like she did out of everything else. (1)
> Hand me my shoes, will you? (2) *She kneels down and hands them to
> him* (3) (looking down at his feet) (4) You're coming with me aren't
> you? (5) She (he shrugs) hasn't got anyone else now. (6) I . . . need
> you . . . to come with me. (7) *He looks into her eyes, but she turns away
> and stands up.* (8) *Outside the church bells start ringing.* (9) (p. 62)

Here the sequence of deictic orientations is marked using Serpieri's
notation to demarcate the changes of reference. It is clear that each
change of referent does not emanate from the speaker alone, as in the
third which is a stage direction referring to Alison. Similarly the bells
which signify the urgency of Alison's decision are not part of the
deictic orientation of the speakers. Whether the seventh section is, in
fact, one orientation, as marked, or three is not decided for us by
following Serpieri's theory, but has to be decided first in order to
apply it. As Kristeva argues, the theory constantly begs the question
of the identifiable semiotic units of the text and needs to be modified.

The creative use of semiotic principles found in drama underlines
the difficulties which any theory of drama as representation must
encounter. If the signifiers of the drama are used in an original
fashion which can only be fully understood by examining the text
closely, then they cannot easily represent signifying practices which
exist elsewhere. Barthes suggests that at first sight some 'analogical'
representations of reality: drawings, paintings, cinema and the theatre, appear to have no code. Where the resemblance is strong, there
is a simple one-to-one correspondence with existing objects. The
absence of a semiotic code can seem to indicate straightforward
representation. Bakhtin, however, clarifies the sense in which the
absence of a code implies the originality of the message: 'Semiotics
prefers to deal with ready-made messages by means of a ready-
made code, whereas in living speech, messages are, strictly speaking, created for the first time in the process of transmission, and
ultimately there is no code.'[25]

There is, in other words, no system of rules independent of the message itself which explains all its semiotic functions. Creative writing such as drama is, therefore, rather like Artaud's performance in that it does not reproduce conventions which exist elsewhere but instead originates new practices. If this is so then the playwright cannot act as an Author-God who ensures that the message is decoded exactly as it was intended, since there are no rules for the audience to follow in any decoding process. The reluctance of playwrights such as Beckett and Pinter to comment on the meaning of their own texts is, perhaps, in part, a recognition of the fact that what they have written is not susceptible of 'interpretation' by any established procedures.

Psychoanalytic theorists have pointed out that illusionist drama which invites the audience to witness life as they know it, is a version of the Lacanian mirror stage in which the audience perceive a complete identity between what they see and themselves: '. . . the realist theatre relying on illusion actually invites the spectator's gaze and encourages him to read the proffered text naively, as a mirror-image of a pre-existing world.'[26] Elizabeth Wright reads Freud as proposing that the theatre fulfilled two functions, the release of wish-fulfillment through conscious identification with a central figure, and the creation of a private 'neurotic space' in which the spectator is covertly encouraged to identify with a surrogate neurosis.[27] As Philippe Lacoue-Labarthe observes, this implies a break with Aristotelean theories of mimesis, since a reality is produced 'outside representation' altogether.[28] Rather than portraying an existing neurosis, the theatre is the occasion for the creation of the phenomenon and hence cannot be the *imitation* of an action.

Audrey McMullan, in 'The Eye of Judgement: Samuel Beckett's Later Drama', takes up the question of the status of dramatic representation and argues that Beckett abnegates his own authority as a dramatist while nonetheless directing our attention to the issues which surround the questions of representation and identity in the theatre. Once the mirror-phase is over the nature of the Symbolic order is called in question. The audience is free to react to the resulting play of concepts, yet the text itself determines what Derrida calls the 'playing space'.

DRAMA AS CARNIVAL

Bakhtin rarely mentions drama, yet his concept of the carnivalesque illustrates many of the characteristics of drama where the playwright is absent. In the classical satires on which Bakhtin modelled his theory, the author was not personified but instead orchestrated a dialogue amongst a group of characters who often revealed their ludicrous natures through their dialogic relations. Serpieri's comments on drama echo this situation: 'The drama "narrates" through the direct interplay of utterances, i.e. it is not the narration of facts *from* a particular perspective but the unfolding of a dynamic development of speech acts.'[29] Todorov also observes how, according to Bakhtinian theory, 'drama shares the properties of the novel'.[30] Like the novel, drama is composed of many voices which are not those of the writer. In Bakhtin's own words, 'The author of a literary work (a novel) creates a unified and whole speech work (an utterance). But he creates it from heterogeneous, as it were alien utterances.'[31] In Bakhtin's terms, therefore, all writers are, as he comments, dramatists to some extent, since no writer can claim absolute ownership of all the languages he or she employs in the text, but must work with the utterances of others.

Another Bakhtinian concept which is ideally suited to the study of drama is that of the 'utterance', a speech act which must be understood from its precise context in a dialogue. In *Look Back in Anger*, when Jimmy is informed that Alison has lost the child she was carrying, Jimmy remarks, 'It was my child too, you know. But (he shrugs) it isn't my first loss.' Alison's reply is, (on her breath) 'It was mine.' (p. 92) Bakhtin would argue that Alison's line, if taken out of context, could mean any number of things. What defines its precise import is its relationship to the remark by Jimmy which precedes it. In this case the subtext of Alison's remark would probably be that she is angry with Jimmy for failing to sympathise with *her*, and she is aware that he is not as considerate as he constantly insists. Whereas Jimmy cannot resist reminding her that he has met death before, Alison's retort underlines his egocentricity in doing so. Alison's line could not convey such a meaning outside this particular context, however, since the use of the word 'mine' deliberately echoes Jimmy's use of the possessive.

The notion of the utterance is therefore of much greater importance for the performers of the play than that of speech-acts, since, as Bakhtin remarks, 'A purely linguistic (and purely discrete) description and definition of various styles within a single work cannot reveal their semantic (including artistic) interrelations.'[32] Intonation, for example, a vital aspect of performance, belongs to the utterance, not to the sentence. Speech-acts take the linguistic form of the sentence as the fundamental constituent of meaning, yet the context of utterance can significantly alter the *prima facie* illocutionary force.

Irony, for example, is difficult to accommodate in the Austinian theory of speech-acts, since it is a necessary condition of various acts that they are performed 'sincerely'. This is an assumption that often begs vital questions. When Jimmy Porter and Alison indulge in their playful game of bears and squirrels, Jimmy remarks to Alison, 'You're very beautiful. A beautiful, great-eyed squirrel.' Shortly after this he adds, 'How I envy you.' (p. 34) Whether this is meant seriously or not, the linguistic form of Jimmy's line will remain the same. The decision as to whether Jimmy genuinely does envy Alison has to be made before the sentence can be recognised as either a positive or negative assertion. There is no fundamental speech-act which can be inferred from the sentence which will help to solve this problem. Derrida pointed out in his protracted debate with speech-act theorists that the assumption that the speaker is sincere rules out a great many contexts in which language is used meaningfully without serious intentions, such as on stage, in a poem, or in a soliloquy.[33]

Meaning in a carnivalesque text is, therefore, derived from the dynamics of dialogue rather than handed down to us by the playwright from a superior position of knowledge, yet this does not mean that the playwright forgoes all possibility of acting as the guiding influence on the text. Bakhtin describes the apparently paradoxical situation whereby, 'the author is outside the world depicted', yet 'the author occupies a position precisely in this real dialogue and is defined by the real situation of the day'.[34] The resolution of this paradox depends on the recognition that the characters do not speak *for* the playwright; his or her own position is not represented in their speech. Despite this, however, the dialogues can be so organised that we are confronted with the dialogic relations which the playwright wants us to consider. All dialogues are, according to the theory of the utterance, constituted for the benefit of a third party in addition to the participants, the 'superaddressee'. The person to whom a reply is addressed may not fully comprehend what it implies, as in the example of Alison's reply to Jimmy's comment on her pregnancy. The dialogue is meaningful and becomes coherent, however, when viewed from beyond the immediate context of utterance. Audiences occupy the position of superaddressee when, for example, they en-joy the position of spectators of dramatic irony. In this sense the playwright is a figure who is active in determining the reception of the text in accordance with current attitudes, the 'real situation of the day' in which judgements are made.

In social carnival everyone is encouraged to participate and yield to the spirit of popular desire which is celebrated. The event is therefore, to some extent, a means of undermining authority which exists by virtue of its ability to dissociate itself from practices on which it sits in judgement. Bakhtin's language theory paves the way for the carnivalesque text by similarly undermining any sense of an authoritative set of meanings of words which exist outside the text itself. Any attempt to stabilise meaning runs up against the carnival spirit. Peter Griffith, in 'Bakhtin, Foucault, Beckett, Pinter', traces the ways in which carnivalesque 'absurd' texts, where context is often obscure, release words from their usual meanings, yet still recall the social practices of the world outside the text. In particular he empha-sises the Foucauldian theory that where discourse is in dispute, a struggle for power ensues. The absurd texts under discussion therefore say a great deal about existing social struggles, since as Foucault remarks, 'History constantly teaches us that discourse is not that which translates struggles or systems of domination, but the thing by and for which there is struggle.'[35]

THE AUDIENCES OF DRAMA

If recent theory has begun to shift the emphasis in criticism towards the context of utterance, the actual situation in which discourse is produced, then drama demands special attention be paid to the location in which it is performed and the composition of the audi-ence. Barthes' reader who suddenly enjoys a new-found freedom in the absence of an authoritarian, 'theological' author, is 'without history, biography, psychology; he is simply that *someone* who holds together in a single field all the traces by which the written text is constituted.'[36] The anonymous reader becomes a functional device by which the text's unity is relocated not in its origin (the author) but in its destination (the reader). Barthes cites Greek tragedy as an example of a form in which the characters fail to understand the linguistic ambiguities which become apparent to the audience and reveal the tragic dimension to them. In a similar manner to Bakhtin,

Barthes suggests that dramatic discourse is structured with the likely response of a superaddressee in mind, and this third party is able to appreciate the gaps and contradictions in the discourse of characters. Elizabeth Freund is amongst the theorists who have noted that this shift in emphasis seems to confer on the reader the status of an encyclopaedic entity who is able to make sense of the codes of the text from an illimitable knowledge. The reader or audience member therefore becomes a site of 'intertextuality rather than intersubjectivity'.[37]

Modern drama, with its plurality of audiences and venues, cannot presume such an ideal spectator with such a wealth of cultural and ideological foreknowledge on all occasions. It was the probable diversity of responses to culturally-encoded signifiers that led the New Critics to rule out signifieds which might be derived from the subjectivity of readers from the concerns of literary cricitism. W. K. Wimsatt, for example, rests his case on the following distinction:

> One of the most emphatic points in Stevenson's system is the distinction between what a word *means* and what it *suggests*. To make the distinction in a given case, one applies what the semeiotician calls a 'linguistic rule' ('definition' in traditional terminology), the role of which is to stabilise responses to a word. The word 'athlete' may be said to *mean* one interested in sports, among other things, but merely to suggest a tall young man. The linguistic rule is that 'athletes are necessarily interested in sports, but may or may not be tall'.[38]

Wimsatt's argument transforms the reader into a skilled lexicographer who is able to restrain the impulse to explore signifieds and instead contents themselves with the referents of words, their indisputable 'meaning'. Wimsatt's motive for maintaining this position is most likely that without some criterion for distinguishing between signifieds which derive from quirks of personal history and those which derive from the text, there could be no way of producing readings of literature. The most likely candidate for the criterion which would enable such a distinction to be made, is the intention of the writer, and this, for Wimsatt, offends against the doctrine of the Intentional Fallacy. Thus, although Wimsatt might be said to free the reader from the strict dominance of the author, he nonetheless relegates the reader to the role of an interpreter who is compelled to understand the text in accordance with pre-established linguistic rules. Barthes allows the reader the freedom to compose textual unity with the aid of semiotic principles as well, yet both he and Wimsatt assume a complete competence on the reader's part and seem to imply that they are obliged to remain faithful to some notion of textual unity which precedes their reading. It appears as if the tyranny of the author gives way initially to the tyranny of the text in constraining the reader's freedom.

If the 'ideal reader' of reader-response theory is yet another fiction which only serves to consolidate the notion of a prior authorial intention, then theory still has to discover the status of the truly liberated reader or audience. One such attempt is made by Louis Althusser in his critique of Brechtian theatre. Althusser insists that 'the play itself *is* the spectator's consciousness': drama must be judged by its likely effects on the audience rather than by some abstract aesthetic proposed by the author. In defining the role of the audience, Althusser discusses two models of audience participation. The first is the Brechtian ideal whereby the spectator is 'outside the play, judging'. Althusser dismisses this theory on the grounds that 'The play can no more contain the 'Last Judgement' on its own story than can the spectator be the supreme Judge of the play.'[39] It is impossible to take up a position outside ideology in order to act as a dispassionate judge with infallible insight into the text. The other model which is rejected is the supposed attitude of the audience in the classical theatre, whereby the audience identifies with the struggles of the central heroic figure. Althusser points out that identification is a psychoanalytic concept which does not take account of the multitude of factors which the audience bring to the theatrical experience. He maintains that there is as much of an ideological struggle on stage as there is outside the theatre, and there is no reason to suppose that the ideology of the performance text will be readily accepted by a diversity of people with different interests and ideologies.

The route out of this particular dilemma for Althusser is to propose that the play creates an internal distantiation from ideology: rather than escaping altogether from ideology, the play creates its own mechanisms for enabling a reflexive attitude to occur which causes the audience to complete the text by reference to their own ideological leanings, thereby achieving a degree of 'self-recognition'.

Look Back in Anger offers some moments of this kind, especially at the end of the play where Alison finally breaks down. When he is confronted with Alison's extreme distress, Jimmy says 'Don't. Please don't.... I can't —' (p. 96) Whether Jimmy is showing a new-found tenderness towards Alison and should be understood as implying that he cannot endure her anguish, or whether he simply wishes to avoid any further emotional extremes and is simply avoiding the issue, is a matter for the audience to decide. The play momentarily compels the question to be raised and by its textual incompleteness leaves room for the audience to actively confront both their own and the text's ideology by supplying the missing links in the discourse.

Althusser's theory suggests that a playwright needs to take account of the actual audience he or she will reach and structure the text in accordance with the knowledge and ideology they bring to the theatre if audiences have the task of completing the play themselves. Rick Rylance, in 'Forms of Dissent in Contemporary Drama and Contemporary Theory', examines the influence of theory on playwrights such as Howard Barker and Howard Brenton and concludes that these two leading political dramatists depend on the existence of the very audience whose values they criticise most. John McGrath, however, is represented as a dramatist who deals more directly with the actual nature of his audience and is conscious of the theatre as a social context in which communication can take place. Rick Rylance argues that self-indulgence in theory obscures the most worthy political motives and that it is McGrath who shows how theatre as a political *event* can best be achieved.

'WHAT DOES IT MATTER WHO IS SPEAKING?'

In Howard Brenton's play *H.I.D. (Hess is Dead)* a group of academics are engaged to rewrite the history of Rudolf Hess's life in the manner which the authorities prefer. The academics argue that their interpretation is 'an encoding of the truth. . . . Our statement is a construct. Like any sentence or photograph.' Raymond, the character who is investigating the death, realises that they are invoking the theoretical principle that language has no meaning in itself, but that meaning is produced by individuals. His derisive response is, 'How Goebbels would have loved modern literary theory.'[40] If there is absolutely no truth, then the struggle to impose a consensus view will be won by the powerful. Similarly, if playwrights cannot exercise some degree of control over the eventual reception of their text, then their work can be appropriated and forced to serve ideological interests to which they are opposed. A sceptical view of literary theory such as Raymond's, is that by leaving the text entirely open to readings of all kinds, it neutralises any commitment on the part of the playwright.

David Hare has expressed a similar dissatisfaction with theory in an account of his days at Cambridge. When structuralism was fashionable, he describes the general opinion that 'the writer was only a pen. The hand, meanwhile, was controlled largely by the social and economic conditions of the time.' Later, however, Hare records that when he inquired whether he had regained control of his own work, he was informed, 'Mostly. But not entirely.'[41] Hare is referring to the emergence of poststructuralism: as Robert Young writes, 'this denial or death of the subject in Saussure, and hence structuralism, has precisely led to its reappearance – not as a unified consciousness, but structured by language.'[42] For Barthes there appeared to be no need to consider any characteristics of the author, since 'it is language which speaks and not the author'. What was at issue for Barthes was not the actual existence of people who wrote, as Karl Miller has suggested, but whether the resulting text was an expression of their individuality which was beyond public scrutiny.[43] If the text somehow expressed the contents of a writer's mind, then that mind alone held the key to the meaning of the text. Structuralism's answer was to deny that the text was an expression of individuality at all: the meaning of language lay entirely in social conventions. Poststructuralism, however, proposed that the text was the product of the author, but that his or her language was the very form of their subjectivity and not a reflection of a mental state which preceded it. Subjectivity was structured in language and the text therefore reveals it.

The advent of contemporary theory, then, need not necessarily lead to the situation where dramatic text can be invoked to prove any position whatever. For poststructuralists, the author reappeared, not as the sole source of a text's meaning, its inaccessible point of origin, but as the presence implied by the form of the text itself.

Foucault, however, carefully qualifies the author function by examining the use of the term in contemporary society as a complex function of discourse. In the case of modern drama the notion of authorship is often particularly difficult to establish. John McGrath tells us that *The Cheviot, the Stag and the Black, Black Oil* was the product of collaboration and independent research by members of the 7:84 company. Some parts arose from improvisation and adaptation. As Foucault asks, what is a work? Would a written record of a rehearsal constitute a part of this particular work? If the work cannot be independently identified then how are we to attribute authorship? More problems arise in the case of adaptations of other authors' works as when Tony Harrison produces a free translation of Racine's *Phaedra* set in colonial India. Who then can lay claim to authorship? Foucault's answer is that the author in such cases is 'a certain functional principle by which in our culture, one limits, excludes and chooses; in short, by which one impedes the free circulation, the free manipulation, the free composition, decomposition, and recomposition of fiction'.[44] John McGrath, for example, serves as a figure by which we judge how the text of *The Cheviot* is to be read so that it conforms with his beliefs and with other texts for which he was responsible. Foucault argues that a culture in which fiction was not limited by the figure of the author would be 'pure romanticism', and the consequences would be wholly unacceptable. The 'author' in the Foucauldian sense is, therefore, not the orginator of all the discourse which is attributed to him or her, but merely a means of organising it coherently.

In his introduction to *The Mysteries* Tony Harrison defends his new version of the traditional plays on the grounds that they were originally created by a series of adaptations themselves.[45] He invokes a Foucauldian principle in declaring that absolute originality is not the essential characteristic of authorship, but that his own work is original in its own way – perhaps as part of the Harrison dramatic oeuvre which includes other imaginative translations of existing works.

Foucault cites Beckett's remark, 'What does it matter who is speaking?' as a way of emphasising that the author's discourse can be understood without an intimate knowledge of the person who produced it. What is important is not who the author is, but what he or she wrote. The author may therefore create a consistent persona in their work which can be inferred from discourse, but this does not necessarily imply that he or she can determine exactly how the persona is interpreted. If the author's character is embodied in discourse, then it belongs to the symbolic order of language with its vast unconscious network. As Derrida says: 'before me the signifier on its own says more than I believe that I mean to say'.[46] As David Hare remarked, therefore, the playwright may have been resurrected as a significant figure in the understanding of dramatic texts but not with complete authority over their reception. In the final three chapters the authors offer readings of particular texts with reference to the concept of the playwrights' intentions and discuss the extent to which they are realised.

Adrian Page, in 'An Age of Surfaces: Joe Orton's Drama and Postmodernism', refers to the critical accounts of Orton's plays which read his work as the expression of an intention to shock or offend his audience and argues that his best-known works are significantly more complex. The postmodern features of Orton's work when read theoretically, reveal that they are more than a simple realisation of the desire to take revenge on society and illustrate the dilemmas which confront the postmodern subject rather than merely celebrating his freedom to cause mayhem both on and off stage.

Jane Thomas takes Caryl Churchill's relationship to Foucault as her theme and considers the extent to which Foucauldian readings of her plays are possible given that she acknowledges her debt to his theories in the writing of her play *Softcops*. 'The Plays of Caryl Churchill: Essays in Refusal', reassesses Churchill's political intentions by reading the texts as illustrating Foucauldian theories of the dynamics of power relations rather than directly challenging the status quo with a radical political agenda.

Trevor Griffiths and Wendy Wheeler, in 'Staging the Other: a Psychoanalytic Approach to Contemporary British Political Drama' consider the ways in which the overt political intentions of dramatists such as Hare, Brenton and Griffiths are subject to unconscious transformations in the act of writing over which they may have little control. They pose the question of whether a self-consciously political theatre is, in fact, possible when an unconscious desire to re-stage the primal scene seems to intervene in the presentation of political ideology.

Notes

1. *Image-Music-Text: Essays Selected and Translated by Stephen Heath* (Glasgow: Fontana, 1977), p. 146.
2. Ibid., p. 147.
3. *Literary Theory* (Oxford: Blackwell, 1983), p. 51.
4. *Criticism and Ideology* (London: Verso, 1978), p. 64.
5. See 'Performance as an 'Interpretant' of the Drama', in *Semiotica* 64–3/4 (1987), p. 211.
6. *The Field of Drama* (London: Methuen, 1987), p. 155.
7. *Writing and Difference* (London: Routledge, 1978), p. 234.
8. Ibid.
9. Ibid., p. 185.
10. Ibid., p. 188.

11.   See 'The Language of Crisis in British Theatre', in Stratford-Upon-Avon Studies 19, *Contemporary English Drama*, ed. C.W.E. Bigsby (London: Edward Arnold, 1981).

12.   *Writing and Difference*, p. 191.

13.   Peter Szondi, *Theory of the Modern Drama*, edited and translated by Michael Hays (Cambridge: Polity Press, 1987), p. 8.

14.   Ibid., p. xii.

15.   Bennett, Boyd-Bowman, Mercer and Wollacot (eds), *Popular Television and Film* (London: BFI, 1981), p. 217.

16.   'TV Drama: the Case Against Naturalism', *Sight and Sound* 46 (1977), p. 101.

17.   *The Field of Drama*, p. 80.

18.   'The Revenge of the Author', *Critical Quarterly*, Vol. 31, no. 2, p. 8.

19.   *The Semiotics of Theatre and Drama* (London: Methuen, 1980), p. 168.

20.   *How to do Things With Words* (Oxford: OUP, 1962), p. 121.

21.   *The Semiotics of Theatre and Drama*, p. 48.

22.   *Sexual/Textual Politics* (London: Methuen, 1985), p. 152.

23.   Toril Moi (ed.), *The Kristeva Reader* (Oxford: Blackwell, 1986), p. 77.

24.   'Reading the Signs: Towards a Semiotics of Shakespearean Drama', in John Drakakis (ed.) *Alternative Shakespeares* (London: Methuen, 1985), p. 133.

25.   *Speech Genres and Other Late Essays*, trans. Vern W. McGee (Austin: University of Texas Press, 1986), p. 147.

26.   Elizabeth Wright, *Postmodern Brecht: a Re-Presentation* (London: Routledge, 1989), p. 56.

27.   Quoted in Elizabeth Wright, *Psychoanalytic Criticism: Theory in Practice* (London: Methuen, 1984), p. 35.

28.   Quoted in Wright, *Psychoanalytic Criticism*, p. 35.

29.   *Alternative Shakespeares*, p. 122.

30.   *Mikhail Bakhtin: The Dialogical Principle* trans. by Wlad Godzich (Minnesota: The University of Minnesota Press, 1984), p. 90.

31.   *Speech Genres*, p. 115.

32.   Ibid., p. 112.

33.   Quoted in Christopher Norris, *Deconstruction: Theory and Practice* (London: Methuen, 1982), p. 110.

34.   *Speech Genres*, p. 116.

35.   'The Order of Things', in *Untying the Text: a Post-Structuralist Reader*, ed. Robert Young (London: Routledge, 1981), p. 57.

36.   *Image-Music-Text*, p. 148.

37.   *The Return of the Reader* (London: Methuen, 1987), p. 80.

38.   'The Affective Fallacy', in *The Verbal Icon: Studies in the Meaning of Poetry* (Norfolk: Methuen, 1970), p. 22.

39.   'The "Piccolo Teatro": Bertolazzi and Brecht', in *For Marx* (London: NLB, 1977), p. 148.

40.   *H.I.D. (Hess is Dead)* (London: Nick Hern Books, 1989), p. 47.

41.   *Guardian*, 3–4 June 1989, p. 2.

42.   *Untying the Text: a Post-Structuralist Reader* (London: Routledge, 1981), p. 13.

43. See Karl Miller, *Authors* (Oxford: OUP, 1989), Chapter XIV.
44. 'What is an Author?', reprinted in Paul Rabinow (ed.), *The Foucault Reader* (Harmondsworth: Penguin, 1984), p. 117.
45. See the Preface to Tony Harrison, *The Mysteries* (London: Faber, 1985).
46. *Writing and Difference* (London: Routledge, 1981), p. 178.

2

'The World Made Flesh': Women and Theatre

JUDITH THOMPSON

In the introduction to her study of *Feminism and Theatre*, Sue-Ellen Case states that her project was 'exciting and frightening to write – exciting, because I had never seen the project tried before and frightening because of the many political decisions that had to be made while writing'.[1] She goes on to say that, in her view, the backbone of her book lies in the suggested reading and the bibliography (p. 3). I associate myself very strongly with these two statements: I, too, do not see that the relationship between feminism and theatre has really been tackled before, and I find myself similarly pleading that the use of what I am writing is to point in what seem to me to be interesting directions. I only have the space of a chapter; what I am attempting to do here, therefore, is to raise questions and issues which I have no time or space to answer, but which seem to me to be important, whether you are interested in theatre, in feminism, or in both.

As in most areas of cultural production, women in theatre are notable primarily for their absence – both as 'authors' of 'texts', and as producers or directors of performances. In her introduction to the first volumes of the Methuen series *Plays by Women*, Michelene Wandor states that 'between the years 1956–1975, only 17 out of 250 produced plays at the Royal Court Theatre (known for its championship of new writing) were written and/or directed by women'. According to the *British Alternative Theatre Directory* of 1981, 'women represent about 15% of all playwrights' (though these statistics are based on information sent in by the playwrights themselves, and one could certainly imagine that women are less likely to register themselves in this way for a number of reasons). Wandor further points out that 'this figure is not represented in commercial play publishing' – a crucial distinction.[2] Any glance at the contemporary scene would suggest that not much has changed since 1956. A tiny proportion of the plays produced by the National Theatre or the Barbican is written by women, and even fewer have women directors. The same statistical model is followed in contemporary issues of *Time Out*, and, to a slightly lesser extent, at this year's Edinburgh Festival.

Women's comparative absence from the theatrical scene is further emphasised in critical histories of the period. From John Russell Taylor to Catherine Itzin, the history of theatre from the 1950s onwards would seem to have been singularly lacking in any input by women writers or directors. In arguing for some kind of a renaissance for English theatre in the 1950s and 1960s, Taylor has sections on 18 named playwrights, two of them women.[3] In plotting 'stages of the revolution', in 1982, Itzin's list of playwrights includes 14 male writers and only two female ones, though she does also discuss 17 theatre collectives, some of which were formed and run by women.[4] Most recent accounts of the history even of political theatre include women writing for theatre only as one amongst many kinds of 'alternative theatres'. Sandy Craig's *Dreams and Deconstructions*, for example, includes a chapter on 'Feminist Theatre', alongside chapters on 'Community and Ethnic Theatre', 'Theatre in Education', 'Political Theatre' and 'Children's Theatre'.[5] Itzin is typical of most theatre historians in finding the crucial names for discussion to be Osborne, Pinter, Arden, Wesker, Mercer, Hare, Brenton, Griffiths, McGrath, Gooch, Barker, Edgar – and Caryl Churchill! And in suggesting that 'the phenomenon of Women's Theatre is something that can no longer be regarded as a minor development', Susan Bassnett-McGuire implicitly draws attention to the fact that women's use of theatre, or their *perceived* use of theatre, has historically been that it is, as it were, 'on the fringe' of things.[6]

One could be forgiven, then, for thinking that women have had no significant voice in British theatre in the last thirty years. Indeed, as Case points out, because there has never been a significant number of extant dramatic texts written by women available for study, theatre history – even feminist theatre history – has recorded an astounding absence of women's voices from the Greeks onwards. There have been, recently, of course, the exceptions to this rule – Churchill, Pam Gems, and, before them Littlewood, Jellicoe and Delaney, have 'made it' into the lists of 'successful' writers – or, at least, of writers whose names are likely to be recognised by those interested in theatre. Indeed, until the advent of Wandor's series of *Plays By Women* in 1982 (or 'Plays *For* Women', as my local bookstore repeatedly insisted on calling it), one would be forgiven for thinking that women simply didn't write for, or use, theatre at all. The same paucity of representation is, of course, clearly evident in other forms of cultural production (women writing for and directing films and television plays, for example), though this is not the case in the same way when it comes to novels, where women writers have for more than a decade had access to publishing companies devoted to the promotion of women's writing, or poetry, which has historically been seen as an appropriate form of articulacy for women (even if not much of what they produced was ever published).

My aim in this chapter is to suggest that, far from being a cultural form which is inaccessible to women (even though this may, for any number of historical and cultural reasons, have been the case in terms of established theatre practice, and is certainly the case in terms of the construction of a dramatic 'canon'), theatre can be seen as an extremely important medium for women writers – in its intricate ability to subvert, or even dispense with, linearity and the illusion of 'concrete realities' (such as gender roles), in the ways in which it can appeal directly to living people, unmediated through the *written* word, and in its multiple abilities to articulate, or embody, what is 'normally' thought of as 'incoherent'.

I should, perhaps, point out that my use of the term 'theatre' (as opposed to 'drama', or even 'plays') is deliberate, since, for the purposes of this chapter, my interest is not so much in published texts, but precisely in the fact that 'theatre' cannot be written down, that there is a crucial difference in writing for theatre, and writing novels or poetry. 'Cultural Studies' is still, in many institutions of higher education, regarded with some suspicion as a legitimate area of research and debate (and has had, therefore, the freedom of creating its own parameters of discussion and its own terminology), but plays have traditionally been regarded as 'texts' which *could* be 'interpreted' in various ways, and much criticism of drama has taken on the terminology applied, in traditional literary criticism, to written texts. Apparent connections between written 'text', 'author', and 'meaning' are, of course, most apparent in the case of the jewel in the cultural and ideological crown, Shakespeare, who any A-level student or first-year undergraduate will tell you is important because he 'understood human nature' (including 'female nature'), and will write in terms of 'character' and 'reality' in exactly the same convinced fashion they will of such issues in novels. Plays, therefore, have been subject to the terminology of traditional literary criticism in ways which other cultural forms have not – primarily because there *is* something readily available which can, in the classroom, be called a text, in that it is written down.

It is not my purpose here to engage in discussions of theories of signification in the theatre (such as the work undertaken by Keir Elam, Esslin or Derrida). These are clearly crucial issues, which feminists need to negotiate with, use, and develop. My concern is to concentrate on the *event* of theatre, and the ways in which I think women have done, and could continue to, use this to make visible a world which other cultural forms cannot reach (or at least, cannot reach in the same way). Drama, as studied in the classroom, may have been subsumed within the essentialist notions ascribed to the written text: in practice, it has never performed this way.

In her introductory chapter to *Sexual/Textual Politics*, Toril Moi attempts a rehabilitation of Virginia Woolf into feminist thinking, using as her main reference-point Elaine Showalter's discussion of *A Room of One's Own*. Moi's argument with Showalter is based on the accusation Showalter makes of Woolf's 'elusiveness', her 'impersonality' and refusal 'to be entirely serious, denying any earnest or subversive intention'. For Showalter, Woolf 'refuses to reveal her own experience fully and clearly, but insists on disguising or parodying it in the text', obliging Showalter to point out for us that '"Fernham" really *is* Newnham College, that "Oxbridge" really *is* Cambridge, and so on'. Moi points out that the only major theoretician Showalter refers to is Lukàcs, whose real interest was in the realist novel, who described himself as a 'proletarian humanist', and who stated that his project was 'to construct the complete human personality and free it from the distortion and dismemberment to which it has been subjected in class society'.[7] Moi's case here is that, while clearly not a 'proletarian humanist', Showalter is adopting a liberal humanist position, which causes her to think in terms of 'the autonomous self' and 'authentic experience', to reject any technique which appears to her to give a 'hazy' account of 'real' female experience, and to see the narrative strategy of *A Room Of One's Own*, with its use of 'repetition, exaggeration, parody, whimsy, and multiple viewpoint' as contributing only to an impression of 'strenuous charm'.[8] Moi goes on to argue that 'remaining detached from the narrative strategies of *Room* is equivalent to not reading it at all', and that Woolf, along with Lessing, 'radically undermines the notion of the unitary self'.[9]

My purpose in citing Moi here is to draw attention to the fact that while much, if not most, criticism of plays still insists on a view of 'character' as central, such notions of an 'essential human nature', to which theatre can bear witness, is fundamentally alien to the workings and practice of the vast majority of drama. Even feminist theatre criticism can insist that the most important function theatre can perform in the hands of the feminist writer is to produce strong female characters with whom the audience can 'identify'. As Helen Keyssar put it, 'drama has thus traditionally urged us to know ourselves better, to search our histories and to *reveal* to ourselves and others who we "really" are'. As a consequence, 'the essential characteristics of feminist drama seemed to be the creation of significant stage roles for women'.[10]

This notion of character, with its underlying assumptions both about a unitary self, and the problems it generates in terms of assumed gender roles, is certainly uncharacteristic of the way in which women have written for and used theatre during the last thirty years. Theatre is, essentially, a place of the corporate creation of illusions. Despite the fact that drama has been recruited into the echelons of the liberal humanist traditions of 'Literary Criticism' in the twentieth century, being read as texts, studied for exams, and presumed to mean something, it simply does not, in practice, work like that. Plays don't, in fact *mean* things, they *do* them – or, as Case puts it, 'a playwright is a *maker* of plays, not necessarily a *writer* of them'.[11] Discussing the same area from a rather different perspective, J.L. Styan states the following:

> When the spectator looks at the stage, he [sic] does not see a character – he sees a man or a woman, youth or age, a smile or a frown, an arm raised or a finger extended, a figure walking or dancing. Nor does he hear words – he hears song or speech, a low tone or a light one, a whisper or a shout, a quick speaking or slow rhythm or silence itself. . . . We pay attention to the actor's face and figure, with or without mask and costume, his gesture and movement, with or without props: his voice and its tone, rhythm and pace – even a change of pace must signal a new perception. . . . All these sensitive attributes speak to us before we take in the meaning of the words the actor utters.[12]

Despite a reliance on binary oppositions, this passage seems to me to contain a crucial comment on what theatre *does*, and how it works. It is only incidentally 'written' – it is rather *made*, co-operatively, including a large team of people (not least of whom are the audience), and it is not, primarily read either, but experienced. And audiences do not experience 'character' – or even, necessarily, gender roles. Such analytical constructions are what you use when engaged in the ideological practice of literary criticism, not what you experience when involved in a theatrical performance.

In the remainder of this chapter, I want to discuss notion of character, gender roles, articulacy and linearity, and to suggest how women dramatists have used and could use theatre to make their own world 'flesh' in the theatre. My later reference points will be the theory of Artaud and Brecht, and the work of especially of Anne Jellicoe. But in order to position this, I want to engage in a brief discussion of some of these issues in relation to the two 'classic' periods of theatre – ancient Greece and Renaissance England.

It is easy, of course, to see how drama formulates important notions of gender roles. Greek drama assumes female sexuality to be dangerous to the male-dominated family, and thus, by extension, to the newly-formed city state. Phaedra, in Euripides' *Hippolytus*, sees suicide as the only way of protecting the honour of her husband's family (and therefore her own worth and value), because she has fallen in love with her stepson. What is important here is not the 'character' of Phaedra, but the choice of a plot which enacts the agreement of women with patriarchal values. The end of the play is wholy concerned with the reconciliation between father and son. Phaedra is forgotten, and the play ends as it began with the divine presences, Artemis and Aphrodite (both female), fighting for their respective male favourites. Clytemnestra, in the *Agamemmnon*, is positioned in a situation which is also associated with treachery and subversion at home (and therefore within the state) because she has taken a lover while her husband has been fighting for the honour of the polis (and sacrificing a daughter and capturing and raping Cassandra on the way). The *Oresteia* ends with the establishment of the principle of the importance of male life above the life of women – a conclusion reached by the inevitability of the plot line, but endorsed by the democratic vote of the elders, the goddess of wisdom, Athena, and by the Furies, who voluntarily surrender their former powers and agree to become 'the kindly ones', subservient to the state, and blessers of hearth and home. Female sexuality is thus seen as dangerous, not only to family honour, but to state security and to cooperative survival: it must be made to seem part of a 'natural' male order by the action of the plays. Male sexuality, however, is posited as being normal and necessary, and justifiably usable in terms of the furtherance of male honour and the good of the state. The Trojan war was, after all, fought to regain one man's 'stolen' woman.

None of this, as Aristotle pointed out, is a question of character, but rather of plot: plays did not imitate people, but life. What is active here is the shaping of the audience's experience, the communal acting-out of parameters which the audience is being encouraged – indeed *led* – to accept as 'normal' and 'right'. Greek theatre, with its unique mixture of religious and civic functions, mapped for a newly emerged people what their history, practices, and recent experiences meant. Its purpose was, in its own way, to 'write the world', and its strong dependence on a linear plot, and a sense of fate and inevitability, were crucial to the task. It is true that, especially in the plays of Euripides, the voice of the chorus could be, and was, used to voice the nearness of chaos and anarchy under the surface of Athenian civic life, but it is still true that the dynamics of Greek plays effect a corporate movement towards a rational justification and an emotional recognition of the present order. Hence the importance of such notions as 'reversal' and 'recognition', both of which imply the existence of a universe of fixed meaning. Hence, also, the context of the term 'catharsis': within those huge arenas, on the occasion of a religious festival, a large proportion of the population of the polis is led, step by inevitable step, and collectively, to the breathing of a sigh of anguish and relief which says 'AH! Yes! – *this* is how it is'.

English Renaissance drama, on the other hand, far from enacting 'the way things are', or 'explaining' the reasons for them, vociferously articulates the fact that no one knows what is going on. From Marlowe's megalomaniac overreachers, who decide to rewrite the universe, to the heroes and heroines of Middleton and Ford, with their desperate implosion into self-gratification, the figures in Renaissance theatre constantly batter themselves against the walls of a universe whose parameters not only restrict their movements, but simply don't any longer make sense. Women, in the plays of this period, are inevitably caught up in this process, and there are many critics who would argue for their strength and independence – even their equality with their male counterparts. But here again, theatre enacts notions of gender – in this case, the growingly obvious necessity to exclude women from the possibilities offered by developing capitalism. Female characters can, and do, signify purity, and thus the preservation of patriarchy: female chastity is high on the agenda of topics for discussion from *The Spanish Tragedy* through *The Tempest* to *'Tis Pity She's A Whore* and *The Changeling*. But while there are many female characters with strong and active parts to play in the plots of Renaissance drama, most of those who achieve anything encounter some kind of degendering. Lady Macbeth is stronger than her husband, but 'unsexes' herself. Shakespeare's comic heroines, so consistently more intelligent – and more active – than their lovers, can be effective only in their disguise as males. Isabella in *Measure for Measure*, one of the most passionate and articulate of Renaissance heroines, is a nun (a change introduced by Shakespeare from his source material which has signally failed to find Isabella any support from twentieth-century critics and directors, who constantly describe her as 'frigid'). There are women of passion and articulacy – and notable courage – in Renaissance plays, but if they are 'good', they tend to signify chastity, or else be effective in the world only when adopting male guise of some sort as a prelude to marrying the man of their choice, or if they are 'bad', they are typified by a tendency to lust, infidelity, murder, and, in the end, self-destruction. (One interesting exception here seems to me to be the Duchess of Malfi, who causes total havoc not by adultery, or lust for power, but merely by falling in love, marrying, and having children. Both her brothers call for her death as a punishment for this 'crime', one goes mad as the result of its accomplishment, and her murderer, a mercenary, undergoes a strange change of heart after her death and attempts, unsuccessfully, to rescue her husband. The Duchess's courage and integrity, in the face of torture and death-threats, and her rigorous insistence on being what she is – a mother – seem too much for any of the male characters to handle.)

Again, it is clear that traditional notions of 'character' do not begin to account for what is being enacted in these plays. Female 'characters' embody, not essential human nature, but aspects of contemporary power relations, and attempts to codify these into gender roles in a rapidly changing economic world. Unlike Greek drama, Renaissance plays are not concerned to formalise 'realities', but rather, to embody and articulate uncertainties and changes. Ambiguities about women are rife in the social consciousness and questioning enacted by Renaissance drama. Women are certainly as articulate as men – indeed, they defeat them in terms of argument, and purposefulness, many times. Hermione, for example, conducts her own defence, convinces everyone on the stage, with the exception of Leontes, and exposes her husband for the jealous, irrational and dangerous fool he is. Isabella subdues Angelo partly because he is smitten with sexual desire, but the language she is given to speak, and the arguments she uses, are as consequential and logical as his own, and in fact, defeat him both in terms of logic and of ethics. Similarly, Portia proves a successful exponent of the law in defeating Shylock. And certainly, Portia, Viola and especially Rosalind are wittier, more articulate, and more *effective* than their male lovers. Nevertheless, this articulacy and effectiveness in the world at large is not as straightforward as it would seem. In the case of the comedies, it is part of a movement towards marriage, and thus, as Rosalind knows full well, the resignation of personal effectiveness (even Isabella is uncomfortably subjected to this fate at the end of *Measure for Measure*, though she does *not* verbally consent). In the case of the tragedies, female effectiveness in the public world is almost always associated with self-will, which must be, and is, punished, as being a challenge to social order. In the plays of the late Renaissance period, notably those of Massinger, one can discern a movement towards the trivialisation and marginalisation of women, in that they appear interested only in marriage, the latest fashion, and so on, and are simply not seen on the great stage of the state at all. In *The City Madam*, for example, the women's rebellion against what is now very clearly a male-run capitalist world is posited as laughable from the beginning; the arguments between the old (impoverished) aristocracy and the 'new money', represented respectively by Lacey and Plenty, are instantly forgotten when both are confronted by the outrageous demands of their future wives for control of finances and personal autonomy. The women are duly brought to heel at the end of the play by the threat of being sold into the white slave trade, and humbly accept the familial and economic – and ethical – authority of their husbands.

There is one more point to make when thinking about women and their functioning in Renaissance drama, and that, of course, is that they were not represented on the stage by female actors. When the audience saw Lady Macbeth chiding her busband for his unwillingness to act and declaring that she will unsex herself, or Rosalind flirting with Orlando, or Vittoria conducting her own defence in the trial scene in *The White Devil*, they *actually* saw, and were in the presence of, men. The apparent liberty of many of the women in

Renaissance plays is, in many ways, ambiguous. As Sue Ellen Case argues, their wit and strength – and, indeed articulacy – could be read as a symptom of contemporary fascination with homosexuality, so that the actions of female characters are merely a form of titillation.[13] Women's power to act in the world comes from challenging the system, which results in punishment (almost always acknowledged by the woman to be justified), from their signification of innocence (in which case they win), or from the temporary adoption of male identity as a prelude to marriage.

Both Greek and English Renaissance drama give women powerful voices, but they are voices which, in different ways, are subsumed within a male world. In both periods, women are regarded with suspicion. What is being enacted is, in fact, the silencing of women, or even their willing compliance with male-ordered social 'norms'. That is what the shape of the plays does to the audience. Greek drama is quite clear about this: it is writing the world in an authoritative way, which relies on the strongest possible link between cause and effect. Renaissance drama is considerably more chaotic and ambiguous, but it still, in the end, constructs women as either challenging male authority, and therefore being punished, or submitting to it and endorsing its ideals. In both cases, it is not necessarily the words female characters say that count: it's the picture of the world that is being created between author, players, and audience. Theatre 'means' what happens in the auditorium. This, of course, is its strength.

What, then, have contemporary women users of theatre done to audiences?

Writing on *The Sport of My Mad Mother*, Anne Jellicoe wrote that her play was about 'incoherent people – people who have no power of expression, of analysing their emotions. They don't know why they're afraid; they don't even know they are afraid'.[14] Much of her play takes the form of rituals of various forms, and of 'nonsensical' chanting, which rises to such a pitch that at one point Dean, the liberal 'audience-identification figure', calls a halt on the proceedings so that everyone can calm down.

We'll now have a little peace – a little tranquillity. I'm serious. I'm calling a truce for one minute. For one whole minute nobody up here is going to do anything and you can all relax. Nothing's going to happen up here. Nothing at all.[15]

Direct address to the audience is not, of course, in itself new. But what Jellicoe is doing to her audience in this play does seem to me to be interesting, in a number of ways. *The Sport of My Mad Mother* 'makes flesh' an invisible world, the world of the dispossessed teenager, whose life is essentially expressed in terms which cannot be incorporated in 'normal' ways. The play was a box-office failure, because no one knew what it 'meant'. Jellicoe had something to say about this.

> I think the word 'meaning' shows exactly what is wrong with people's attitudes. If they were to ask 'What is this play about?' it would be a better approach. . . . Most playgoers today are not used to taking anything direct in the theatre. What they do is transform it into words and put it through their brain. For instance, there is a scene in my play where Caldaro is knocked out, and the Teds stand him on his feet, wrap him up in newspaper, cavort round him, chanting until they get to a pitch of ecstasy when they tear the newspaper off him. Now in this action there are hardly any words that make sense – there is nothing your intellect can take in. If you sit watching and say 'What does this mean? What does this mean?', you're not going to get anywhere; but if you allow yourself to be excited by the visual action and the gradual crescendo of noise underlying this, you may begin to appreciate what it's about . . . so many plays tell you what is happening the whole time. People don't act angry; they tell you they're angry. Now, my play is about incoherent people. . . . And all this is directly shown, instead of being explained.[16]

Implicit in this is the notion that something is being 'bodied forth' in Jellicoe's play which is not explained, or necessarily, explainable. It is a play that puts the incoherence of teenagers' lives on the stage in apparently 'incoherent' form. There are two interesting comparisons to make here with Jellicoe's fellow-playwrights at the Royal Court, Osborne and Arden. Jimmy Porter, of course, spends the entire course of *Look Back in Anger* not only acting out, but explaining in meticulous detail the fact that he is bored. He may lack some powers of political analysis, but he can certainly talk. In contrast, John Arden was criticised for *Serjeant Musgrave's Dance* (admittedly by Bernard

Levin) because there seemed to be no clear 'meaning' to the play. 'Why is it fully one and a half acts before we have any idea of what is going on? . . . the suspicion grows that Mr Arden actually regards clarity and directness as a vice . . . '.[17] Levin – and apparently Osborne – seem to feel that theatre should work primarily through the intellect, an attitude Jellicoe explicitly rejects. As John Russell Taylor pointed out of *The Sport of My Mad Mother*:

> When staged it makes extraordinary demands on the playgoer schooled in the traditional techniques of the English stage; he [sic] expects the play he sees to be, in effect, written mainly for the ear, with the eye required to act on its own just once in a while when it may notice a bit of business and aid the mind to deduce some logical significance for it. But here is a play which assaults (the word is used advisedly) both eye and ear, and makes very little appeal to the intellect at all.[18]

The importance here lies in the terms 'schooled', 'traditional', 'mind', and 'logical'. Osborne fits this model, Jellicoe, Delaney and Littlewood do not, and most women's writing for the theatre since has not done so either. It is the form of the play that audiences and critics found difficult with Jellicoe, not the content. It is something of a commonplace in twentieth-century theatre criticism to oppose the theories of Artaud, the mystic and ritualist, and Brecht, the analyst and demonstrator. Both challenged the contemporary social and political functioning of theatre, though they did so for different reasons. Artaud used the analogy of theatre and plague; he saw theatre as a communal acting-out of subconscious social and political forces. Theatre acts as a 'revelation', though Artaud sees this as revelation of 'a latent undercurrent of cruelty through which all the perversity of which the mind is capable, whether in a person or a nation, becomes localised'.[19] His objections to Western drama was that it did not sufficiently utilise the capacity of theatre to enact and embody the traumas that were affecting Western society. Instead, Western drama had lost any connection with current issues in its obsession with explanations and verbalisation, and had become merely 'a form of pleasurable relaxation' in which problems which were not worth solving were intellectually posited and intellectually answered in ways which would not change audiences. His contrast was, like Yeats, the stylised theatre of the East.

The Balinese theatre was not a revelation of a verbal but a physical idea of theatre where drama is encompassed within the limits of everything that can happen on stage, independently of a written script. Whereas with us, the lines gain the upper hand and theatre as we understand it finds itself restricted by them. Thus theatre is a branch of literature, a piece of vocal language, and even if we admit a difference between the lines spoken on stage and those read by the eyes, even if we confine theatre to what goes on between the cues, we will never succeed in divorcing theatre from the idea of script production.

This notion, the predominance of lines in theatre, is deeply rooted in us and we view theatre so much as just a physical reflection of the script, that everything in theatre outside the script, not contained within its limits or strictly determined by it, appears to us to be a part of the staging, and inferior to the script.[20]

Like Jellicoe, he expresses a deep suspicion of theatre which is imagined to work primarily through verbalisation – through 'lines' (or 'the word'). For Artaud, theatre acts on something much more 'primitive' and collective, and the shrinking of theatre to the writing of plays which 'talk about things', or which can be seen by their audiences as 'talking about things', and which do not incorporate their audiences into collective, non-verbalised experience, he put down to the decadence of the West (and a possible sign of future catastrophe!). His answer to this state of affairs, the 'Theatre of Cruelty', was designed to smash what he saw as the complacent bridging of art and aesthetics, the de-politicisation of writing, and the 'literarification' of theatre. No one who sat through one of his plays was going to forget the *experience*.

Brecht, while he would certainly not have seen eye to eye with this theatrical model, thought little more of his contemporary drama, or its effectiveness with audiences, than did Artaud.

Let us go into one of these houses and observe the effect which it has on spectators. Looking about us, we see somewhat motionless figures in a peculiar condition: they seem strenuously to be tensing all their muscles, except where these are flabby and exhausted. They scarcely communicate with each other; their relations are those of a lot of sleepers, though of such as dream restlessly because, as is popularly said of those who have nightmares, they are lying on their backs. True, their eyes are open, but they stare rather than see, just as they listen rather than hear. They look at the stage as if in a trance: an expression which comes from the Middle Ages, the days of witches and priests.[21]

Epic theatre, with its rejection of linear development and its adoption of montage, an episodic shape, and its concept of 'demonstration', of alienating the audience, is designed for a very different political purpose from anything Artaud had in mind – but I am not so sure that they disagreed about the potential power of theatre as a cultural and ideological force. Like Artaud, Brecht saw twentieth-century theatre as having become very little more than an elitist, polite form of rehearsing social norms. Even naturalism, in the hands of Ibsen, and the banging of doll's house doors, simply elicited a polite liberal tut-tutting, and theatre could, potentially, do much more than this. It could change people's thinking *because* it was a live medium, which confronted an audience with an acting-out (in his case, a very deliberate acting-out) of issues which the audience had to attend to, of events which they knew had happened. While analysis of events is crucial in Brechtian theatre, it is still true that he chose theatre as his medium, rather than the novel, or more obviously analytical political forms. It was what you could do to an audience that interested him – what you could force them to be witnesses to. His theatre derives its strength from the fact that, for example, you see Mother Courage come on stage riding on her waggon with Kattrin, her two sons in harness, at the beginning of the play, and at the end you have to watch her pull it out again, on her own – *and* you have seen everything that has happened in between. You've seen her lose each of her children, one by one, you've seen the waggon go through its good days and its bad days, full of goods and shiny, and weather-beaten and empty. The shape of the action – what you are confronted with as a live audience – compels you to make the connection. Nothing needs explaining (as, for example, Jimmy tries to do in *Look Back in Anger*). We do, of course, have commentary, for example in the form of Mother Courage's *song* of 'The Great Capitulation'. In one scene, there is no dialogue at all. We simply watch Courage and Kattrin haul the waggon on to the stage, where they stand listening to a song about the passing of spring and winter issuing from the interior of a peasants' cottage, and then we watch them move on, dragging the waggon behind them. Dialogue and character are, here, used not as identification markers, but very clearly as *needing deciphering* by the audience. Being witnesses to the action of the play, we have no option.

Artaud and Brecht differ markedly from each other both in the kinds of invisible world they use theatre to make visible and, necessarily, in their theatrical techniques. Brecht wants his audience emotionally separated from the action: he wants it sitting up and taking notice. Artaud wants his audience surrounded by the action and the experience of the play, increasingly unable to distinguish between 'reality' and 'illusion', since this is the only way in which theatre can have its proper purgative effect. But they nevertheless have interesting similarities. Both deny the supremacy of character, both would argue that articulacy in drama is not dependent upon the spoken word, and both argue strongly that theatre is a collective experience. Women writing for theatre have drawn on both possibilities, though they have changed and adapted them for their own purposes.

Jellicoe makes an interesting beginning point. Initially, she would seem to draw more on Artaud, in that in plays like *The Sport of My Mad Mother* and *The Knack*, she uses the occasion of theatre to involve her audience in experiences they might not understand, and which are certainly not explained, but simply thrown in the audience's face. The action she dramatises certainly cannot be contained within 'normal' speech patterns – or even within a constant relationship between stage and audience. Jellicoe relies heavily on the use of ritual, whether it be the ritual of perming one's hair or of dancing round a totem pole or gang fights, which have no clear rhyme or reason about them, but are simply experienced as a kind of inevitability – like changes in the weather. But she also uses the Brechtian device of having a musician on stage who is only tangentially 'within' the play and who at times gets involved in the action and at times 'accompanies' it. And while Dean can be seen as some sort of 'normative' figure, his hold on 'normality' becomes increasingly fragile. The following two actions come within less than a minute of each other towards the end of *The Sport of My Mad Mother*, when Dean is finally 'confronting' Greta. They are, I think, worth quoting at length.

> DEAN: There is a far more moral reason why you should protect Cone, why the strong should protect the weak; to act otherwise is below human dignity – don't you see? Every time anyone does anything cruel or immoral he betrays mankind. I'm not a religious person, at least I'm not a Christian, a church-goer, but this is what I feel – I can't see any reasons for men being on this earth, but since we are here, we men, we must try and become

better, we must seek to become better and better, to help to create order, truth and love. It's so easy to slide into chaos – don't you see that? You're intelligent and strong – surely you understand?

DEAN: I don't care if it worries you! I don't give a damn! You're going to hear. Somebody's got to get it into that thick cruel skull. Don't interrupt me! No self-control! No discipline! What's a world without serenity, without mutual assurance, a bedrock of mutual trust, of laws and decencies you can rely on? Be quiet! All the things decent men have striven for, all the high aims; learning, philosophy, morality . . . moral discipline, a moral philosophy of responsibility that each man hammers out for himself and tries to live by.

GRETA: For crying out loud, I'm off —

DEAN: You're not.

GRETA: I am.

(Greta starts to go, he pulls her down.)

DEAN: You're stopping.

GRETA: Rough stuff.

DEAN: Yes.

GRETA: Just you remember it's a pregnant woman you're pulling around.

DEAN: Pregnant! Pregnant woman! You pregnant! You're not fit to have a child. What'll your child be? What'll its life be?

GRETA: Rough.

DEAN: You're disgusting! You destroy people. You eat them, you eat them. A boy, your friend, trusts you, and you just toss him off. . . . You obscenity! You gross thing! Man/woman, cruel! Unstable! Frigid!

GRETA: Frigid?

DEAN: Yes frigid! No love, no true morality, no giving, all taking! You eat men, you eat them, well, you shan't eat me! You shan't devour me! You and your kind – how dare you? Look at me! Look at me! What have you got to say?
(pp. 164–5)

Greta doesn't actually have anything much to 'say' at all: after involving Dean in an increasingly ritualised chant, centring on the repetition of the words 'kill', 'bash', 'lash', 'suck', 'knock', 'bang', 'feel' etc., she calmly gives birth behind a sheet on stage, and ends the play examining the baby 'with lively interest' (p. 168).

There is much one could say about the ending to this play in terms of its language usage – the automatic associations in Dean's speeches between maleness, understanding, knowledge, morality, and the responsibility for order, for example. But what seems to me to be important here is the speed at which Dean flips from being author-ity-figure, associated (at least in his own mind) with civilised values, to a hysterical woman-hater. He most certainly doesn't just tell you he's angry but acts it. The language is, of course, violent, and so are his actions, but it is his world which, in the end, is expressable only in ritualised form, and which finds itself silenced by the birth of Greta's child. Verbalisation dependent on 'male' norms of its mean-ing is, here, part of a world which cannot maintain its own para-meters in the face of other kinds of reality – and it's the dynamics of the action, the physical relation of actors to audience, the fact that the audience is both, at times, assaulted, in terms of sensation, and at times given a 'breather', as it were, where it can attempt to match the beliefs it came in with to what it has been experiencing, which mark the play's highly experimental nature. You are in the immediate presence, as a member of the audience, of the illogicality and power of male violence against women, and of a women's essentially *non*verbal being – and strength.

In a lecture on 'Some Unconscious Influences in the Theatre', Jellicoe writes at length of the importance of ritual and myth as ways of understanding what happens in theatre. She also talks about the fact that the same production, never mind the same text, *means* – or, rather, *is* – a totally different thing at each performance. She de-scribes seeing *The Knack* in various provincial locations when it was on tour, and thinking on one night it really wasn't a very good play, on the next that it was obscene, and in the next town discovering how innocent it was. 'The play', she says, 'will indeed be a different play, in Bath or London according to the audience with whom we see it.'[22] It seems to me wholly understandable that Jellicoe should have departed from West End theatre in order to work in commu-nity theatre, given her interest in theatre as a collective event. The work she has done recently in collaborating with the inhabitants of towns and cities in 'writing' their own history is a natural extension of her early work: it is a communal 'making visible the invisible' - not just facts about the past, but the creation of it from the perspec-tive of the present. People can write histories of communities and read them: creating and enacting this is another ball-game altogether.

Brechtian theatre, of course, makes visible 'society's casual network',[23] and the applicability of this to women writing for the theatre hardly needs to be pointed out. But there are other ways in which women have used theatre to make visible their world – Churchill's *Vinegar Tom* enacts the ease with which women who were felt to be a threat were cast in the role of witches in the medieval period, and she writes (perhaps with some degree of satisfaction) that several members of the audience had to be helped, retching or fainting, from the auditorium in the 'pricking' scene, and that most spectators insisted on believing that dummies were used in the hanging scene.[24] If 'mankind cannot bear too much reality', then theatre is an extremely effective way of getting them to witness images of it. Similarly, plays can be written about breast cancer, and its effect on families, about rape, about battery, about child-abuse – as of course they can about any form of injustice and oppression. My point is that theatre is a unique medium for such marginalised groups to use. Precisely because audiences do *not* see 'character' on the stage, but people, or signs of people, they are a sitting target for whatever you want to do to them. You can make them observe, you can make them laugh, suffer, cry, hold their breath – *think* – respond in any number of different ways. Perhaps, most importantly, women can put themselves on the stage – their history, their oppression, their humour, their experience, their *bodies* – they can, to quote Augusto Boal, 'reassume their protagonistic function in the theater and in society'.[25] They can, quite literally, 'embody themselves'.

Notes

1. Sue Ellen Case, *Feminism and Theatre* (London: Macmillan, 1988), p. 2.
2. Michelene Wandor, *Plays by Women*, Vol. 1 (London: Methuen, 1982), p. 11.
3. John Russell Taylor, *Anger and After* (London: Pelican, 1962).
4. Catherine Itzin, *Stages of the Revolution* (London: Methuen, 1980).
5. Sandy Craig (ed.), *Dreams and Deconstructions: Alternative Theatre in Britain* (Ambergate: Amber Lane Press, 1980).
6. Susan Bassnett-MacGuire, 'Towards a Theory of Women's Theatre', in Herta Schmid and Aloysius Van Kesteren (eds), *Linguistic and Literary Studies in Eastern Europe*, Vol. 10, 'Semiotics of Drama and Theatre' (Amsterdam: John Benjamin, 1984), p. 445.

7. Toril Moi, *Sexual/Textual Politics* (London: Methuen, 1985), pp. 2–3.
8. Ibid., p. 8.
9. Ibid., p. 7.
10. Helene Keyssar, *Feminist Theatre* (London: Macmillan, 1984), p. xi.
11. Case, p. 29.
12. J. L. Styan, *Drama, Stage and Audience* (London: Cambridge University Press, 1975), p. 145.
13. Case, pp. 19–27.
14. Quoted in *Anger and After*, p. 67.
15. *The Sport of My Mad Mother* (London: Faber, 1985), p. 124.
16. Quoted in *Anger and After*, p. 67.
17. Bernard Levin, *Daily Express*, 23 October 1959.
18. *Anger and After*, p. 66.
19. Antonin Artaud, *The Theatre and its Double* (London: Caldero, 1970), p. 21.
20. Ibid., p. 50.
21. Bertolt Brecht, 'A Short Organum on the Theatre', in John Willett (trans.), *Brecht on Theatre* (London: Methuen, 1964), p. 187.
22. Anne Jellicoe, *Some Unconscious Influences in the Theatre* (Cambridge: Cambridge University Press, 1967), pp. 9–10.
23. Bertolt Brecht, 'The Popular and the Realistic', in John Willett (trans.), *Brecht on Theatre*, p. 109.
24. Caryl Churchill, 'Afterword', in Michelene Wandor (ed.), *Plays for Women*, Vol. 1, p. 42.
25. Augusto Boal, *Theatre of the Oppressed* (London: Pluto Press, 1974), p. 119.

3

Popular Drama and Realism: The Case of Television

CHRIS PAWLING and TESSA PERKINS

Undoubtedly one of the most important debates in twentieth-century literary criticism has been the contest between defenders and opponents of realism. Whilst this debate is central to the understanding of narrative forms in general, it is probably correct to argue that the realism/Modernism controversy has found its most coherent expression in the theory and practice of drama. From the Brecht/Lukàcs debate on expressionist theatre in the thirties, through to the debates of the seventies, in *Screen* and elsewhere, about the 'radical' conventions of a TV series such as *Days of Hope*, there has been a longstanding concern with the relationship between drama and that disputed terrain commonly labelled as 'reality'. This chapter will begin by reexamining the realism/Modernism debate before moving on to an examination of four examples of television drama in the light of our conclusions about: (a) the strengths and weaknesses of these opposing theoretical positions; (b) the efficacy of posing the questions facing contemporary television drama in terms of such a seemingly fixed dichotomy.

Although it has serious limitations, one of the best starting-points for a discussion of this kind is still Colin MacCabe's attack on naturalism, or what he terms the 'classic realist text'. In an essay entitled 'Realism and the Cinema: Notes on some Brechtian Theses', first published in *Screen* in 1974,[1] MacCabe highlighted what he saw as a crucial difference between a naturalist-inspired Hollywood narrative cinema and an alternative tradition of revolutionary Modernism which had its origins in the 'epic' theatre of Weimar Germany.

For MacCabe, and other proponents of what might be termed the *Screen* approach to film and television, Brecht and Piscator represented a popular, anti-illusionist art which deliberately undermined the ideological and aesthetic 'closure' of the classic realist text.

By employing the radical technique of the *'Verfremdungseffekt'*,[2] Brecht introduced a space between the spectator and the events on stage which allowed the former to step back from the action, rather than being drawn into the 'illusion' of the play through a process of emotional identification with the actors/protagonists. This process of 'estrangement' was an important device, not only aesthetically but also politically. Its political importance lay in the fact that the destruction of the artistic illusion of the naturalist theatre was held to be a necessary precondition for allowing the audience to become thinking, *political* subjects who would be able to make independent judgements on the action developing in front of them. It was this process which was politicising – which produced *political* subjects.

Brecht's emphasis on form and its supposed effects became the linchpin of MacCabe's argument while 'content' tended to be ignored. On the whole for MacCabe, if the content of radical theatre was still significant it was decidedly the junior and weaker partner. MacCabe argued that naturalism was dominated by a heavily 'closed' narrative discourse, which tended to elide contradictions and fix the subject in 'a point of view from which everything becomes obvious'. This position, which MacCabe terms 'dominant specularity', seduced the viewer by offering the illusion that he/she could observe events from a privileged transcendent standpoint, effectively outside of history. The illusion was maintained at the formal level because the narrative discourse in the realist text acted as a 'metalanguage' which was superior to the other discourses by virtue of its 'transparent' nature which seemed to achieve 'perfect representation'. Whereas the other discourses within the narrative were 'material' in that they were clearly the products of a particular 'point of view', the narrative discourse simply 'allowed' reality to 'appear' and denied its own status as 'articulation'. Thus, whereas the spectator of a play or film could test the 'materiality' of a character's version of events by comparing his/her discourse with that of the other characters, one was not invited to question the *overall* framework of a narrative discourse which tied the fiction together and which was the only point of entry into the diegetic world of the text. Indeed, one was persuaded not to question the process of the narration itself, because to do so would be to break the illusion of superior detachment which resulted from identifying with the privileged position of the author.

MacCabe argued that the classic realist text could not be progressive because it substituted one form of domination for another. Even if the content was critical of the dominant ideological discourse in society, the aesthetic form still relied on an unquestioning identification with a point of view and, hence a subject position which was not open to question, or contestation. Thus the main function of political art, which must be to encourage the audience to engage in a struggle to transform existing reality, was inevitably undermined if it left them as passive consumers of pre-digested truths, in the form of a 'correct' political line:

> All this by way of explaining that the classic realist (a heavily 'closed' discourse) cannot deal with the real in its contradictions and that in the same movement it fixes the subject in a point of view from which everything becomes obvious. There is, however, a level of contradiction into which the classic realist text can enter. This is the contradiction between the dominant discourse of the text and the dominant ideological discourses of the time. Thus a classic realist text in which a strike is represented as a just struggle in which oppressed workers attempt to gain some of their rightful wealth would be in contradiction with certain contemporary ideological discourses and as such might be classified as progressive. It is here that subject matter enters into the argument and where we can find the justification for Marx and Engels's praise of Balzac, and Lenin's texts on the revolutionary force of Tolstoy's texts which ushered the Russian peasant onto the stage of history. Within contemporary films one could think of the films of Costa-Gavras or such television documentaries as *Cathy Come Home*. What is, however, still impossible for the classic realist text is to offer any perspective for struggle due to its inability to investigate contradiction. It is thus not surprising that these films tend either to be linked to a social democratic conception of progress – if we reveal injustices then they will go away – or certain *ouvrieriste* tendencies which tend [sic] to see the working class, outside any dialectical movement, as the simple possessors of truth.[3]

For MacCabe the four-part TV drama series *Days of Hope* transmitted by the BBC in 1975, was a case in point. *Days of Hope* covered a decade in the history of working-class struggle – the period 1916 to 1926 – through the lives of three characters: Sarah Hargreaves, her husband Philip – a pacifist in the Great War, and afterwards a Labour MP – and her brother Ben – a soldier with the army in Ireland in the early twenties and, later, a member of the Communist Party. In essence, the series was a study of the heroism of the working class and its inevitable betrayal by a bureaucratic, reformist leadership. Although the narrative purported to set up a dialogue between reformism (Philip) and revolution (Ben, Sarah) there was never any real contest between the two positions, since the only way of *understanding* the experience of the working-class was to identify with Ben, who acted as the 'major articulation between viewer and screen'. Each stage of Ben's development, from naive squaddy to politically-aware revolutionary, was portrayed as a logical response to what the viewer observed on the screen whereas Philip's refusal to abandon his reformist position was 'simply *unrealistic*', since his politics were presented 'without any visual evidence to explain their origin or form'. Thus the rationale of the drama, its logical *terminus ad quem*, emphasised 'Ben's position as true (coincident with what we have seen) and Philip's as false (non-coincident)'. This was particularly evident in the final episode where Sarah was seen to side with her brother, against both her husband and the 'reformism' of the Labour Party.

In attacking *Days of Hope*, MacCabe was trying to highlight the weaknesses of a 'progressive' drama which he saw as being limited through being tied to what he termed an 'empiricist' concept of reality. For the authors of *Days of Hope* the history of the working class was not a changing entity, which was constantly debated and reconstructed in the light of contemporary considerations and experience. Rather it was a suppressed 'truth', which had been hidden by dominant versions of history and was simply waiting to be recovered by a faithful reconstruction of the past. But, while *Days of Hope* aimed to raise political consciousness by recovering a lost 'memory' of political struggle, it still operated through a petrified view of history and a passive relationship to its audience. For in true 'classic realist' style, it *demonstrated* the truth of a revolutionary view of history by aligning the viewer with a single point of view which suppressed unresolved contradictions. Hence one was finally won over by a process of *identification* with those figures in the drama who had supposedly matured to a point of revolutionary insight.

MacCabe's critique of naturalist political drama had a certain force and logic and it is not hard to see why it was so influential with a section of the critical intelligentsia (especially those gathered round the magazine *Screen* in the 1970s). However a number of reservations were expressed about MacCabe's definition of realism and writers such as Raymond Williams and Colin McArthur[4] argued that *Screen* was in danger of espousing an overly formalist aesthetic which was unable to deliver any model for a radical drama with a broad, popular appeal. Instead, one was left with an elitist *avant garde* art which seemed to concentrate exclusively on exposing the artifice of all institutionalised art, including popular culture, and the political discourses on which it rested. Thus, the alternative to *Days of Hope* was a cerebral, anti-illusionist art – a formalist version of Brecht – which fetishised 'distanciation' and refused any of the 'pleasures' of the aesthetic domain. In particular, the refusal to countenance a progressive drama based on forms of emotional identification between audience and characters was debilitating in that it inevitably meant that the vast majority of popular television drama was automatically categorised as reactionary. The popular appeal of TV dramas such as soaps or sit-coms could only be lamented. Furthermore MacCabe's model presupposed a monolithic audience producing a single reading. The work of Richard Dyer, Terry Lovell and others on the politics of 'pleasure' in *Coronation Street* [5] suggested the possibility of a more sophisticated approach.

However, it would be as simplistic to reject MacCabe's critique of naturalism out of hand because of such weaknesses as it was to accept it without reservation. If it did nothing else, the debate on 'realism' in the 1970s encouraged crucial questions to be formulated about the nature of 'progressive' drama and about the inherent properties of visual media such as film and television. The identification of television's 'naturalistic effect' was timely. Stuart Hall commented: 'The utopia of straight transmission, or the 'naturalistic fallacy' in television, is not only an illusion – it is a dangerous deception.'[6] Hall's critique was echoed in a lecture given by Dennis Potter to the Edinburgh Film Festival in 1987:

> Most television ends up offering its viewers a means of orientating themselves towards the generally received notions of 'reality'. The best naturalist or realist drama, of the Garnett-Loach-Allen school, for instance, breaks out of this cosy habit by the vigour, clarity, originality and depth of its perceptions of a more comprehensive reality. The best non-naturalistic drama, in its very structure, disorientates the viewer smack in the middle of the orientation process which television perpetually uses. . . . It shows the frame in the

picture when most television is busy showing the picture in the frame. I think it is potentially the more valuable, therefore, of the two approaches.[7]

Potter's own popular television dramas, such as *Pennies From Heaven* and *The Singing Detective,* have made use of a variety of estrangement devices/effects to 'disorientate' the viewer, and his plays mix the techniques of *avant-garde* theatre with popular culture (melodrama, popular song, detective stories, etc.) in an unsettling manner.

One of Potter's favourite devices, which has almost become a cliché, is to disturb the illusionism of naturalist drama by cutting from a moment of intense dramatic dialogue to a comedy review routine. Thus the conventions of a bourgeois realism, based on individual histories or interpersonal conflicts, are suddenly dispensed with and realist 'characters' turn into 'artists' in a popular review or chorus (an effect reminiscent of that created by Joan Littlewood in *Oh! What a Lovely War*).

Potter's dramas are clearly intended to involve the viewer in a more active process of engagement with the image on the screen, so that the meaning of the play is the outcome of a creative dialogue. At the same time he seems to be implying that it is not possible to use drama to document history without interrogating the very process by which historical memories are reconstructed and circulated in a mass-mediated culture. So, for example, the use of popular songs from the thirties in *Pennies From Heaven* is not simply a decorative device, a form of 'background' designed to aid the realist effect of the drama. Rather these songs become a crucial medium for articulating those hidden desires and fears which constitute the suppressed imaginary universe of the central characters, while at the same time functioning like dreams in 'censoring' the realm of personal desire and containing it within a discourse of sentimentality and banality. Thus Potter seems to be arguing that in order to unlock the 'meaning' of the thirties and experience it 'from the inside', one must focus on the contradictory ways in which reality was *imagined*, in and through popular culture, rather than the means by which it was *documented*, at the level of newsreels or formal history.

Potter's television dramas are important because they try to explore the disjuncture between ideology and experience in terms of a formal rupture of dominant codes, including those of naturalist drama. However, as interrogations of popular memory, Potter's plays are constrained by a tendency to concentrate on the struggles of isolated individuals. Thus although the Bob Hoskins character in *Pennies From Heaven* seems to be representative of a social type (the salesman), his own personal development is rarely articulated with the wider collective experience of his class – his struggles (like those of the 'hero' in *The Singing Detective*) are presented as those of a unique and privileged individual with whom we are in the main encouraged to identify. Since the other characters are cardboard cutouts who hardly engage our sympathies at all and the contradictions which have been revealed to us by Potter's anti-naturalist strategies do not seem amenable to solution, Potter's work may leave audiences with an apathetic sense of despair.

By contrast in *The Cheviot, The Stag and The Black, Black Oil* John McGrath tells an equally critical story but does so with very different effects. In the debate about the classic realist text *The Cheviot* was often cited as *the* example of what progressive television drama could be like. In many respects it is easy to see why this should be the case, nor would we disagree with it as a verdict. The general consensus about *The Cheviot* seems to be that it is immensely enjoyable, thought-provoking and *energising*. And it is this that makes it particularly interesting in this context – because in at least two respects it adopted strategies that MacCabe's analysis suggested were inherently unprogressive.

Firstly, as we discussed above, MacCabe argues that a closed text cannot be progressive because it leaves the audience as 'passive' consumers of pre-digested truths. A crucial part of MacCabe's argument about *Days of Hope* centres on his claim that its authors adopt a particular view of history and that this view of history entails a passive viewer and a passive viewer is synonymous with an apolitical one. However, we shall argue that *The Cheviot* adopts a very similar view of history but that this does not necessarily produce a passive viewer. Secondly, and relatedly, MacCabe argues against the use of realist forms, and for aesthetic strategies which show the 'frame in the picture', which reveal to the audience the constructedness of the work. Although at first sight the form taken by *The Cheviot* makes it seem as if it would fall unproblematically into the anti-naturalist camp, and McGrath's known opposition to 'boring realism' would tend to confirm this, in fact *The Cheviot* relies heavily on precisely those realist strategies of which MacCabe is so critical, the strategies which lead the audience to adopt the authorial point of view.

The Cheviot is a unique combination of dramatic and filmic forms which defies simple categorisation. At one level it can be described as a documentary about a performance given by a travelling theatre company (7:84) in the Highlands. The performance is a presentation in words and music of the history of the Highlands – 'a story with a beginning, a middle but as yet no end'. The performance takes place in what appears to be a community centre in an isolated part of the Scottish Highlands. The Audience is composed of local Highlanders. (The Audience is crucial to how this piece functions and we will return to this below.) The first two-thirds of *The Cheviot* mainly take the form of a record of parts of a particular evening's performance and *that audience's reaction to it.* However, the television audience is not simply watching a record of a stage performance. In the television adaptation of McGrath's play, filmed material is also used. So at times we slip from watching a burlesque music-hall performance on the stage to watching a historical reconstruction on film which is more or less 'naturalistic'. (It is this combination of styles and forms which makes *The Cheviot* so unique.) Interestingly this slippage between media is hardly disorientating at all. Its function does not seem to be to 'disturb' the viewer or make them 'question' what they see. On the contrary. What could be an extraordinarily confusing jump from a music-hall sketch about two rather shabbily but flamboyantly-dressed Victorian gentlemen to a film of two Victorian men on horseback, riding across the Scottish countryside, is beautifully 'managed' by the techniques of continuity editing – strategies developed in the service of realist cinema. For example, although the men's costumes are different the voices are the same and the soundtrack is continuous; shots of the audience are used to conceal the jump from 'stage' to 'film'.

The final part combines the music-hall-type acts with conventional documentary footage. The 'historical reconstruction' which was used to 'illustrate' what had happened, (for example, during the Clearances) is replaced by filmed interviews with people involved in the oil industry in Aberdeen today. The whole feel of the piece changes in this final section. Much less time is spent in the community centre watching a performance, and the role of the 'Audience' is considerably reduced. They do not become a part of the performance in the way they are in the first part. The style of the piece as a whole ranges from the exuberance of music hall through the solemnity of the illustrated talk in the local library to the excitement of a political rally.

However, it is clear that this is not the version of Scottish history which we learn (or fail to learn) in school. The story we are being told is being told from a different point of view – it is being told from the point of view of the people of the Highlands, rather than the owners. The suggestion is that this alternative interpretation of history is the one implicitly and unconsciously held by the Scottish people – by the Highlanders we see watching the performance – and that this is the true version – the version that was waiting to be told, in just the same way as MacCabe argued *Days of Hope* was offering the one true version. This is one reason why the Audience in *The Cheviot* is crucial.

The Audience takes the place of the central character in a more conventional drama. These people are the heirs and descendants of those whose history we are seeing re-enacted. We have witnessed their 'recognition' of the validity of this version of history. They are used throughout to give authenticity and validity to the actors. They act as guarantors of McGrath's history; there are no dissenting voices; we are shown no shots of members of the Audience looking bored rather than amused or shocked or sad or interested. The Audience is a collective subject with whom we identify as strongly as with any individual. Nor are we ever invited to query the status of this 'Audience' in the Highlands. The well-developed techniques of realism which conceal the editorial hand and lead the reader/cinema audience to believe that we are being 'shown it as it really happened' are employed here as skilfully as in any ordinary realist text. We never doubt that the Audience's reaction that we are witnessing is a reaction to what we have just been shown a second before. It does not occur to us that this laughter might have been dubbed on later or that that man's sad expression was not a reaction to what has just been said but to something completely different. Furthermore the boundaries between actors and the Highlanders 'then' and Highlanders 'now' are extremely fluid and at times disappear altogether. In one sequence, the actors have been giving accounts of examples of resistance; they tell of the celebrations which took place to mark the occasion and we see film of people dancing round a bonfire. Of course the people we see dancing, who for the moment we believe are peasants, are actually actors. At the same time the actors (now in their role as commentators/masters of ceremony) start to dance and fetch members of the Audience on to the stage to join in the dancing. These two celebratory dances merge and it is impossible to tell as you watch it on television which is 'then' and which is 'now' and who are the actors and who the Audience. 'Then' and 'now' actors and Audience, have all become part of a collective identity, and the television audience is swept into this ecstatic moment celebrating resistance.

The importance of the Audience as a mechanism of emotional involvement may explain why, for many people, the play seems to flag in the final documentary section which seems less successful. In that section most of the material consists of filmed interviews and consequently there are few shots of the Audience and its reactions. The element which has been the primary vehicle of our emotional involvement in this complex interplay of discourses, has been removed and we are faced with a much more simple and conventional structure – a quite long section of visually uninteresting documentary footage (interviews) interspersed with a few interventions from the actors which provide the explanatory framework within which to interpret the interviews. While previously there has been a great deal to watch and to make sense of, in the final section we have relatively little to do, our energy dissipates and there is almost a sense of loss.

The Cheviot is unique in the sort of active involvement it demands of its audiences (i.e. both the Audience in the theatre and the television audience) but it is not the case that at the end of the performance the audiences are 'free' to produce their *own* interpretation of Scottish history: nor has the TV audience at any point been encouraged to do so. On the contrary they have been offered an alternative interpretation of Scottish history which is produced as much by a single point of view as the one which it is replacing and it has been produced so we have hardly noticed how this discourse has become dominant. It seems only 'natural' that the upper classes are the figures of fun – the burlesque characters; and it seems equally 'natural' that the peasantry are only ever presented 'realistically' and respectfully. It is the upper classes who are rendered as stereotypes and the peasantry who, by contrast, are treated with respect. What the peasantry say or claim is demonstrably 'true' while what the upper classes say is generally shown to be false. For example the claim by Lord Sutherland that no one has suffered during the Clearances is accompanied by shots of derelict and burnt-out settlements; and in the midst of this dereliction stands Dunrobin castle, the only building that remains intact. If this were a straightforwardly 'realist' text there would be nothing remarkable about this – what is remarkable is that in a text which does use some anti-illusionist devices realist strategies can still be used to great effect.

One of the achievements of *The Cheviot* is the production of a dynamic popular drama which combines naturalist and non-naturalist forms and manages to be engaging and emotionally uplifting. Although McGrath and his co-workers employ anti-illusionist devices, they manage to avoid the pitfalls associated with more formalist approaches to the notion of an 'open' text. For McGrath it is clearly important to offer political direction and ways of thinking through the contradictions raised by his dramatised history of the Scottish people. This means moving beyond a form of 'aesthetic' debate to a position where it is possible to investigate 'the dynamic of social change and transformation.'[8] To this extent, *The Cheviot* has much in common with *Days of Hope*, even if McGrath is not wedded to documentary realism in the same way as Allen, Garnett and Loach.

However, it is debatable whether all forms of political drama can maintain this kind of political optimism and certainty. One does not have to share MacCabe's critique to see that the notion of a political drama which is based on the appeal to a unitary historical subject, the working class, may seem less credible in some contexts than others. Thus, whilst McGrath's play draws on the continuing radical republicanism of Scottish history, a dramatist like Alan Bleasdale is faced with a different set of objective circumstances in attempting to capture the developing consciousness of the Liverpool working class in the 1980s.

Bleasdale's television drama, *Boys from the Blackstuff* was first broadcast by the BBC as a single play *The Blackstuff* in November 1981. Bleasdale was then commissioned to produce a series of five plays which were transmitted on Sunday evenings at 10.30 p.m. on BBC2 – hardly 'prime-time' viewing! The first episode, 'Jobs for the Boys' was broadcast in October 1982 and viewing figures soon registered unusually high interest for a drama spot at this time, so that the whole series was repeated almost immediately, in January 1983, on Tuesdays at 9.25 p.m. on BBC1 in the *Play for Today* spot. While Bleasdale insisted that *Boys from the Blackstuff* was not intended as an overt political statement,[9] a number of critics pointed out that, although the series did not necessarily address 'the dynamics of social change and transformation', it was militant in the way it exposed the plight of the unemployed and forced society to acknowledge its complicity in their fate, 'simply in speaking this sorrow out loud'.[10]

But *Boys* did not just tap the conscience of concerned sections of the society at large, it also seems to have gained an immense popularity with the people of Liverpool itself. Bleasdale's clever use of the

Liverpool footballers Graeme Souness and Sammy Lee in the night-club scene of 'Yosser's Story' helped to enhance the local appeal of that particular episode, and Yosser's refrain of 'Gi'us a job' was soon echoing round the Liverpool Kop. Above all, *Boys from the Blackstuff* was able to evoke a certain resonance, by the way in which it captured the spirit of a particular time and place, the crisis-ridden Liverpool of the early 1980s. The 'subject' of the drama was not simply the 'Boys', but Liverpool itself as a city under intense pressure. So the location shots of the derelict docks or the demolition of the Tate and Lyle refinery in 'George's Last Ride', were not just signifiers of a generalised backcloth of dereliction, but acted as *specific* records of the concrete destruction of people's working lives at that particular moment in time. This, then, was no dramatic recreation for visual effect, but actuality footage of Liverpool's devastation as it occurred, brick by brick.

As a result, *Boys from the Blackstuff* does not evince the quality of confidence and jauntiness which characterises *The Cheviot*. While the narrative explores the situation of the Liverpool working class as a collective subject, the group of 'Boys' who act as the microcosm of the class are not presented as a united entity with a concrete political vision. Rather they appear as separate individuals whose trajectories are plotted against a seemingly overwhelming background of chaos and despair. At times Bleasdale hints at the need for a collective memory of political struggle and in the final episode, 'George's Last Ride', the death of the old militant docker becomes a lament for the decline of traditional socialist ideals. Yet George's last defiant statement – 'I can't believe there is no hope, I can't'[11] is uttered against the backdrop of the deserted Albert Docks and at this point the visual narrative discourse seems to reiterate the overall 'truth' of the narrative, as articulated by the younger Chrissie, that George's dreams are merely fairy-tales, the stuff of 'Cabbages and Kings'.

Later on in the same episode, after George's funeral, Chrissie and his friend Loggo end up at a pub in a scene which rapidly deteriorates into bedlam and farce. The setting is a bricolage composed of various emblems from an older, more optimistic Liverpudlian past, with John Lennon's 'Imagine' playing on the jukebox and an ex-waiter 'Ronny Renaldo' whistling 'If I were a Blackbird', almost unnoticed by the rest of the bar, in a parody of old-time musical hall. It seems as if even the humour which has been Liverpool's saving grace in the past can no longer contain the awful tensions which are building up in the city, so that the scene takes on a macabre, semi-surrealistic air. The landlord, who is popping pills and drinking doubles all the time he is serving, eventually breaks when yet another 'redundancy party' arrive to drown their sorrows and he is last seen tottering across the road with his whisky glass still in his hand. Finally, the conventions of visual realism are dispensed with entirely when the redundancy party throw 'Ronnie Renaldo' through the window of the pub and he lands on the pavement, completely unscathed, still sitting on his chair and singing cheerfully. At this point it seems as if the codes of realist drama have broken down completely and that we are moving in a world which is visually, as well as metaphorically, a 'bad dream'.

What we witness here is, however, not some 'carnivalesque' disruption of realist narrative codes which opens the text to a moment of liberatory 'excess', *à la Bakhtin*. Rather, it acts as a visible demonstration of the overall message of *Boys from the Blackstuff*, that sentimental images of Liverpool and a traditional working class no longer accord with reality. What is enacted in the pub scene can be read as a 'transparent' visual metaphor for the seemingly undeniable 'truth': that chaos has entered the soul of Liverpool. There is, then, in Colin MacCabe's terms, a 'coincidence' between the visual and verbal discourses of the text, so that the visual madness being paraded in front of the viewer is immediately underscored by Chrissie's ironic aside: 'There isn't a soul there who is certified. They are all sane people'.[12] (The implication is that such madness is not freedom at all, but the product of terrible circumstances.)

We seem to be moving towards a position where *Boys From The Blackstuff* would be seen as fulfilling MacCabe's criteria for a 'classic realist' text, rather than a 'progressive' or 'Revolutionary' drama. After all, Bleasdale does not offer his audience a completely 'open' text with a plurality of narrative voices and, despite the excursions into surrealism and the absurd, there is no *major* disjuncture between the non-realist visual codes of the text and the search for some *meaning* at the heart of contemporary reality which unifies the narrative. Thus, like McGrath, Bleasdale utilises a mixture of realist and non-realist conventions to produce a drama with a dominant 'message', although the final prognosis of *Boys from the Blackstuff* seems at first sight to be much more pessimistic than that of *The Cheviot*.

Yet it would be wrong to leave *Boys from the Blackstuff* with the implication that it is a completely 'closed' drama, devoid of dialectical contradiction and productive dialogue. The danger of an overly formalist criticism, of the kind proffered by MacCabe is that it tends to develop rather crude indices for measuring the 'progressive' nature of literary or visual texts. For to fetishise the notion of aesthetic 'distanciation', and to argue in favour of texts in which the questioning of a traditional realist narrative viewpoint becomes the main point of articulation for the meaning of the text, is to lose sight of more subtle mechanisms for rendering the complexities and nuances of meaning.

This can be demonstrated by returning to our analysis of 'George's Last Ride', where closer inspection shows that the narrative may not be as clear and 'resolved', as we have tended to imply. Earlier we commented that the discursive devices adopted in the dock scene seemed to undermine George's socialist vision and reinforce a dominant narrative perspective, based on the assumption represented by Chrissie, that socialism was a 'dead' issue. Yet, if one places this scene in the context of the rest of the play, the issues seem to be more complex and unresolved and we are faced with a 'dialogical' text in which different 'voices' enter the arena, even if the final effect is not formally as spectacular as MacCabe would wish. Thus, while it is true that the visual narrative discourse of the dock scene undercuts George's speech on behalf of socialism, this must be juxtaposed with an earlier moment when George's wife lambasts their sons for half-hearted and defeatist talk. . . . At this point the camera reinforces Mrs Malone's viewpoint by looking down at her sons from a position of dominance and finishing with a shot of George nodding in agreement. Moreover, although Chrissie pokes fun at George's illusions by undercutting the conversation with playful rejoinders, he is of course present at George's death and he makes a passionate intervention at the funeral to cut aside the pathetic rhetoric of the priest and plead for George's humanism. For all Chrissie's cynicism, he seems to be on the point of assuming George's mantle at the end of the series, as evidenced in the following exchange with Loggo outside the pub:

CHRISSIE: George is dead.
LOGGO: So y've said.
CHRISSIE: Yeah. But George is dead.
LOGGO: I know, Chrissie, I know.
CHRISSIE: But . . . you know what he stood for, don't y'?
LOGGO: What do you mean?

(*Chrissie shakes his head.*)

CHRISSIE: Yea. Well that's dead an' all isn't it?[13]

If there is a 'resolution' to this exchange it is not the same as that of the dock scene. Now Chrissie's irony is directed at those who have forgotten what George stood for (including Chrissie himself until the shock of George's death). Hence one possible reading of *Boys from the Blackstuff* is that George's socialism represents a 'significant absence' from the Britain of the 1980s, even if it is not recoverable at present. Moreover although the narrative seems to be driven by a bleak vision of contemporary reality, it is punctuated at crucial moments by a quality of redemptive humanism. So, whilst the last scene of 'George's Last Ride' shows Chrissie leading the group of battered heroes through a blasted landscape, reminiscent of *Waiting for Godot* (with Yosser, the archetypal tramp, following on behind and rummaging in a dustbin), the final freeze-frame is lit by a beam of sunlight which can be read as signifying optimism and resilience.

Of the four dramas we have chosen to discuss, *Tenko* appears to be the most like a 'classic realist text'. There are no moments of distanciation – we are never encouraged to see the 'frame in the picture'; actors play only one character; the camera style is unobtrusive, the lighting is naturalistic, the sets and costumes appear to be fairly accurate reproductions of the place and time they are representing and so on. On a scale of progressiveness measured by degrees of anti-naturalism *Tenko* would undoubtedly come out as the least progressive. And yet of these four examples, *Tenko* with all its realist trappings was in some respects the most 'open' of the texts, the one which left the spectator with the most freedom to make judgements on the action unfolding before them.

Tenko shared with *The Cheviot, Days of Hope,* and *Pennies from Heaven* a desire to give a different account of a particular part of the past. Like them it constituted an intervention into the field of History. *Tenko* was inspired by Lavinia Warner's and John Sandilands' book *Beyond the Wire* which told the largely untold story about women who were imprisoned in Japanese internment camps in Sumatra in the Second World War. As the authors comment at the beginning of the book, this story is not only

a conventional story of hardship and suffering and danger, but [it can also be seen as] a singular experiment: a 'laboratory' in which there was a great deal to be learned about women. Long before it became fashionable to examine women for their strengths rather than their weaknesses, to ask what they are able to accomplish rather than underlining what they cannot, here was a case-history with all its elements neatly laid out.[14]

Unlike the other dramas we have discussed, *Tenko* was a serial rather than a one-off play. It was a serial which eventually ran to three series and a 'Christmas Special'. And unlike the others it was written by two women, Jill Hyem and Anne Valery, although it was produced and directed by men. Hyem and Valery were called in by the BBC after the first two episodes had been written by a man. 'They were, in effect, handed a cast of characters without history, motivation or charm and asked to continue the story' (*Guardian* 27 November 1984). Having agreed to do it Hyem and Valery were determined to avoid simply reproducing another war-yarn but with women as the central characters. They wanted to 'unpick the cliches of wartime experience'. In the *Guardian* interview Anne Valery comments in particular on their determination to resist the typical class stereotypes: 'You know, like the chirpy cockney chap in all PoW dramas who was always tugging a mental forelock, had a cheery philosophical remark for all occasions and died in the penultimate episode, sacrificing himself for an officer. What appalling nonsense.' They also wanted to use the opportunity to investigate racism which they did primarily through the Eurasian character of Christina. They decided to concentrate 'not on the heroics but on the day-to-day minutiae of distress and survival. And we showed how it is easy to be heroic for an hour, very difficult to be heroic for a year.'

In the whole series there is only one, minor attempt to escape. There are occasional instances of resistance to the Japanese captors, but these are not particularly significant, narratively speaking. The women do not all become feminists or socialists. *Tenko* is not about 'exceptional' women doing miraculous things we never knew they did, but more, as the authors of *Beyond the Wire* said, about:

Women obliged to express themselves according to their true natures, not in conformity with some imposed pattern. Women forced to set up their own structures, devise and apply their own politics and social order and discipline. . . . Women supporting and relying on each other, constantly testing the notion of sister-

hood, and able to compare it with its male equivalent.
. . .

All this under interminable stress: there was hunger, sickness and fatigue to contend with, and men beyond their worst imaginings, literally their masters in every aspect of their lives and backed up by rifles and bayonets. Ironically, it can now be seen that what was illuminated by the women's imprisonment, was its exact reverse – Women's Liberation.[15]

Hyem and Valery adopted a strategy of systematically breaking down the stereotypes which were established at the beginning of the series so that at least in part the first series seemed to be partly about stereotypes of women. This breaking-down of stereotypes foregrounded them as stereotypes, thus constituting a sort of auto-critique, but also had important consequences for audience involvement. While at the beginning of the series some fairly conventional types were established along class and age lines – for example Sylvia, Marion and Rose as the three middle/upper class British women. At the beginning Sylvia is outrageously racist, excessively patriotic and snobbish. But we are shown surprising things about her, ways in which she is both strong and vulnerable, and after a few weeks it was hard not to admire her capacity for resistance and her ability to change. Gradually she becomes understandable, acceptable almost, someone with whom we can at times identify. This process of unveiling the characters to the audience and of confounding audience expectations happens with most of the main characters. There are no heroes and even the villains (Mrs Van Meyer and Verna) are eventually shown to have redeeming characteristics.

The consequence of this approach is that from week to week the audience's sympathy tends to shift around between a number of characters; at times a favourite character would do something totally unacceptable or an unfavoured one would reveal some surprising quality. For instance, in the second series two of the stroppiest women were Dot and Blanche and since they very often held the most 'oppositional' view of things they were probably very attractive characters for many of the audience. But when it was found out that it was Lillian who had betrayed Rose in order to get food for her son, Dot and Blanche decide to wreak their own revenge and they attacked Lillian and cut off her hair. This produces a moment of considerable emotional confusion for the audience. Dot and Blanche's violence is both shocking and admirable; Lillian's crime is both

unforgivable and a pathetic sign of the madness to which her situation has reduced her. Lillian is neither a particular likable *nor* dis-
likable character; but for a few weeks the audience has watched as
her anxiety about her son's health changed from being a 'reasonable'
one to being one which (at one level only) is totally unreasonable
and neurotic. But what Lillian has been doing in her desperate all-
consuming attempts to ensure that her son Bobby has enough food,
is what all women have been taught to do as 'good' mothers. What
we see in Lillian is a woman acting out the pages of a child-care
manual. And so what we see in Lillian's collapse is the contradiction
she is faced with: to be loyal to her fellow-prisoners or to get food for
her child at all costs. And while we might not condone her betraying
Rose it is equally hard to condone Dot and Blanche's behaviour even
though at some level the audience must have wanted to do something similar to Lillian during the previous weeks as she became
increasingly pathetic and irritating. We are not given an easy answer
but nor can we evade the question; rather the authors force us to
address the issues the characters were addressing: how would we
feed our child? How would we punish Lillian?

What Hyem and Valery managed to do then was to find ways of
exploring 'the major moral and ethical issues which confront
humankind – euthanasia, abortion, suicide (and the Catholic Church's
position on them) and homosexuality' without producing an obviously 'correct line' on them. In this respect *Tenko* provided what
MacCabe claimed the classic realist text could not provide: it demonstrated the contradictions but left the audience to sort them out –
and, more importantly, to feel the need to sort them out.

In some important respects *Tenko* was more like a soap opera than
a war film. Firstly, its narrative concerns were the everyday lives of
the prisoners rather than their heroic activities and it was not organised around one single war-type story – such as an escape or trek or
conflict between the forces of good and evil; instead in the course of
the serial there were several stories and often two or three were in
play at once. Secondly, it did not have one or two main characters
whose feelings and views received privileged status and who became the main objects of identification, but rather a dozen or so
central characters all of whom were equally important and none of
whom were obviously the most likable or reasonable. None of the
characters ever achieved dominance either in terms of narrative time
devoted to her or in terms of becoming the holder of the authorial
voice. There was no uniquely privileged individual whose con-

sciousness was more sharply tuned or whose *angst* more finely-honed. No one's suffering was more important than anyone else's. The characters changed and grew, but they did not do so at the expense of other characters as is so often the case (consider for example *The Singing Detective*).

While it might seem that this is an insignificant matter, we would argue that such decisions can have important consequences. The sort of world produced by *The Singing Detective* is a world in which the individual is the sole bearer of truth surrounded by thoughtless, stupid, cruel, etc. people. In such a world the possibility of any form of collective action is not only inconceivable but also undesirable – why bother? By contrast the world which *Tenko*, and *The Cheviot* produce is a world in which the characters are on the whole respected and in which relationships with others are to be valued. In such a world collective action would be a meaningful option.

Perhaps the final point to be made about *Tenko* is that it demonstrated that popular forms such as soap operas do have considerable potential, and that there are no hard and fast rules about what will make a popular serial. Much to the surprise of the BBC *Tenko* was immensely popular – with men as well as with women. During the second series it was reported that viewing figures had risen to 14 million, four million higher than the figures for *Dynasty*, and approximately half the audience was estimated to be male. While some of its popularity with men might have been for dubious reasons (for example pleasure at seeing women as victims) it is hard not to agree with the view that its popularity mainly stemmed from the much more complex characterisation given to the women than is usual. What we would point to here is the argument that representations of women are generally much more stereotypical than are those of men, who are more likely to be presented as fully-rounded, complex individuals. Part of the pleasure of a series like *Tenko* was to offer the audience women they could respect and believe in. That men apparently responded as strongly to these different representations is surely extremely encouraging. However, to make this as a positive claim in support of *Tenko* may seem a little odd in the context of a debate about realism. Are we not simply falling into the trap of believing it is possible to 'show it as it really is', or 'show women as they really are'? Here it is worth remembering Richard Dyer's comment that 'for groups – the working class, women, blacks, gays – who have been excluded from culture's system of representation in all but marginal or demeaning forms the call for an end to identification figures is, if nothing else, premature.'[16] What this suggests is that what counts as progressive in one context is not necessarily progressive in another. In order to produce a useful way of thinking about what constitutes progressiveness we have to adopt a less rigid model than that offered by MacCabe.

CONCLUSION

One of the problems of talking about progressive drama is that we are always implicitly talking about 'effects' but the claims we are making about effectively are based on unspecified, and probably unexamined, assumptions. Undoubtedly one of the strengths of MacCabe's initial intervention was that he did at least try to describe what constituted progressive drama and identify the processes by which drama has effects.

MacCabe's model of the classic realist text established a set of equivalences between on the one hand a type of text and on the other a type of reader. This can be described graphically as follows:

Text	*Effect*	*Verdict*
Classic realist	Passive reader	Non-progressive text
Anti-naturalist	Active reader	Progressive text

The text 'produced' the reader and the type of reader produced led to a verdict about the progressiveness of the text. The model implied that only one form – the anti-naturalist, avant-gardist – had any real progressive potential. Popular realist drama such as soap-operas or sit-coms were assumed to posit a passive reader.[17] It is clear now that this notion of passive reading was altogether too simplistic and monolithic, and that MacCabe conflated three different processes which should have remained analytically separate.

Firstly, the term 'passive reader' refers to the ease with which audiences can make sense of a film or drama. The question it raises is, to what extent are conventional forms broken in order to distance the reader from the text and to make reading problematic? The more distancing effects there are, the more 'active' the reader has to be. Secondly, the 'passive reader' can be seen as a function of the notion of a hierarchy of discourses in which one emerges as the dominant one, and all contradictions are elided. For MacCabe this is an inherent feature of the classic realist text whereas we have argued that it is possible to have a realist text in which this does not happen. We have argued that while *Tenko* is realist in the sense that it is perfectly easy to understand (thereby implying a passive reader) it nonetheless leaves the reader with many contradictions and unresolved issues to think about (thereby implying an active reader). By contrast *The Cheviot* is more difficult to make sense of (active reader in sense 1) but leaves the reader little option but to adopt the position of the author (passive reader, sense 2). These two senses of 'passivity' both refer to the act of reading.

However, all readers are also involved in other activities and it is in the effects of texts on people as political beings that we are really interested. MacCabe's model implied that 'passive reader' was synonymous with political indifference or apathy. The third sense of 'passivity' then concerns what happens, or is deemed likely to happen, after the act of reading is over – when the credits roll. Has new knowledge or new energy been produced? Has the experience produced a new way to think or experience our own lives? Was it an enabling or a disabling experience? The assumption behind MacCabe's model was that only the anti-naturalist text would be capable of stimulating the production of new knowledge and avoid reproducing old forms of domination. It is perhaps here that MacCabe's argument seems most clearly to need reformulating in the light of specific texts.

In a recent essay Lawrence Grossberg has argued that 'theory in cultural studies can only be measured by its relationship to – and its enablement of strategic intervention into – the specific practices, structures and struggles of its place within the contemporary world'.[18] Thus, a theory's ability to 'cut into the real' (to use Benjamin's image) is measured by the political positions and trajectories it enables in response to the concrete contexts of power it confronts. We would argue, in a similar vein, that the 'progressiveness' of television drama, or any other cultural practice, cannot be established in an abstract fashion as the outcome of a set of ahistorical, formalist categories. Rather, one should look to the ways in which *particular* strategies enable *particular* audiences to make sense of their experience and hence to engage in concrete struggles to transform themselves and the world they inhabit. This means breaking with the notion that 'progressiveness' can be equated with any one *form* of drama – whether realist or Modernist – and moving to a position where it is possible to identify the inherent possibilities and potentialities of a variety of forms including naturalism.

Each of the texts we have considered can be assessed in this light. If these arguments are accepted then it is essential that we stop viewing texts in isolation as if their meanings were all contained within narrowly-defined boundaries and recognise that the meanings of a text derive in part from the context, the time and the place, in which it is consumed. The *contemporary* relevance of *Days of Hope* had less to do with whether it gave new insight into the past in a purely archival sense than to do with the connections it enabled readers to make between 1926 and 1974. Here it seems essential to insist on the importance of the context of viewing. In the early seventies the references to the General Strike of 1926 and to the Depression had a shocking resonance which could not but affect the way in which a drama was received and understood. In this sense it cannot be considered to be a 'closed' text because it reached out and addressed the present by provoking debate and conflict; it could not but be used by readers as a means of thinking about their present.

Similarly while *Boys from the Blackstuff* did not offer a direct political solution to the crisis of the early eighties, and presented an extremely depressing picture of Liverpool, this depression was not an excuse for resignation but rather a reminder that we do need hope and a vision of the future. While the text is open and dialogical, to the extent that it allows the audience to inhabit different subject positions and to identify with conflicting responses to the crisis, it constantly returns to the question of action and the need for change. Thus the narrative is driven by a debate about socialism and Bleasdale implies that the search for a collective subject of history is crucial, even though socialism must remain a 'significant absence' from the Britain of the early eighties. By contrast both *Tenko* and *The Cheviot* offer us a collective subject as the source of emotional identification here and now, *within* the narrative. Significantly both leave one feeling *energised* and optimistic.

Unfortunately the same cannot be said of Dennis Potter's dramas, *Pennies From Heaven* and *The Singing Detective*, where, contrary to what MacCabe's model predicts, the anti-naturalist techniques do not prove to be politically enabling. While we would accept that Potter's plays do offer important insights, for example into the workings of popular culture, these insights are grounded in a political position that seems oddly conservative and defeatist. The only conclusion which is open to the viewer at the end is to accept that there is nothing one can do to change the world – indeed it seems as if the only 'reality' is the ironic detachment of an elite band of superior intellectuals who have seen through the illusions of 'traditional' politics including those of the left. All one can do is enjoy the 'spectacle' of contemporary reality and delight in its absurdities.

This brings us to the final comment we would make on MacCabe's model of cultural practice and its relationship to the arena of social and political life. One of the most surprising things about MacCabe's piece is that although the terms 'progressive' and 'revolutionary' are key terms, and it feels as if there is a Marxist position somewhere behind the argument, there is in fact no actual politics there. We are told that art is concerned with 'the irreconcilable contradictions of life over and beyond the particular contradictions of the class struggle' and that it will be 'ill at ease in the class struggle, always concerned with an area of contradiction beyond the necessity of the present revolution'.[19] Yet this 'area of contradiction' is only described in the vaguest and most general terms ('the ineliminable contradictions of the sexes, the eternal struggle between Desire and Law')[20] and one is left with a gestural politics which is more concerned with the universal and timeless features of human existence than with concrete political struggle. It seems as if the 'prison house of language' looms larger than the fight against social and economic injustice in capitalist society. But, as our analysis of Potter has shown, an artistic or political strategy which concentrates exclusively on the interrogation of discursive forms and the 'frame in the picture' may not prove to be particularly enabling. Instead, radical art and politics must find ways of utilising textual innovations to address the specific needs of particular audiences in concrete historical situations. Only by uniting the levels of form, content and context in this fashion can radical texts act as 'resources of hope', encouraging individuals to become *active* in the struggle to transform the present and build the future.

Notes

1. Reprinted in *Theoretical Essays: Film, Linguistics, Literature* (Manchester: Manchester University Press, 1985), pp. 33–57.
2. Sometimes translated as 'alienation effect', but more accurately rendered as 'estrangement effect'.
3. Colin MacCabe, op. cit., p. 44.
4. See Raymond Williams, 'A Lecture on Realism', *Screen*, Vol. 18, no. 1 (Spring 1977) and 'Realism and Non-Naturalism' (Edinburgh International Television Festival, 1977); Colin McArthur, 'Days of Hope',

Screen, Vol. 16., no. 4 (Winter 1975/6) and *Television and History* (London: British Film Institute, 1978).

5.   See Richard Dyer et al., *Coronation Street* (London: British Film Institute, 1981).

6.   Stuart Hall, 'Television as a Medium and Its Relation to Culture', cited in G. W. Brandt (ed.), *British Television Drama* (Cambridge: Cambridge University Press, 1981).

7.   Dennis Potter, 'Realism and Non-Naturalism' in *Official Programme of the Edinburgh International Television Festival* (1977), p. 37.

8.   G. Murdoch, in *Media, Culture and Society*, 1980, no. 2, p. 152.

9.   *BFI Dossier: Boys From the Blackstuff* (London: British Film Institute, 1983), p. 19.

10.   Ibid., p. 23.

11.   Alan Bleasdale, *Boys from the Blackstuff*, ed. David Self (London: Hutchinson, 1985), p. 253.

12.   Ibid., p. 273.

13.   Ibid., p. 272.

14.   See Lavinia Warner and John Sandilands, *Women Beyond the Wire* (London: Hamlyn, 1982), p. 15.

15.   Ibid., p. 15.

16.   Richard Dyer, *Stars* (London: British Film Institute, 1979), p. 184.

17.   This view of popular drama and its inevitably passive reader has since been challenged on a number of fronts and it is clear that this notion of the passive reader is basically untenable.

18.   Lawrence Grossberg, 'It's a Sin: Politics, Post-Modernity and the Popular' in L. Grossberg (ed.), *It's a Sin* (Sidney, 1988), p. 9.

19.   Colin MacCabe, op. cit., p. 45.

20.   Ibid., p. 50.

4

Shelagh Delaney's *A Taste of Honey* as Serious Text: A Semiotic Reading

EDWARD J. ESCHE

A Taste of Honey has a rich stage and publishing history. It was a success when first performed by Theatre Workshop, in the Theatre Royal at Stratford, London on 27 May 1958; and soon became a 'smash hit' when it transferred to Wyndham's Theatre, London on 10 February 1959. In the same year, the play made the transatlantic cultural leap to New York; it has since never left the theatre as a performance text and continues to receive professional revivals.[1] The play is still in print as a script on both sides of the Atlantic,[2] but it has undoubtedly gained its widest popular dissemination through an adapted film version.[3] American financiers initially offered to back the film if Audrey Hepburn played the leading role of Jo,[4] which is an indication of what a hot cultural property the film was perceived to be. The play text achieved true canonical status in the early eighties with widespread school syllabus selection. The two decade time-lag here is hard for me to explain beyond the obvious observation that the eighties brought us back to problems of mass unemployment and homelessness. Perhaps detailed work on which examination boards selected the play and when might net some more precise answers, but whatever the explanation the canonisation was completed in the eighties with the publication of student texts and accompanying study notes volumes.[5] The play has, however, not caught the attention of academe: we are now over thirty years away from the first appearance of *A Taste of Honey*, and as far as I can discover, only one article has been written which was devoted entirely to the play.[6] There have, of course, been numerous 'mentions' of it in book studies and articles on modern British drama, but it has not been given the serious academic attention as a cultural product in its own right which is usually accorded to similar works of such initial and sustained success. This chapter begins to redress that imbalance by providing an approach to the play through a limited (and sometimes questioning) application of the soft semiotics recently articulated by Martin Esslin.[7] It concludes by claiming the stature of tragedy for the reading that emerges, not because the play fits a mould in a Greco-Elizabethan tradition, but because the term 'tragedy' has been hijacked to that tradition for far too long; I want it back, and with it the status of seriousness accorded its object.

CRITICAL BACKGROUND

The following is a typical example of comment on *A Taste of Honey*:

> [The play] feels spontaneous but it is also ingenuous and inconclusive, with some dreadfully artificial lines. However, it is very haunting, in parts beautifully written, and with a deceptive structural toughness that goes beyond the use of music-hall technique, the direct address to the audience, and the episodic form of a variety act. It is easy to see why the play has become one of the staples of secondary-school English classes; engaging and easy to read, it remains exactly what it was – a play written by a young person about a world in which adults are suspicious and grasping and the young are self-absorbed and looking for independence. The cult of youth was in the ascendant as well as the cult of working-class style.[8]

This is damning with faint praise indeed, and a model of most of the criticism the play has received since its creation. It is fraught with traditional impressionistic responses. The vague generalities of praise ('spontaneous', 'haunting', containing 'structural toughness') are more than countered by the equally vague citings of limitation ('dreadfully artificial lines', 'in *parts* beautifully written'), and the final judgement is conclusively dismissal: the play remains fodder worthy only of the secondary-school syllabus, which is understandable because, after all, it was written by a '*young* person' and continually reveals the limitations of the 'cult of *youth*'. The phrase 'it remains exactly what it was' authoritatively places the work as little more than an historical document unworthy of resonances accorded to (it is implied) 'better' writing – the ability to move somehow outside of its time. So much for *A Taste of Honey*. The curious thing about this thumbnail response is its tone of received opinion: we all know this to be self-evident – but do we? Where are the original arguments which might have established or even proved these conclusions?

A search through the critical history, even as scarce as it is, reveals that early comment was lively and varied. Lindsay Anderson, one of the leading theatre and film directors of the day, noted the Brechtian playing of Avis Brunnage which 'managed most skilfully to combine the broadest, eye-on-the-gallery caricature, with straight-forward, detailed naturalism',[9] while Colin MacInnes, that fine sociological recorder of the fifties, remarked that 'The play gives a great thirst for more authentic portraits of the mid-twentieth-century English world'.[10] Raymond Williams, Britain's most influential literary critic, actually singled out *A Taste of Honey* as the most effective example of the general characteristic of all the new British drama in the fifties, which he described as a new sound or new wave of feeling, 'that of a general restlessness, disorganization and frustration'.[11] Clearly, the play engaged some of the leading minds of the time, but for whatever reasons, and one may well be that most theatrical revivals have stressed (in my view quite inappropriately) the naturalistic possibilities of performance,[12] the variety of critical response has simply not survived. What has come through to us is something much more limited, another strain of criticism which existed beside, sometimes even within the same critical writings as the ones just cited. In this argument the play is first and foremost about characters in relation to their world. Jo, for instance, is often described as having a 'working-class resilience that will always pull her through';[13] more generally, life goes on 'with a boisterous appetite for tomorrow'.[14] Delaney herself seems to support such a view when she refers to the characters' ability to 'take in their stride whatever happens to them and remain cheerful'.[15] So, the 'feel' or 'impression' of the play becomes comfortable: it had 'a feeling for life that [was] positive';[16] 'It deals joyfully with what might in other hands, have been a tragic situation'.[17] There is an overwhelming consensus in the critical writing that the play is an example of cheery chaps, or rather chapesses, muddling through a difficult world, and, by extension, cheering us spectators with their resilience. But I teach *A Taste of Honey* to third-year degree students of all ages and backgrounds at Anglia College, and their fascination with the play rests in other, less centrally-addressed areas of interest. Not a single student in my experience comes away from the play thinking that they have seen or read a cheery or cheering text, and neither do I. The following is an attempt to offer a critical reading (and it is only one) which somehow accounts for personal responses so vastly different from received critical opinion.

SOFT SEMIOTICS

Martin Esslin is humble about the claims of a semiotic critical theory: 'this *semiotic* approach is, basically, extremely simple and practical'.[18] He is fairly distrustful of the extreme claims of semiotics as a critical tool, but highly supportive of it as a way of explaining precisely how drama achieves its effects.[19] He offers a general compilation of various theories for use, stressing what is similar; thus the idea of *which* semiotic theory we need to address does not really arise. Esslin's approach, his soft semiotics, can be applied to *A Taste of Honey* to clear away broadly impressionistic responses to the play and replace them with explanations of specific responses which will in turn accumulate to an interpretation based on a reasoned argument. But we should approach the exercise with caution, because as we break the 'total image down into the separate items of information that have been present, and convert the multidimensional instant impression into a linear sequence of separate ingredients', we should remember that 'for each member of the audience this impact of the image, at any given moment, will be different, simply because different people notice different things in a different sequence' (Esslin, pp. 36–8). In other words, the reception given to separate bits of information will vary from spectator (or reader) to spectator. Of course, there is a question begged here: how are we receiving the bits of information? The text that we address in most cases is a script, but with a play it could well be a workshop version,[20] a professional production or even a film adaptation. It is a curious fact that most criticism written on a play of many years' popularity is usually based upon a script with a remembered or projected view of professional performance. That is what I am about to do in this chapter, but I wish to stress that such an approach is *not* the only one, and certainly not a privileged one. Finally, the 'script' in the case of *A Taste of Honey* masquerades as stable, but we know that it was not when first presented for performance: we know that it underwent considerable collective revision,[21] the precise amount of which will remain a mystery until further research. And even as we look at the printed text today, it may appear to be stable, but it is not. What, for instance, is the precise meaning of 'Music'? The choice a director (cerebral or professional) makes determines the reading of the action, but we shall come to that later.

Esslin divides the signs of drama into six different groupings for purposes of his discussion: icon, index, symbol; the frame; the actor; visuals and design; the words; music and sound. The first of these is a set of basic signs first articulated by Pierce as early semiotic theory.[22] An icon is a sign that represents exactly what it signifies: a table on a stage is an icon of a table in reality. An index is a type of sign which derives its meaning from a relationship of contiguity to the object it depicts (Esslin, p. 44): a frightened look is a gesture that could be described as an index because it points to something causing the fright. A symbol is a sign which derives meaning entirely from convention: the colour of white, for instance, is a Western symbol of purity or happiness, whereas it is an Oriental colour symbol of mourning. I will return to the notion of the frame later. The next four areas are what will concern us for most of what follows. We will be applying each of the four groups of signs which Esslin notes to *A Taste of Honey*. Incidentally, he claims that the order in which these groupings are presented corresponds precisely to the weight each has in the dramatic spectacle; so, for instance, the visuals are always of more weight than words in the decoding or communicative process of interpretation.

THE ACTOR

'The actor is the iconic sign *par excellence*' (Esslin, p. 56) which we read on at least three levels. First, s/he is a 'real person'; second, s/he is a transformation made up and trained to appear to be the fictional character that s/he is playing; third, s/he is the 'fiction' itself, for which s/he stands as a representation. So Jo is, on this first level, the real actress Caroline Milmore (in the case of the recent Royal Exchange Theatre Company revival). On the second level, Jo is the fictional character of that name in *A Taste of Honey* being played by Caroline Milmore, who has been made up to appear an adolescent and who uses her acting expertise to interpret the character. On the third level, Jo becomes the fiction for which she stands; the job of critic is to identify precisely what that is and how its meaning is established. On this level the sign Jo is a blending of everything in the script and everything in the actress that contributes to the por-

trayal on the stage. There may also be a further category of signification: Jo may become a representative of a class of individuals for
which she stands (adolescent working-class girls, buoyant female
spirits, etc.), but this level, although a corollary of the third, seems to
me a limitation of meaning to merely one of many interpretations,
though of course class typicality is a strength which has appealed to
critics such as Piscator, Brecht and Lukàcs.

The actor has at her/his disposal a wide range of techniques and,
for lack of a better word, accidentals to create her/his fiction. Among
the techniques Esslin lists vocal interpretation, facial expression,
gesture and movement, make-up and costume (pp. 63–4). Accidentals
would include various uncontrollable things, such as involuntary
responses (blushing, a twitch of the eye), unintentional suggestiveness (voice timbre may suggest hardness to a member of the audience). Most of this is very difficult to address as I am mainly reacting
to and writing about the published script, but we should always be
aware of the possibilities available to us. Esslin probably underesti-
mates the role of accidentals in semiotic encoding because the line
between what is controlled and what is uncontrollable is a blurred
one: it becomes absolutely broken when we consider suggestiveness
associated with accidentals such as skin pigmentation (an Asian Jo),
mobility (a handicapped Jo) or accent (an Irish Jo). Again, I make my
choice and try not to pay any attention to accidentals here; I apply
theory severely and comment only upon the technical aspects that
are embedded in the script. One of those is certainly movement, and
in particular, entrances and exits. Quite often the characters dance
on and off stage. This can be read iconically as simple dance movement; it can be read also as an index pointing to its own noteworthi-
ness because it is an unusual form of entering or leaving most
spaces; finally, it can be read as a symbol indicating that we are not
in the realm of naturalistic drama, but rather in something much
more akin to an eclectic style somewhere between Brechtian technique and naturalism.

One of the aspects of the actor-as-sign that Esslin does not address
fully is that of the body. He does mention that as a fiction Juliet is
supposed to be beautiful; it does not matter if the actress who might
play her is not beautiful – the spectator will understand her as
beautiful nevertheless (p. 58). But he does not attempt further explanation of sexual signification. For instance, take the example of one
actor slapping another in the face. If a male strikes a male, or a
female strikes a male, or even a female strikes a female, we may have

(broadly speaking) a similar response, but if a male strikes a female, the action probably registers more violently to us than the other three combinations. Why? Because of the sexual codings of the bodies administering and receiving the blows: the sex of each makes a large difference to our reactions. Similarly, the sex of the body, in this case that of Jo, is charged with meaning, the most important of which in the play may well be its procreative function, because, during the play that body changes before our eyes as it swells through pregnancy; by the final curtain, the body is in labour and about to give birth. In feminist criticism, this particular sign of the actor's sex is probably of more importance than any other. One feminist critic, Michelene Wandor, notes that 'the gender bias in this play is reversed from that of most other plays', and concludes, rather lamely, that 'the family of women appears to be the one constant factor, but even that is fraught . . .'.[23] It is clearly much more than fraught, as we shall see, but we should recognise that here again, possibilities of interpretation exist. Feminist critics rarely address this play, but when they do it is with the understanding that the central mother–daughter relationship is at worst 'problematic' and at best 'loving'.[24] As we shall see, this strain of feminist reading wilfully neglects some of the social concerns which are at the heart of the play and directly *determined* by that central female relationship, but such is criticism: ours is a wilful practice.

Wandor reiterates an important point originally made by MacInnes about character grouping. She notes that the female characters carry our main interest in this play; the male characters seem to come and go, attaching or disengaging themselves from the central pair.[25] The play opens with the entrance of a mother and daughter, which is a pairing that is highly charged, if only because of the absences it might suggest. The grouping points to a family, but the father is missing. The absent male coupled with the squalor of the set might indicate a single-parent family. As we follow this particular sign-system of character-grouping through the play, we watch it disintegrate (as Helen leaves Jo for Peter), re-form near the end of the play (when Helen comes back to the flat after she has been thrown out of Peter's house) and then disintegrate again at the very end of the play (when she leaves Jo in the first pangs of labour to get a drink). The mother and daughter grouping thus breaks twice, and the second time it occurs at a weighted, some would maintain the most weighted moment of the play – at the end. The fact that the moment is also one that is heavily charged for the female body (when it begins labour

for the first time) is crucially important. I have never directly experienced this moment, but most (not all) women I have spoken to
about it describe this time as a moment when they need support. In
the play script (and we cannot fantasise here about what may or may
not happen afterwards), Jo gets no support: she is abandoned.[26] The
simple charting of the sign-system of character grouping defines the
female relationship between Jo and Helen as one of abandonment,
and we can only conclude at those final moments that Jo is left
isolated because there are no other alternative character groupings
possible, such as those we saw earlier in the play between Jo and
Jimmie or between Jo and Geoff.

VISUALS AND DESIGN

The most important visual aspect of *A Taste of Honey* is its set.
Throughout the entire play we are in a cheap, rundown flat in
Salford in the 'today' of 1958. In semiotic terms, what is a realistic set
is of course not the thing itself, but a sign for *what may be* a realistic
type of flat in Lancashire, and that type of flat must be read as
squalid. The set in turn codes the bodies on it; if it is squalid, then
those on it are probably too poor to be anywhere else, or at the very
least, must have a definite reason for inhabiting that space. One
other thing that we can say with certainty is that this set clearly
defines itself as other than the comfortable space we inhabit in the
theatre as we view the play. The set does change throughout the
performance, from the filthy squalor of the opening, to the inhabit-
able organisation after the arrival of Jo and Helen, to the comfortable, almost homely atmosphere created by Jo alone and afterwards
with Geoff.

Another important set of visual signs in the play is the properties.
Two of them deserve specific attention: the drawings and the flower
bulbs. Jo's drawings are mentioned twice, and both times they function as indices pointing to the character as interested in art; considering the setting, such activity might be thought out-of-the-ordinary.
But the props also function as symbols indicating both times that
they are mentioned that Jo has a potential for creative work, even if
it needs to be developed, as Geoff says. Of course, one of the points
of the drawings is that they remain static: they are not added to or
developed, and thus the potential that they indicate is never realised. The flower bulbs are another set of properties in the play,

probably the most conspicuous. Jo brings them to the flat to plant because she likes flower boxes. As icons, they are simply flowers, but they are also indices pointing to a major difference between Jo and Helen, that of aesthetic taste. Jo would rather try to decorate her environment with varieties of pleasing colour. (The shading of the light bulb can be read in exactly the same way.) The bulbs also take on further meanings of symbol when they are discovered by Geoff much later in the play, hidden under the sofa in the flat. At that point, they are dead. Quite clearly, they are symbols of, again, the potentiality of growth, and through growth, of the potentiality of beauty. The two properties work as reinforcements of each other, and both indicate processes that end in exactly the same way: in failure and loss – the bulbs die and the drawings are relics of an activity that we never see taken up again.

WORDS

Words and articulation are the privileged areas of the literary critic, but they are often far less powerful as signs in drama than either actors, actions or properties. Esslin consistently emphasises the 'principle of the primacy of the actor and action' (p. 75), and he is absolutely correct to do so. There is nothing controversial about this. Jimmie *says* that he will come back to Jo, but he does not; we then read his behaviour, not by what he said but by what he did, by the action, not the words of the play. But many (one might even say most) critics have been reluctant to read the fiction that is 'Jo' in the same way; her words and words about her are regularly given primacy over the other signs of the play. She *says* she is independent, but the signs of the play point in exactly the opposite direction.

Again, Esslin's simplicity is admirable in stating a position for the examination of words in plays: 'in drama the meaning of the words ultimately derives from the *situation* from which they spring' (pp. 86–7). So, language is never straight; it must be read in a variety of contexts. In *A Taste of Honey* Delaney seems to be using the technique of paralleling similar phrases and thoughts to generate meanings. Peter's arrogant assertion to Helen when proposing marriage is, 'You can't afford to lose a man like me' (p. 17), which parallels Jimmie's assertion to Jo later in the play: 'There isn't another man like me anywhere. I'm one on his own' (p. 36). And both men abandon the women to whom they pledge allegiance, thereby proving that the positive value that they seem to be claiming for themselves is entirely spurious. Jo too asserts her own uniqueness immediately after Jimmie's lines quoted above and later when she is with Geoff: 'There's only one of me like there's only one of you', and Geoff agrees, 'We're unique!' (p. 50). But are the confident assertions that these two attractive characters in the play make any more creditable than those made by the two unattractive male characters? In Geoff's case it is hard to be sure, but Jo proves to be one in a pattern. Again, we have to look to parallels for meaning.

Jo is clearly frightened of becoming like her mother, and is pleased when Jimmie tells that she is not at all like her (pp. 37–8), but in the first scene of the play when we see them both together, there is a parallel of action: shortly after we hear Helen reminisce about her first job 'in a tatty little pub' (p. 12) we hear Jo say that *she* wants to get a job in a pub, which will be her first job. Much later in the play, Geoff warns Jo that she may turn out exactly like her mother, which Jo denies (p. 72), but the action of the scene underscores Geoff's observation that she already is similar in many ways. Just before the exchange between the two characters, Jo has become frightened and has asked Geoff to hold her hand. She reminisces about her earlier life when she 'used to try and hold my mother's hands, but she always used to pull them away from me' (pp. 71–2). Then when Geoff tells her that she and her mother are similar, '*She pushes his hand away*' (p. 72). Jo's action is a direct parallel to that of Helen. And there are larger parallels of action, the most important probably is that of the two pregnancies. We are told that Helen became pregnant with Jo after her first sexual experience (pp. 43–4); similarly, we see that Jo has become pregnant with her child after her first sexual experience. Clearly, Jo's claim for uniqueness cannot be proven on the level of these parallel actions of behaviour.

MUSIC AND SOUND

There is no musical notation in any of the published scripts of *A Taste of Honey* currently available. Stage directions in the scripts simply refer to '*Music*', which can obviously be quite versatile and entertaining, but which also remains as vacant of meaning as those in most Shakespearian texts. Clearly, a director has a range of options as to how the music works in any given performance, and since this area of the script is utterly malleable, I do not propose to discuss it at length. Sounds are a slightly different matter. There are plenty in the script, ranging from standard situations of farce, such as offstage business of exploding a gas cooker or tumbling through pots and pans, to something altogether more resonant. At the end of the play Jo goes into labour, and as she does she screams in pain. After the scream, a stage direction tells us that *'Children sing outside.'* Again, the actual words or rhyme being sung would encode this stage direction in a variety of ways, but since that information is not specified, we can only, in fact, concentrate on the stage direction itself. It is a sound quote from earlier in the play, where we heard it twice in the same scene between Geoff and Jo. In the first instance (p. 54), it triggered a general discussion about child neglect, and in the second instance (p. 57), it forms an ironic background to Geoff's attempt to 'start something' with Jo. In both cases the children's singing underscores Jo's pregnancy and the future it will bring, a future which combines the fact of the physical presence of the child and also the possibility that it may join the crowd of 'filthy children' making the sound. Thus the final image, of the female body in labour and deserted quite literally as Helen flees the flat for a drink, must be read against these sounds.

THE FRAME

We can now challenge several of the interpretations offered for *A Taste of Honey* by considering the idea of the frame. Framing devices exist in a variety of forms, and they all place the play in a context which generates expectancy in us as spectators/readers. The performance space itself is often a potent frame: going out to a West End theatre creates a different set of expectations from going out to a town hall in Lancashire. The acting company is another important frame: we would expect that a play done by The Women's Theatre Group would emphasise women's concerns, while we would not necessarily make that assumption if the same play was being presented by, for instance, The Royal Shakespeare Company. Reviews also function as powerful frames: raves create the expectation of 'good' theatre, while slatings do just the opposite. And there are probably many more frames which set various contexts for us (including that created by publishing a play in a student edition), but one of the most important frames in literary criticism remains that of genre. Unlike many critics, I think that such labels are important. The 'biggest' and most 'important' label has traditionally been that of 'tragedy', and with it the inference that the tragic play contains highly serious matter. We saw that Kenneth Tynan's impression was characteristic of the received reading of the play: 'It deals joyfully with what might in other hands have been a tragic situation.'[27] But in the reading that is outlined above, the notion of joy and cheeriness has no place, mainly because I avoided discussing the element of the jokes. The jokes are often very funny, but most of them are verbal signs, and are, according to Esslin, not necessarily as heavily weighted in their meaning as some of the other signs I have been discussing. Now Tynan, more clearly than any other critic, articulates avoidance of an issue I want to address: he tells us that he has chosen to avoid using the term tragedy for the play. He begs a huge question: what would a tragic situation look like in this play? I believe it looks like the situation in which Jo finds herself at end of the play.

Arthur Miller defines the tragic figure, and by extension her/his situation, as one who 'engages . . . questions . . . whose answers define humanity and the right way to live so that the world is a home, instead of a battle-ground or a fog in which disembodied spirits pass each other in an endless night'.[28] Those kinds of questions are raised directly at the end of *A Taste of Honey*. The limited semiotic reading of the play that I have offered exposes a pattern of overall action that could be described as cyclical,[29] accompanied by a downward movement – Jo repeats the pattern of her mother and various symbols of growth end in ruin. The tragic experience is not necessarily just of Jo as class typicality (although that aspect is included), but it is, again, of the fiction that she represents, and that fiction is of an individual *young* woman trapped in a downward spiral of social and economic decay. The most chilling feature of this tragedy is that it is repetitive, and, again, not simply for Jo. As she screams in the pain of labour, the process, the cycle of single mother trapped in poverty with its inherent possibility of neglect, may be starting all over again for the child about to be born. Such action is a clear and powerful articulation of abuse breeding abuse; the jokes simply serve the function of papering over or disguising a pattern of social fracture, and thereby deepening rather than negating the tragic experience. There is resilience and humour throughout, but there is no solution offered to the cycle of decay.

WAYS FORWARD

This article has only scratched the surface of an extremely rich and complex play worthy of detailed and extended study. Let us hope that we will cease to read comments such as that the play has no 'ideas', or that it has 'no clear-cut message';[30] but much more needs to be done. In particular, the historical context needs to be more fully charted; I suspect that Jo's claim for uniqueness could be justified on the grounds of her choice of a black sailor and a gay art student as male companions. What criteria (or opportunisms?) were at work in Joan Littlewood's choice of Delaney's script for performance by the Theatre Royal? The Brechtian influences also deserve much further examination; a study of the first musical score would be of major importance here. And as we all watch the intoxicating events in East Europe, notion(s) of class typicality will engage our thought. The question of speech prefixes is fascinating: 'Helen' is one which wears a dubious weight of history; 'Jo' is sexually indeterminate; 'Boy' is extraordinary when applied, as it is in the play, to a black man. More work needs to be done on performance generally with such a rich revival history. Finally, why has the play 'resided' on school syllabuses and not been addressed in any substantial way by the higher establishments of education and academe?

Notes

1. Including those by The Royal Exchange Theatre Company, Manchester, first performance 2 March 1989, Director Ian Hastings, and by the Nottingham Playhouse, first performance 25 January 1989.
2. Shelagh Delaney, *A Taste of Honey* (London: Methuen, first published January 1959, new edition April 1959) and Shelagh Delaney, *A Taste of Honey* (New York: Grove, 1959).
3. *A Taste of Honey*, screenplay by Shelagh Delaney and Tony Richardson, directed by Tony Richardson (1961).
4. Pam Cook (ed.) *The Cinema Book* (London: British Film Institute: 1985), p. 49.
5. Shelagh Delaney, *A Taste of Honey* (With a Commentary and Notes by Glenda Leeming), Methuen Student Editions (London: Methuen, 1982); Shelagh Delaney, *A Taste of Honey*, ed. Ray Speakman (London: Heinemann, Methuen, 1989) in The Hereford Plays series: Susan Quilliam, *A Taste of Honey* by Shelagh Delaney (Harmondsworth: Penguin, 1987) in Penguin Passnotes; John Jenkins, *A Taste of Honey* by Shelagh Delaney (London: Pan Books, 1988) in Brodie's Notes.

6.   Arthur K. Oberg, 'A Taste of Honey and the Popular Play', *Wisconsin Studies in Popular Literature* (now *Contemporary Literature*) 7, 1966, 160–67.

7.   Martin Esslin, *The Field of Drama: How the Signs of Drama Create Meaning on Stage and Screen* (London: Methuen, 1987).

8.   Colin Chambers and Mike Prior, *Playwrights' Progress: Patterns of Postwar British Drama* (London: Amber Lane Press, 1987), pp. 37–8.

9.   Lindsay Anderson, *A Taste of Honey*, Review in Charles Marowitz, Tom Milne, Owen Hale (eds), *New Theatre Voices of the Fifties and Sixties: Selections from* Encore *Magazine 1956–1963* (London: Eyre Methuen reissue, 1981), p. 80; reprinted from *Encore*, 1958.

10. Colin MacInnes, 'A Taste of Reality' in *England, Half England* (London: MacGibbon & Kee, 1961), p. 206; reprinted from *Encounter*, April 1959: for new cultural mappings of the fifties see also Rick Rylance (ed.), *Ideas and Production: A Journal in the History of Ideas*, 'Culture and Experience in the 1950s', Vols IX–X.

11. Raymond Williams, 'New English Drama' in John Russell Brown (ed.), *Modern British Dramatists: A Collection of Critical Essays* (Englewood Cliffs, New Jersey: Prentice-Hall, 1968), pp. 32–3; reprinted from *Twentieth Century*, CLXX, no. 1011 (1961), 169–80.

12. See Helene Keyssar, *Feminist Theatre* (London: Macmillan, 1984), p. 42.

13. Anderson, p. 79.

14. Kenneth Tynan, *A Taste of Honey*, review in Gareth and Barbara Lloyd Evans (eds), *Plays in Review 1956–1980: British Drama and Its Critics* (London: Batsford Academic and Educational, 1985), p. 66; reprinted from *The Observer*, 1 June 1958.

15. Methuen Student Edition, p. xvii.

16. MacInnes, p. 205.

17. Kenneth Tynan, in *A Taste of Honey*, Royal Exchange Theatre Company Programme (Manchester, 1989), unpaginated; reprinted from *A View of the English Stage 1944–1956* (London: Methuen, 1984).

18. Esslin, p. 10.

19. See Keir Elam, *The Semiotics of Theatre and Drama* (London and New York: Methuen, 1980) for such extreme claims.

20. For an excellent discussion about workshop practice, see Simon Shepherd, 'Acting Against Boredom: Some Utopian Thoughts on Workshops' in Lesley Aers and Nigel Wheale (eds), *Shakespeare in the Changing Curriculum* (London: Routledge, forthcoming).

21. See John Russell Taylor, *Anger and After: A Guide to the New British Drama* (London: Methuen, 1962; revised 1969), pp. 131–2 and Howard Goorney, *The Theatre Workshop Story* (London: Eyre Methuen, 1981), pp. 109 and 112.

22. One of the best introductions to semiotic theory is Kaja Silverman, *The Subject of Semiotics* (Oxford and New York: Oxford University Press, 1983), which includes explanations of these terms based on Pierce's own *Collected Papers*, pp. 19–25.

23. Michelene Wandor, *Look Back in Gender: Sexuality and the Family in Post-War British Drama* (London and New York: Methuen, 1987),

pp. 41–2.

24. For instance, see Wandor, pp. 39–43 and Keyssar, pp. 38–43.

25. MacInnes, p. 205; Wandor, p. 40; Keyssar, p. 39.

26. For readings that do not view the ending as despair see Williams, Wandor and Keyssar.

27. See note 14 above.

28. Arthur Miller, 'Introduction' to *Collected Plays* (New York: The Viking Press, 1957), p. 32.

29. See Oberg, p. 164 for the hint of repetition that has led me to note this pattern.

30. Taylor, p. 132 and Leeming, Methuen Student Edition, p. xvi, respectively.

5

The Eye of Judgement: Samuel Beckett's Later Drama

AUDREY McMULLAN

Beckett's dramatic works, particularly the later plays, with their shadowy figures continually failing to complete the narrative which they are compelled to utter under the searching stare of the theatrical spotlight, seem to stage the ruins of representation, and yet bear witness to the continuing force of its laws. Deconstructionist theory argues that these laws are rooted in the hierarchical framework of classical metaphysics, which has determined the construction of self and other, truth and falsehood, presence and semblance, as well as the quest for knowledge and meaning.[1] Many of Beckett's later plays seem to be founded on a conflict between the disintegration of this framework, and the repeated attempts to enforce authority through the positions of perceptual mastery and judgement which representation, the theatre in particular, appears to offer.

It is in their interrogation of the apparently fixed boundaries and categories of traditional representation that certain discourses of contemporary literary theory can provide a relevant context for an investigation of Beckett's dramatic practice. I shall be referring principally to theories of deconstruction and psychoanalysis, in an attempt to analyse Beckett's investigation of the positing of authority through the order of representation, and the strategies used in his plays to frame or disrupt this order.

Instead of the hierarchical structure of binary oppositions ordered in relation to the central place of the Logos, Derrida substitutes the concept of a decentred structure, where there are no fixed points of reference or certainty, producing a dynamic and unlimited play of meaning between terms:

Henceforth it was necessary to begin thinking that there was no

82

centre, that the centre could not be thought in the form of a present-being, that the centre had no natural site, that it was not a fixed locus but a function, a sort of nonlocus in which an infinite number of sign-substitutions came into play.[2]

The emphasis on interplay radically challenges the assumption of any definitive position of authority from which to determine truth, meaning or knowledge, since there are no longer any privileged terms. On the one hand, Beckett's plays frame the attempt to assume a central position of authority in relation to the representation and judgement of self and others – his theatre often features tyrannical creators who attempt to exert control over the body or text of their creatures.[3] However, Beckett also plays with and questions such apparently polarised roles. A recurrent pattern in his plays is the establishment of binary positions (self and other, torturer and victim, performance and narrative) which are subsequently undermined through the performance.

The theories of Julia Kristeva help to create a link between the destabilisation of positions of knowledge, meaning and power in Beckett's work, and his equally characteristic destabilisation of structures of identity. Kristeva links the assumption of a position of identity from which perception and judgement can be determined with the order of representation or the symbolic order, which includes the laws of language:

Although they intervene at different levels in phenomenological reflection, *seeing* and *judging* prove to be at one in positing the transcending Ego, which will posit transcendental intention and intuition. A *posited* Ego is articulated in and by *representation* (which we shall call the sign) and *judgement* (which we shall call syntax) so that, on the basis of this position it can endow with meaning a space posited as previous to its advent.[4]

Such positions of perception and judgement, however, are only made possible through a process of separation from what Kristeva describes as the semiotic order or the *chora*. The semiotic corresponds to the stage when the child is still intimately connected through the drives to the mother's body, and constitutes a dynamic space where the borders between self and other are fluid and shifting:

the drives, which are 'energy' charges as well as 'psychical' marks, articulate what we call a *chora*: a nonexpressive totality formed by the drives and their stases in a motility that is as full of movement as it is regulated. . . . We differentiate this uncertain and indeterminate *articulation* from a *disposition* that already depends on representation, lends itself to phenomenological, spatial intuition, and gives rise to a geometry. . . . Neither model or copy, the *chora* precedes and underlies figuration and thus specularisation, and is analogous to vocal and kinetic rhythm (p. 26).

The process whereby the subject is separated from 'the semiotic motility . . . which fragments him more than it unifies him in a representation' (p. 46), is initiated through visual identification with the mirror-image of the body. This identification anticipates the subject's assumption of the signifying position of the 'I' within language. However, psychoanalysis emphasises that the separation which enables the subject to represent and signify him/herself also divides the self between his/her position within the symbolic, and that part of the subject which remains unrepresented, and continually renews or animates the *process* of representation and 'signifiance': 'the semiotic *chora* is no more than the place where the subject is both generated and negated, the place where his unity succumbs before the process of charges and stases that produce him' (p. 28).

Beckett's theatre can be seen as the site of a similar confrontation between the attempt to assume a position of control and judgement in relation to the visual and verbal representations of self and the laws of representation in general, and the opening up of a space anterior to the construction of the roles posited by representation, including those of author, character and spectator or judge. Beckett's drama therefore not only frames the ruins of authority, but stages the drama of a subjectivity which escapes or exceeds the codes of representation, questioning in the process the languages and limits of theatre itself.

Theatre has been seen as the art form where the laws of representation are most firmly rooted. Keir Elam describes dramatic representation as the creation of 'a fictional dramatic world characterised by a set of physical properties, a set of agents and a course of time-bound events'.[5] Mimesis therefore plays a particularly important role in theatre. Alessandro Serpieri describes dramatic relationships – between characters or between characters and objects or the space of the stage – as being established '*through deictic, ostensive, spatial relations. From this derives the involving, engrossing force of the* theatrical event . . . because the theatre is mimesis of the lived, not the detachment of the narrated'.[6]

According to this model, theatre can be seen as presenting the audience with a ready-made world, miming or imitating the model of a universe created and in all material respects abandoned by an absent creator who yet remains the guardian of the truth or meaning of the created world. Derrida points out the 'theological' implications of such theatre in his essay on Artaud, entitled 'The Theatre of Cruelty and the Closure of Representation':

> The stage is theological for as long as its structure, following the entirety of tradition, comports the following elements: an author-creator who, absent and from afar, is armed with a text and keeps watch over, assembles, regulates the time or the meaning of representation. . . . He lets representation represent him through representatives, directors or actors, enslaved interpretors who represent characters who, primarily through what they say, more or less directly represent the thought of the 'creator'.[7]

Theological theatre not only emphasises the authority of the creator, but casts the audience in the role of perceiver and judge, with the performance or performers on trial. It therefore requires various levels of competence or mastery on the part of the creator, director, actor and audience,[8] but in order for us to believe in the illusion of presence and mastery, theological theatre seeks to deny its artifice, the processes through which it is both produced and perceived.

However, much experimental drama from Jarry's *Ubu roi* to contemporary performance artists has been concerned precisely with rejecting such a definition of theatre. Indeed, Kristeva's distinction between the symbolic and the semiotic can be seen as paralleling the distinction sometimes made in performance theory between theatre as representation, and theatre as performance: theatre which posits the dramatic universe as an already constituted world, and theatre which emphasises its own processes of production, perception and interpretation: 'As long as performance rejects narrativity and representation, in this way, it also rejects the symbolic organisation dominating theatre, and exposes the conditions of theatricality as they are.'[9] Maria Minich Brewer notes that 'Theatre allows a philosophical discourse to shift from thought as seeing and originating in the subject alone, to the many decentered processes of framing and staging that representation requires but dissimulates.'[10] On the one hand, Beckett exploits the theological structures of theatre, from the absent master in *Waiting for Godot* to the tyrannical figures in *Play, Catastrophe* and *What Where*, but on the other, his emphasis on the spaces, margins and processes of theatre, exposes and undermines the authoritarian eye of representation.

Beckett's later plays do not open upon a world already ordered in a manner corresponding to the organisation of space within a particular society or ideology. Rather they open upon darkness – the pre-symbolic space from which image and then speech will emerge. Beckett thereby emphasises the process whereby the dramatic world comes into being, and shifts the focus from the scene or activity represented, to the processes and conditions of representation. On the one hand, this space acts as a frame: 'No matter what is stripped away of character, plot and setting, on the stage there always persists within the most reduced performance, a residual self-doubling – the stage representing itself as stage, as performance.'[11] On the other, this darkness which remains part of the performance, since the stage image in the later plays occupies only a small area of the stage space, constitutes a continual reminder of that which escapes or eludes the framework of representation. Beckett thus suggests the constructed nature of our attempts to organise time, space, history, or knowledge, and the gap between the verbal and visual systems we use to organise or master reality and identity, and the unrepresentable regions of experience which both elude and threaten such structures.

Space is also used to fragment elements of image and text, preventing the presentation of a totalised structure. Instead, the relations between visual and verbal elements are open to continual reinterpretation. Beckett therefore places emphasis on the interrelated processes of production, perception and judgement: both through his characters' attempts to represent their existence as an image or a narrative in the scene of judgement which constitutes the fiction of the play, and through the structure and texture of the plays which foreground the production of visual and verbal signifying material for perception and judgement by an audience. In other words, Beckett's plays not only exploit but self-consciously focus on the internal dynamic of theatre, and the power relations inherent within that dynamic.

As previously noted, the visual space of Beckett's theatre is non-mimetic, and does not reconstruct a coherent dramatic universe. Rather, the images of Beckett's later plays focus almost entirely on the body. Even the apparently inanimate props that are used, such as the urns in *Play*, the lamp in *A Piece of Monologue*, or the rocking chair in *Rockaby*, are in a close symbiotic relationship with the body. However, Beckett dissociates the body from the usual indexical function of indicating an individual identity, and focuses instead on the body as *image*: produced, signifying, perceived. The bodies in his plays tend to be fragmented and denaturalised, mouths or heads suspended in darkness, the stark lighting and stylised costumes or gestures stressing Beckett's use of the body as visual material, rather than as a centre of identity. Moreover, the frequent separation of body and voice decentres the subject by creating a position of perception and discourse outside of the body, and establishing the body as an *object* of perception (although the body may also fulfil the function of perceiver, as in *That Time*, or the Listener in *Ohio Impromptu*). The body therefore becomes the focus of a struggle for specular possession, as in the psychoanalytic drama of the mirror stage. The dynamic of this theatre of the body becomes a paradigm for Beckett's exploration of theatres of power. I shall focus on three of the later plays, two of which, *Catastrophe* and *Play*, rely on the dynamic of power and subjection, and finally, *Not I*, which is animated by the absence of any position of mastery.

The most explicit dramatisation of the dynamic of power is *Catastrophe*, where a Director is preparing an image of human suffering. His material is the body of the Protagonist, confined to a plinth facing the audience, and subjected to the gaze of the tyrannical Director:

> D: Down the head. (*A at a loss. Irritably.*) Get going. Down his head. (*A. puts back pad and pencil, goes to P, bows his head further, steps back.*) A shade more. (*A. advances, bows the head further.*) Stop! (*A. steps back.*) Fine. It's coming. (*Pause*) Could do with more nudity. (p. 299–300)[12]

Michel Foucault emphasises the importance of the gaze in the discipline and subjection of bodies through surveillance:

> The exercise of discipline presupposes a mechanism that coerces by means of observation; an apparatus in which the techniques that make it possible to see induce effects of power and in which, conversely, the means of coercion make those on whom they are applied clearly visible.[13]

Catastrophe underlines the role of specular mastery in the exercise of authority, and specifically relates this to the processes of representation.

The Protagonist in *Catastrophe* is deprived of speech:

> A (*Timidly*): What about a little . . . a little . . . gag?
> D: For God's sake! This craze for explicitation! Every i dotted to death! Little gag! For God's sake!
> A: Sure he won't utter.
> D: Not a squeak. (p. 299)

His body, his only remaining text, has been stolen from him and turned into pure spectacle in the service of representation. The transformation of the body into visual signifing *material* – the anatomical references, the process of 'whitening all flesh' – is presented as a process of appropriation and subjection.[14] As in psychoanalytic theory the image of the body represents a fixed but alienating identity which cannot express the subject's emotional and physical experience of fragmentation and desire, the body in representation is reproduced as a conditioned image in accordance with the dominant laws, while any attempt on the part of the powerless to speak or gesture is repressed:[15]

> The imposed-upon body is captured and framed in representation. Representation is a coded scene, a framing and fetishising of the body as a whole (an image-pose) or a part.[16]

The body of the Protagonist is not only subjected to and by the gaze of the Director, but offered to the gaze of the fictional audience, whose role is played by the 'real' audience:

> D: Stop! (*Pause.*) Now . . . let 'em have it. (*Fade-out of general light. Pause. Fade-out of light on body. Light on head alone. Long Pause.*) Terrific! He'll have them on their feet. I can hear it from here. (p. 301)

The 'real' audience are, of course, likely to sympathise with the Protagonist, but, because the play foregrounds the power dynamic inherent in its own production, the audience are made uncomfortably aware of the ambiguity of their role. Apparently privileged authors of the gaze which perceives and judges the humiliating spectacle of the Protagonist's suffering, they are rendered conscious of their own collaboration in the subjection of the body offered to their view. At the same time, the play emphasises the extent to which they have been manipulated in order to fulfil that role, and have therefore also been subjected to the mechanisms of representation as spectacle: Artaud's theatre of enslavement. Yet the very interplay of gazes, where that of the audience is reflected in the gaze of the Director, especially when he announces he is going to observe the spectacle from the auditorium, the gaze of the Assistant, and finally, the defiant gaze of the Protagonist, when, against all expectations, he raises his head and returns the audience's gaze, both exposes and deflects the gaze of power. Barbara Freedman sees such a deflection of the gaze as an important strategy in theatre's power to disrupt the frames of representation:

> Theatre is fascinated by the return of one's look as a displacing gaze that redefines as it undermines identity. The spectatorial gaze takes the bait and stakes its claim to a resting place in the field of vision that beckons it – only to have its gaze fractured, its look stared down by a series of gazes which challenge the place of the look and expose it as in turn defined by the other.[17]

In *Play*, the positions of seeing and judging are again closely linked. Three heads, rigidly enclosed in urns, are forced to relate the narrative of their interrelated pasts, as a spotlight moves rapidly from one head to another, extorting speech. The second part of the text emphasises the role of the Light as interrogator, judge and eye:

> W2: Is it that I do not tell the truth, is that it, that some day somehow I may tell the truth at last and then no more light at last, for the truth? (p. 153)

> M: And now that you are . . . mere eye. Just looking. At my face. On and Off. (p. 157)

The Light therefore seems to constitute the principle of law and order which seeks to construct a coherent narrative from the fragmented confessions of the three characters:

> The narratorial voice is the voice of a subject recounting something, remembering an event or a historical sequence, knowing

who he is, where he is, and what he is talking about. It responds to some 'police', a force of order or law ('What "exactly" are you talking about').[18]

Yet any coherence or sequence is frustrated by the very motion of the Light in the process of interrogation, disrupting any visual or narrative continuity. The rapid tempo of the delivery of the text not only removes the expressivity of the voices, but materialises their speech, so that it is perceived 'not as conveying thought or ideas, but as dramatic ammunition'.[19] The role of the audience as voyeurs preying on the dramatic spectacle is overturned as the audience is made aware first of all, of the extreme effort to perceive and understand, which is experienced almost as an imperative to which they must submit, and gradually, of the futility of such an effort, as the repetition of the entire text empties it of any possible core of meaning or truth. There is therefore no question of mastery, either on the part of the interrogating Light or on the part of the audience, who see their own failure to achieve a position of perception and judgement reflected on stage in the role of the Light. Instead of seducing the audience into forgetting their role or denying their gaze through identification with the spectacle, the failure and futility of the roles imposed by representation had become a main focus of the performance.

Play can therefore be seen as parodying the concept of theatre as a privileged place of seeing where truth is revealed in and as appearance. Any hierarchy of authority is rendered meaningless, as torturer, victim and audience are equally imprisoned in a meaningless and apparently endless performance, where not only the characters, but the Light and the audience are forced to repeat their roles. *Play* seems to present the drive to representation as an empty mechanism of power and discipline, devoid of any centre of truth, presence or authority, and yet which continues to operate, and enslave its operators, like a machine out of control.

While in *Catastrophe* and *Play* the suffering of the dispossessed subject is transformed into a masquerade or spectacle, *Not I* dramatises that suffering which signifies itself through its disruption of the authoritative framework of the symbolic. The figures of judge, accused and observer reappear within the text, and are also central to the dynamic of the play:

that time in court . . . what had she to say for herself . . . guilty or

not guilty ... stand up woman ... speak up woman ... stood there
staring into space ... mouth half open as usual ... waiting to be
led away ... glad of the hand on her arm ... now this ...
something she had to tell ... could that be it? ... something that
would tell ... how it was ... how she -- what?
... had been? ... yes ... something that would tell how it had been
... how she had lived ... lived on and on ... guilty or not ....
(p. 221)

Much of the dramatic tension is created through the image of the
trial, reproduced in performance through the positioning of Mouth,
confronting the audience and suspended in the stage darkness,
pouring forth her confession. This framework of constraint – Mouth
can neither shift her position nor escape the light and the necessity to
repeat her story – is contrasted with the uncontrollable stream of
speech 'mad stuff ... half the vowels wrong' she emits.

The text revolves around the four denials of the first person by
Mouth: 'what? ... who? ... no! ... she! ... ', which emphasise
Mouth's refusal to adopt the central signifying position of the 'I'
within language. As in *Play*, Beckett emphasises the association of
the symbolic with law and order and the forces of authority through
the staging of his theatre as a trial where Mouth is compelled to
represent herself. The role of the audience as apparently detached
observers of this coercion and of Mouth's agony is emphasised
through the placing of the silent, detached figure of the Auditor on
stage. The stage space therefore appears at first to correspond to the
space of the symbolic, which establishes clearly-defined spatial relationships between self and other, observer and observed.

The image and speech of Mouth, however, refuses the establishment of visual and verbal order. Mouth is a denial of the specular
image of the body which offers the subject a unified visual representation. Instead, the two lips in continual motion form an image of
lack or absence, like Lacan's 'objet(s) petit a', and disrupt stable
spatial categories: 'this is not an organ which exists solidly in space,
but is itself the space in which solidity and vacancy are produced
and reproduced'.[20] Space is transformed into process, so that the
image of the Mouth becomes indissociable from the *activity* or
function of uttering. The steady flow of speech undermines the
binary opposition and distinction between inside and outside, con-
tainer and contained, essential to the symbolic order: 'The first of the
distinctions effected by the symbolic register of language – the dis-

tinction between interior and exterior – is particularly vital for the "subject"'.[21] The space of judgement originally posited in the play is therefore contrasted with a dynamic space reminiscent of Kristeva's *chora*: 'the *chora*, as rupture and articulations (rhythm), precedes evidence, verisimilitude, spatiality and temporality' (p. 26).

These semiotic rhythms also radically disorder the syntax of Mouth's speech and the conceptual categories necessary for the construction of symbolic representation. Any attempt to establish spatial or temporal distinctions is undermined. Although there appears to be a distinction between the glimpses of what Beckett refers to in the manuscript as 'life-scenes',[22] and the description of Mouth's experiences *after* 'all went out . . . all that early April morning light', and supposedly *leading up to* the actual time of performance, these temporal categories are undermined. The last life-scene to figure in Mouth's speech is that of the old woman, who, after having been silent and as if absent for all of her life, takes to sudden outpourings of speech in public lavatories: 'sudden urge to . . . tell . . . then rush out stop the first she saw . . . nearest lavatory . . . start pouring it out'. This parallels the narrative of Mouth's experience in the dark, which tells of the advent of speech: 'words were coming . . . imagine! . . . words were coming!' This torrent of speech is in turn witnessed by the audience of the play. Instead of remaining spatially and temporally distinct, the description of the life-scenes and the tale of events in the darkness begin to merge into the image or rather *performance* of Mouth ceaselessly reproducing an undifferentiated flood of words.

While the text therefore appears to tell the narrative of an insignificant life and a death one April morning, it in fact continually returns to the moment or process of birth, simultaneously that of the infant – 'tiny little thing . . . out before its time . . . ' – and that of speech. In her book, *Psychoanalytic Criticism*, Elizabeth Wright cites *Not I* as a representation of the primary splitting of the subject which ruptures the pre-verbal choric lack of distinction between subject and other, self and world:

> Mouth is reliving the trauma of the primordial moment when the body senses its split from the Real. The traumatic moment can return in psychosis as the experience of the 'fragmented body', unique for every subject, remainder and reminder of this fracture. . . . For Lacan, narrative is the attempt to catch up retrospectively on this separation, to tell this happening again and again, to recount it: the narrative of the subject caught in the net of signifiers.[23]

However, just as Mouth is another of Beckett's characters who has 'never really been born',[24] *Not I* can also be seen as dramatising the *failure* to achieve the separation necessary to posit oneself, and therefore objects and the world, in language and the symbolic order. This sense of failure is intensified through the dominant image of the trial, where Mouth's release from the agony of speech and the glare of judgement is dependent on the self-representation she is incapable of achieving.

In her essay on Beckett's *First Love* and *Not I*, 'The Father, Love and Banishment',[25] Kristeva argues that Mouth is haunted by the absent father/Father, whose Death is the foundation of all meaning (as the phallus only permits signification through its absence), but from whose presence she is exiled. She is therefore doomed to the pursuit of 'a paternal shadow binding her to the body and to language' (p. 154), even though both body and language, deprived of centre or meaning, are transformed into uncontrolled excrement or waste as Mouth 'gives way violently and publicly to a kind of dialoghorrhea'.[26] Whether the disorder of Mouth's speech is seen as resulting from the disintegration of the paternal body, producing non-sense, or from the undifferentiated flux of the maternal body from which Mouth cannot separate herself, the sense of anxiety which her performance communicates – and produces in the audience – is related to the inability to escape or reject the shadow of paternal authority which maintains the eye of judgement.

Indeed, there is also a contrast throughout the play between the gaze of judgement and the subversion or deflection of that gaze. The confrontation between the subject observed and the observing look characterises the life-scenes narrated in the text. The only time the old woman is described as looking, is when she watches with complete detachment the tears drying on her hand, and when she stares at the bell in the April meadow, as if trying to anchor herself to the visual world as she senses that it is about to slip away. In the scenes in the supermarket and in the courtroom, however, the old woman is observed: 'stand up woman . . . speak up woman . . . ', but returns no gaze of her own – her eyes are empty, 'staring into space . . . '. In the scene in the lavatory, however, the empty look has become a flood of speech which she directs at her auditors – 'till she saw the stare she was getting . . . then die of shame . . . crawl back in . . . '.

Likewise, in the narrative of Mouth's experiences 'in the dark', at first her eyelids open and close, but there is no gaze. Shortly afterwards, however, the word-flood which constitutes her performance on stage, begins. The two lips continually opening and closing recall the description of the eyelids in the text, and indeed, Mouth seems almost to be staring at the audience. However, the gaze of judgement which orders difference, distinguishing between observer and observed, is transformed into an excessive flow of speech which eschews the central, controlling position of the 'I'.

The audience, on the other hand, appear to be cast in the role of judge – privileged and detached observers of Mouth's disorder. Yet Beckett both frames and subverts that role. In the narrated lavatory scene, the audience's gaze is reflected back at them in the image of Mouth's spectators as 'an assembly of gapers in a place of public convenience'.[27] Beckett thereby replaces the gaze of power with the disruptive gaze familiar to psychoanalytic theory: 'The gaze is a discovery that one is seen – that one's look is always already purloined by the Other. . . . Theatre's disrupting gaze reflects any look as already taken; it stages presence as always already represented, and trapped by another's look.'[28]

Beckett further undermines the audience's supposed detachment and authoritative position of perception as they, like the ear and the brain in the text, are unable to hear or understand a large part of Mouth's speech. Yet, unless they leave the theatre, they are unable to escape their role as spectator. Like Mouth, they are held in position by the framework of theatre and the role it casts for them, yet Beckett ensures that the audience are as incapable of fulfilling that role as Mouth is of fulfilling hers. Both are condemned for the duration of the play to the impossible struggle to make sense and order out of Mouth's chaotic stream of speech: 'try something else . . . think of something else . . . oh long after . . . sudden flash . . . not that either . . . all right . . . something else again . . . so on . . . hit on it in the end . . . think everything keep on long enough . . . then forgiven'. (p. 222)

The paradox, and perhaps the power of Beckett's theatre is that, as Kristeva suggests, he retains the framework of authority even as he subverts it. She describes his work as: 'carnivalesque excavations on the brink of toppling over toward something else, which, nonetheless, remains impossible in Beckett. X-ray of the most fundamental myth of the Christian world: the love for the father's Death (a love for meaning beyond communication, for the incommunicable) and for the universe as waste (absurd communication).'[29] Rather than a liberation of theatre, Beckett's stages become scenes of judgement where representation itself, and the power relations inherent within it, are put on trial.

Notes

1. 'In each case, *mimesis* has to follow the process of truth. The presence of the present is its norm, its order, its law. It is in the name of truth, its only reference – *reference* itself – that *mimesis* is judged, proscribed or prescribed according to a regular alternation.' Jacques Derrida, 'The Double Session', in *Dissemination*, trans. Barbara Johnson (London: Athlone Press, 1981), p. 193.

2. Jacques Derrida, *Writing and Difference*, trans. Alan Bass (London: Routledge & Kegan Paul, 1978), p. 280.

3. A number of Beckett's later plays, including *Footfalls, Rockaby* and *Ohio Impromptu*, subvert the framework of authority through using images of maternity and fraternity. The ways in which they depart from the dominant structures of judgement discussed here, however, seemed to me to require a separate analysis.

4. Julia Kristeva, *Revolution in Poetic Language*, trans. Margaret Waller (New York: Columbia University Press, 1984), p. 35.

5. Keir Elam, *The Semiotics of Theatre and Drama* (London: Methuen, 1980), p. 98.

6. Quoted by Elam, p. 113.

7. Jacques Derrida, *Writing and Difference*, p. 235.

8. Elam points out that the construction of the dramatic world depends on the spectator's ability to decipher the codes on which this presented world is based: 'the spectator is called upon not only to employ a specific *dramatic* competence (supplementing his theatrical competence and involving knowledge of the generic and structural principles of the drama) but also to work hard and continuously at piecing together into a coherent structure the partial and scattered bits of dramatic information that he receives from different sources' (p. 99).

9. Josette Féral, 'Performance and Theatricality', trans. Teresa Lyons, *Modern Drama*, Vol. 25, no. 1, pp. 177–8.

10. Maria Minich Brewer, 'Performing Theory', *Theatre Journal*, no. 37, 1985, p. 16.

11. Stephen Connor, *Samuel Beckett: Repetition, Theory and Text* (Oxford: Blackwell, 1988), p. 124.

12. Page references in brackets are to the *Collected Shorter Plays of Samuel Beckett* (London: Faber, 1984).

13. Michel Foucault, *Discipline and Punish*, in *The Foucault Reader*, ed. Paul Rabinov (Harmondsworth: Penguin Books, 1984), p. 189.

14. See H. Porter Abbott, 'Tyranny and Theatricality; The Example of Samuel Beckett' in *Theatre Journal*, Vol. 40, no. 1, March 1988, p. 87: 'The aesthetic and the political are two faces of a single meaning in *Catastrophe*, and they merge in the insight that the political will that seeks to constrain human life to an imagined social order, imprisoning or eliminating those uncontrollable elements that threaten that order, is rooted with the aesthetic will that seeks to dominate the human through formal representation.'

15. The play is dedicated to the Czechoslovakian playwright, Vaclav

Havel, who was placed under house arrest for his subversive writings.

16.   Philip Monk, 'Common Carrier: Performance by Artists', in *Modern Drama*, Vol. 25, no. 1, p. 167.

17.   Barbara Freedman, 'Frame-up: Feminism, Psychoanalysis, Theatre', in *Theatre Journal*, p. 395.

18.   Jacques Derrida, 'LIVING ON: *Borderlines*', in *Deconstruction and Criticism*, ed. Harold Bloom et al. (London: Routledge & Kegan Paul, 1979), pp. 104–5.

19.   George Devine, manuscript notes for the first production of *Play* in England, presented at the Old Vic, London, March 1964. Reading University Library, MS 1581/15.

20.   Steven Connor, op. cit., p. 162.

21.   Anika Lemaire, *Jacques Lacan*, trans. David Macey (London: Routledge & Kegan Paul, 1977), p. 57.

22.   See Reading University Library, MS 1227/7/12/10.

23.   Elizabeth Wright, *Psychoanalytic Criticism: Theory in Practice*, (London: Methuen, 1984), p. 113.

24.   *All That Fall* (London: Faber & Faber, 1957), p. 34.

25.   In Julia Kristeva, *Desire in Language: A Semiotic Approach to Literature and Art*, (Oxford: Blackwell, 1980), pp. 148–58.

26.   Keir Elam, 'Samuel Beckett and the Ars(e) Rhetorica' in Enoch Brater (ed.), *Beckett at 80: Beckett in Context* (New York: Oxford University Press, 1986), p. 138.

27.   Ibid., p. 143.

28.   Barbara Freedman, op. cit., p. 394.

29.   Julia Kristeva, 'The Father, Love and Banishment', p. 155 (see note 25 above).

6

Bakhtin, Foucault, Beckett, Pinter

PETER GRIFFITH

There is one way at least in which the activities of the drama producer and those of the student of linguistics resemble each other: starting with a particular corpus of text (the 'words on the page', so far as drama is concerned), each seeks to go on to build something out of them. What they build, however, is usually something very different in each case. The producer is working from a standard text towards a performance, in which each particular realisation of the text is unique, specific, and unreproducible; the student of linguistics, if following in the major twentieth-century tradition established by the Swiss scholar Ferdinand de Saussure, is looking for some set of regularities, above and beyond this particular collection of utterances. In Saussure's terms, such a regularity constitutes a *langue* or language system underpinning this specific *parole* or instance of language usage. For the producer, then, the text counts as a generality from which the particular has to be derived; for the student of linguistics (if prepared, as many are not, to accord any validity to literature as data) the text is a particular instance from which a regular and abstract language system has to be inductively produced.

Mikhail Bakhtin was a Russian polymath whose writings on discourse, produced over a period of half a century but introduced by translation into the consciousness of the English-speaking world only in the last fifteen years or so, went a long way towards subverting the neat opposition I set out in the previous paragraph. For him the goal of language study was not to discover some abstract set of rules taken to underlie each and every utterance in a given language, but to try to see what was going on during the course of each utterance. If Saussure's system of abstract rules belongs to the realm of the social – a kind of common contract to which people must subscribe before they can begin to speak – it begins to look, then, as

97

if Bakhtin is laying a compensating emphasis upon the individual, who is being held to be the fount and origin of all that is quirky and specific about particular utterances. This is an interpretation that Bakhtin would emphatically reject; he would see it as grounded in the monstrous error of supposing that *langue* = social, whereas *parole* = individual. For him *parole* was social through and through, since the utterances of an individual did not emanate from some deep inner soul – the realm of the psychological, the personal, the individual – and then spread outwards into society – thereby entering the realm of the sociological, the metapersonal, the collective. Instead language begins in the world outside, and is then taken into the individual. After all, we are exposed to utterances before we begin to produce them, and some students of child language acquisition, and in particular the Russian psychologist Vygotsky who was Bakhtin's contemporary, have argued that the early speech of the child precedes, and largely serves to generate, the thought processes that in later life will accompany speech. So the socially-produced individual has its origin outside the biological individual, and Bakhtin's definition of the psyche was that it is something which 'enjoys extraterritorial status in the organism. It is a social entity that penetrates inside the organism of the individual person.'[1]

Just as there is no such thing as 'fresh air', since, if we think about it, every gulp of it is likely to have been in several pairs of lungs before our own, so there is for Bakhtin no such thing as 'fresh speech', since all the words in it are likely to have been used already, and to carry with them traces of various of their previous usages. What *is* new for Bakhtin is the way in which each is used on every new occasion, since out of the various available dictionary meanings some are highlighted and others suppressed, and intonation and other devices enhance this specificity. It is therefore the contextual force of each utterance that is unique – the 'theme', as Bakhtin termed it – rather than the 'words on the page', which may well have been used in that combination millions of times before. There is no 'fresh speech', then, but there are perpetually fresh utterances. In this sense, the language is being remade each time it is used to each specific situation, and abstract and general systems, such as 'the English language', or 'Standard English' are no more than artefacts generated by the observer, a kind of temporarily necessary fiction arising from the process of observation.

There is another sense in which Bakhtin may be imagined as having more in common with the producer than he would with the

Saussurean linguist: each of the first two would be likely to stress the primacy of dialogue. For Bakhtin this relates to the way in which words bear traces of previous uses, and the way in which they slip and slide even within a single conversation, as first one participant and then another struggles to impose one particular set of meanings upon the terms that are in play. 'Heteroglossia' is Bakhtin's term for this competitive process of attempted definition of terms. Even a solitary upon a desert island, in Bakhtin's scheme of things, would be engaged in dialogue, mimicking in self-directed speech all the voices encountered during a more sociable previous phase of existence.

But solitaries are the exception rather than the rule, and when two or more people engage in dialogue the usual processes of conversation resume: each participant attempts to impose, or at least sustain, a definition of reality which may have much in common with, but can never be identical to, that of the co-speaker. Moreover, Bakhtin tells us, within one particular literary convention the narrative takes a hand as well as the participants. This genre is the written equivalent of the Saturnalian feast of Ancient Rome, the Venetian Carnival, or the rites traditionally observed on Twelfth Night, in which the everyday relations of superior and inferior are inverted, and the structure of authority is (depending on your point of view of the process) either subverted or reinforced. The kind of writers that Bakhtin is thinking of are Rabelais, Cervantes, Sterne, Diderot, and indeed Dostoyevsky, of whose novels he wrote an extended study. What I would want to suggest is that this carnivalesque mode is a particular example of the more general point made earlier – language in use demonstrates a struggle for power. It is as though, by putting every utterance in a kind of ironic quotation marks, carnivalesque language is interrogating and subverting the ground of each and every propositional statement. 'If God is dead then everything is permitted' wrote Dostoyevsky in Nietzschean vein, though it is important to remember that his novels went on to reinstate God after all, just as bishop replaces boy bishop once the carnival is over. While it lasts, though, the participants in the carnival are not concerned to be 'true to themselves', or to anything else; what they do is to take a theme and embroider it, in a perpetual and all-encompassing piece of street theatre in which the roles of spectator and actor are played out simultaneously. Just as it is impossible to take a stance somewhere outside the carnival in order to watch it – it has no proscenium arch – so there is no way of interrogating carnivalesque utterance from a ground of pure and detached reasoning.

Carnival, utterance, dialogue, struggle: these are terms that apply to drama as much as they do to the analysis of discourse, and it is time to apply them in this way. One of the reasons why Beckett and Pinter have often been bracketed together is that they are both frequently seen as writing hermetically-sealed dramatic texts which deliberately and wilfully bear no relation to the world outside the play; another version of this criticism is that they create a spurious and ahistorical picture of The Human Condition which neglects existing social conditions and processes. What I want to do is to use some of the concepts that Bakhtin offers to test the strength of these criticisms.

One point at least will be conceded by Beckett's detractors: he self-consciously writes plays which abound in echoes of earlier texts, as well as a cacophony of internal echoes. These echoes, by both replicating and commenting on the processes of language itself, are, I would argue, the point of fissure in the closed circle of the text, or, at least, the means by which that text adopts a stance towards the linguistic and social strategies to be found in the outside world.

> VLADIMIR: Boots must be taken off every day, I'm tired of telling you that. Why don't you listen to me?
> ESTRAGON (*Feebly*): Help me!
> VLADIMIR: It hurts?
> ESTRAGON: Hurts! He wants to know if it hurts!
> VLADIMIR (*Angrily*): No one ever suffers but you. I don't count. I'd like to hear what you'd say if you had what I have.
> ESTRAGON: It hurts?
> VLADIMIR: Hurts! He wants to know if it hurts!
> ESTRAGON (*Pointing*): You might button it all the same.
> VLADIMIR (*Stooping*): True. (*He buttons his fly.*) Never neglect the little things of life.
> ESTRAGON: What do you expect, you always wait till the last moment.
> VLADIMIR (*Musingly*): The last moment . . . (*He meditates.*) Hope deferred maketh the something sick, who said that?
> (*Waiting for Godot*, p. 10)

In the above passage, the two-line exchange beginning 'It hurts?' is identical in form on each of its two occurrences, though the allocation of turn to speaker is different on each occasion. What is going on here is a kind of power play, a childish demanding of attention in which he who complains last complains most effectively, and he who steals the other's formulation holds the trump card. This simple repetition constitutes the most rudimentary form of quotation.

There is one other difference between the two exchanges, though, which concerns the identity of the referent of the pronoun 'it'; a different bodily extremity is envisaged in each case, as the stage business must take care to point out. What we have here, therefore, is identity of linguistic form but not of reference; the same language can be employed to differing ends, or, in Bakhtin's terminology, the meaning remains constant but the theme varies.

A more complex form of internal quotation occurs at the end of the passage, when Estragon's banal kindergarten complaint 'You always wait till the last moment' is repeated, but musingly, by Vladimir. The different processes of utterance point up the heteroglossia, here involving a leap from urology to eschatology. Though perhaps 'leap' is here the wrong word; hereafter, in this play, the two themes are linked. Mandrakes, as the text reminds us, grow at the place of execution, which is also the place of ejaculation, and ejaculation is only another form of utterance, a kind of parodic Last Words from The Cross. The mandrake's shriek represents the only kind of utterance which can not just mean but be.

However, it is not only internal quotations that we meet in the passage quoted above. 'Hope deferred maketh the something sick, who said that?' The immediate answer to Vladimir's query is that the quotation is to be found in Proverbs 13:12. ('Hope deferred maketh the heart sick: but when the desire cometh, it is a tree of life'.) The stage set is of course dominated by a tree, which is or is not the tree of life. Vladimir's inability to complete the quotation is therefore one level in a multiple instance of irony, since the stage set could be held to provide him with the answer. But such an answer would beg more questions than it solved, since it leaves unanswered the question of the status of The Word, monologic rather than dialogic, which seeks to foreclose rather than extend the process of the dialogue.

It is widely recognised that the whole of the play is filled with intertextual references of the kind discussed above, and Beckett has acknowledged his use of Biblical reference as a convenient structuring mythology, whilst at the same time stressing the arbitrariness of his choice – arbitrary, that is, in the linguist's sense of the word, in that there is no necessary connection between symbol and referent, but only a conventional one. What has been less remarked upon is the oddity of the fact that both Beckett and Vladimir are capable of using and abusing quotation. A useful categorisation of varieties of deliberate citation is offered by Michael André Bernstein, in discussing Bakhtin's account of the carnivalisation of language. His first and most common category consists of the author who cites the work of another writer. The second is the character in a work of literature who deliberately refers to a fictional character in an earlier work; Bernstein's chosen example is Stephen Dedalus's frequent and explicit self-comparison to Hamlet. Bernstein's definition of his third category requires to be quoted in full:

> an author who draws upon a particular literary tradition or genre rather than upon any one specific *exemplum*, and whose characters, in order to be locatable within that tradition, themselves also consciously quote from the fictional works that have established the genre's conventions. In this paradigm, aspects of the two other models unite; *both* the author and the characters knowingly use citations and imitation as essential elements of their self-representation.[2]

Since Bernstein is discussing prose narrative in this definition, it is possible for him to make a clear distinction between characters' utterances and the surrounding authorial narrative. Such a distinction is not possible in the same way in a dramatic text, but it is still possible to deploy it in a different fashion by differentiating between conscious and unconscious quotation on the part of the characters. When both the present characters and the absent author use ironic quotation, argues Bernstein, then the irony becomes all-pervasive, and intention becomes impossible to disentangle.

> Now the question is no longer restricted to the choice between a strictly comic or a serious argument, nor is it resolvable by the sleight of hand of labelling the work as a 'comic' presentation of essentially serious themes. . . . Instead, all of these modes co-exist in the discourse of a character who is himself at a loss to know which response is appropriate, a figure whose speech lacks all of the customary contextual cues separating an articulation according to its degree of truth, folly, or humour, but whose own familiarity with the expectations of the satiric genre makes him long in

vain for some stable reference point against which to measure his outbursts.[3]

It is helpful to measure these comments against a fairly typical passage of dialogue from the play:

VLADIMIR: . . . Do you not recognise the place?

ESTRAGON (*Suddenly furious*): Recognise! What is there to recognise? All my lousy life I've crawled about in the mud! And you talk to me about scenery! (*Looking wildly about him*) Look at this muckheap! I've never stirred from it!

VLADIMIR: Calm yourself, calm yourself.

ESTRAGON: You and your landscapes! Tell me about the worms!

VLADIMIR: All the same, you can't tell me that this (*Gesture*) bears any resemblance to . . . (*He hesitates.*) . . . to the Macon country, for example. You can't deny there's a big difference.

ESTRAGON: The Macon country! Who's talking to you about the Macon country?

VLADIMIR: But you were there yourself, in the Macon country.

ESTRAGON: No, I was never in the Macon country. I've puked my puke of a life away here, I tell you! Here! In the Cackon country!

(*Waiting for Godot*, pp. 61–2)

Deprived of the cues normally provided by props or action, and of the processes of memory, Vladimir and Estragon suffer from an imperfect ability to reconstruct the events of the past. For this reason they are obliged continually to reinvent it by means of external and internal quotation, and by a diverting but ultimately random rotation of styles. It has often been remarked, for instance, that much of their dialogic interchange and stage business is derived from the conventions of the music hall, but it is remarkably difficult to determine just which passages do and which do not match up to this description. Their speech is carnivalesque, but it differs from the experience of carnival as defined above in that there is no temporal boundary to the performance of their roles; they cannot properly recollect any time in which they were other than what they now are, whatever that may be, and they face no persuasive prospect of ever becoming anything else. What they are practising, then, is not some Yeatsian remaking of the self; however much they may beat upon the wall, there is no truth out there that is able to obey their call.

Language is memory is power; that is what there is, and all there is.

Both internal and external quotation are forms of repetition, and it was famously pointed out that *Waiting for Godot* is a play in which nothing happens, twice.[4] All language usage, in the Saussurean sense, is repetition, since we are never there when that original social contract is made, if indeed (shades of *Godot*) such an event ever occurred. Saussurean language is like Estragon's boots: it is impossible to tell if it is your own or somebody else's, and it tends to feel uncomfortably tight, though you have to put it on if you want to get anywhere, or even to run around on the spot. Repetition is not, however, a simple return to a pristine original, since, in Bakhtin's sense, each enactment will be thematically different. Repetition-as-quotation is therefore a form of dialogue with the past rather than a re-experiencing of it, and that past can be anything from the sum total of Western civilisation to an imperfect recollection of what we may or may not have ourselves said five minutes before.

Dialogue is of course the norm of Vladimir and Estragon's speech behaviour, and this fact is underscored by the brevity of their utterances and the rhythmic nature of their turn-taking. Their interchanges with Pozzo differ in many ways from their discussion one with another, as we shall see later, but they are nevertheless dialogical in nature. The one passage in the play that is non-dialogical in its apparent nature – and even in its appearance as a squared-off mass upon the printed page – is Lucky's tirade towards the end of Act I. Though precipitated by Pozzo's commands, it is in no sense a response to them, but stands outside the normal processes of conversation as though it were some divinely-inspired oracular utterance. Similarly, its termination is engineered not by any of the normal processes of conversation management, but by physical force of the crudest kind.

Divine speech is expected to be self-identical, non-derivative, and usually cast in the imperative mode. Lucky's speech reads as if it is a series of declarative utterances, even if it is not in practice possible to disentangle any of them, and it is profoundly imitative, as well as iterative, in both overt and more devious ways.

Given the existence as uttered forth in the public works of Puncher and Wattmann of a personal God quaquaquaqua with white beard quaquaquaqua outside time without extension who from the heights of divine apathia divine athambia divine aphasia loves us dearly with some exceptions for reasons unknown but time will tell and suffers like the divine Miranda with those who for reasons unknown but time will tell are plunged in torment plunged in fire whose fire flames if that continues and who can doubt it will fire the firmament. . . . (*Waiting for Godot*, pp. 42–3)

I assume Puncher and Wattmann to be nonce-names of the kind found in *Tristram Shandy*, and the device of using them to be a reference to this work, and to the Rabelaisian tradition from which it stems. The Latin 'qua' is a piece of scholarly jargon instantly made risible by meaningless repetition so that it resembles the quack of a duck. 'Divine apathia' echoes the aesthetic theories propounded by Stephen Dedalus in *Portrait of the Artist as a Young Man*, and the fires of torment are equally recognisable from the hellfire sermon in the same book. Reference to Miranda reminds us not only of Stephen's obsession with Shakespeare, but of the themes of suffering and redemption that abound in the late romances. The unsentenced form of the speech as a whole combines Molly Bloom's stream-of-consciousness chapter in *Ulysses* with the anguished rationality that is Stephen's hallmark. And reference-hunting of the kind I have been practising here can be continued throughout the entire speech. But despite the elaborate interpretative apparatus that can be erected around the tirade, as utterance it lacks all thematic motivation. It is therefore complementary to Vladimir and Estragon's dialogue in affording a parodic *reductio ad absurdum* of the functioning of language; indeed, its irony extends outside the confines of the play to encompass the brief interpretative apparatus I have just offered. Despite appearing to be, in Austin's[5] terms, a set of constative utterances offering statements about the world that can be tested by reality criteria, the speech really asserts nothing whatsoever. But equally it fails to conform to the criteria for Austin's other category, that of performative utterance, by satisfying no felicity conditions whatsoever. Perhaps its ultimate irony, in fact, is that it affords a parody of language usage by breaching all known rules on how to do things with words.

In discussing the dialogue between Vladimir and Estragon earlier, I may have seemed to imply that the relationship between them is a static and equal one. In practice, and as a stage performance should remind us, this is not the case. As they squabble and make up, bully, frighten and cajole each other, there is established a constantly shifting pattern of power and submission, initiative and response. To extend one of Beckett's images, the boot is now on one foot, now on the other. The same variable features characterise, though obviously in a more marked fashion, the pair's dealings with Pozzo, and, *grosso modo*, with Lucky. Lucky is pitied, patronised, deprived of the chicken bones, is comforted – and attacks. Even within the compass of Act I, Pozzo arouses fear, but also incomprehension; he is insulted, even if by accident; he demands attention, but is dependent upon it in order to accomplish seemingly simple tasks of physical and mental coordination. The rope that links Lucky and Pozzo can be seen as emblematic of the economic and political relationship between an exploited and an exploiting class (though I have to say I am also reminded of Samuel Johnson's description of fishing as a piece of line with a worm at one end and a fool at the other); the conversational linkages that variously bind the quartet together are woven of a different stuff. To help in an examination of this material, I want to draw on some of the concepts of power propounded by the French theoretician Michel Foucault.

To begin with, it is important to be clear that, in Foucault's terminology, power is a very different thing from either domination or legal prohibition. Domination is a monolithic affair, usually arising from fixed relationships between large categories of people, and legal prohibition is a method of gainsaying by the state; power is more like a kind of lightning that plays over the scene. Domination might well be the term that we should choose to use of the relationship between Lucky and Pozzo, but Foucault advises us to be cautious about it[6] because of its vacuous generalisation and limitedly negative character – domination can prohibit, but not create. Domination is imposed from above; power, in one formulation of Foucault's, comes from below – that is to say, it can be the creation of a moment, of a word or a glance, even if it can spread outwards and upwards from there. 'Power', said Foucault, 'produces effects at the level of desire – and also at the level of knowledge.'[7] And, just as it is the protagonists' misfortune that they cannot systematically exercise power without resistance, so it is characteristic of their behaviour that the knowledge they painfully acquire cannot be coherently retained.

To illustrate the relevance of the concept of power to the text of the play, we can consider the following interchange:

ESTRAGON (*Violently*): Will you approach! (*The Boy advances timidly.*) What kept you so late?
VLADIMIR: You have a message from Mr. Godot?

BOY: Yes, sir.
VLADIMIR: Well, what is it?
ESTRAGON: What kept you so late?
   (*The Boy looks at them in turn, not knowing to which he should
   reply.*)
VLADIMIR (*To Estragon*): Let him alone.
ESTRAGON (*Violently*): You let me alone! (*Advancing, to the Boy.*)
   Do you know what time it is?

                        (*Waiting for Godot*, p. 49)

In a passage like this the producer has a number of decisions to
make. Some of Estragon's lines are to be delivered 'violently'; does
that mean that his others are to be delivered gently, or merely less
violently? Is Vladimir to be portrayed as kindly, or rather, in the
famous cliché, as the kind of Gestapo officer who offers a cigarette
rather than a blow on the cheek? As the Boy looks from one to the
other, is he to be shown as feeling unable to differentiate between the
two types of power that are being exercised upon him? Is Vladimir's
line 'Let him alone' to be delivered as an intercession or as a com-
mand? Is Estragon thrown off-balance by it, or merely provoked?
These are intensely practical questions for anyone involved in the
business of rehearsal; they graphically illustrate the point that,
deprived as we are in this play of many of the usual cues of social
context, we are more dependent here than in many plays on the
interpretative help offered by stage directions – contrast the typi-
cally tautologous nature of what Shaw often provides in his draw-
ing-room plays, for example. It is in respect of questions like these
that Foucault's conception of power can prove helpful as, in both
senses of the word, a productive strategy, since it deals with the
minute-by-minute action of the play whilst at the same time keeping
a weather eye on the development of its larger themes. The following discussion by Foucault may help to illustrate the point:

   interconnections [between power relations and other forms of
   relationship] delineate general conditions of domination, and this
   domination is organised in a more or less coherent and unitary
   strategic form; . . . dispersed, heteromorphous, localised procedures of power are adapted, re-inforced, and transformed by these
   global strategies, all this being accompanied by numerous phenomena of inertia, displacement, and resistance; hence one should
   not assume a massive and primal condition of domination, a binary

structure with 'dominators' on one side and 'dominated' on the
other, but rather a multiform production of relations of domination which are partially susceptible of integration into overall
strategies. . . .[8]

Another of Foucault's areas of concern that is of direct relevance to
a theatrical production is his insistence that power is something that
concerns the body. 'Body' is an intensely and revealingly ambiguous
word; it can be used to denote something highly abstract – 'a body of
men', 'a body of laws' – or to refer to corporeal existence. Foucault's
historiographical studies have shown that this abstraction and this
concreteness are but two sides of the same coin, so that laws and
attitudes pertaining to the monarch's person are transferred, in the
evolution of legal codes, to the concept of the state.

Though the physical condition of all four protagonists forms a
constant theme throughout the play, Pozzo is the one most conspicuously concerned with his bodily well-being, and the one who deteriorates most strikingly, just as he is the one most conspicuously
dominant, and the one who most dramatically loses many of the
advantages of this dominance. He attends to his various needs and
pleasures with chicken, tobacco, and vaporiser; all Lucky's para-
phernalia is designed to assuage, assist, and delight his master. Yet
at the same time Pozzo is more aware than the others of threats
posed to his physical and mental well-being at the level of abstract
systems: his fears for the loss of his watch and the stopping of his
heart concern the operation of that great abstract system, time, and
during his appearance, blind, in Act II, his greatest fear is that he
may by ill chance be appearing before 'the Board' – a noun which,
like 'body', combines reference to the abstract and the concrete, as
Oliver Twist also discovered.

Some of Foucault's comments on the relationship between power
and the body seem particularly illuminating in respect of Pozzo's
predicament and behaviour:

Mastery and awareness of one's own body can be acquired only
through the effect of an investment of power in the body: gymnas-
tics, exercises, muscle-building, nudism, glorification of the body
beautiful. All of this belongs to the pathway leading to the desire
of one's own body. . . . But once power produces this effect, there
inevitably emerge the responding claims and affirmations, those
of one's own body against power, of health against the economic

system, of pleasure against the moral norms of sexuality, marriage, decency. Suddenly, what had made power strong becomes used to attack it. Power, after investing itself in the body, finds itself exposed to a counter-attack in that same body.[9]

Foucault is describing a rising curve of bodily well-being, in which the sense of physical health and comfort poses a challenge to existing personal and social relationships. It is Beckett's strength to have depicted the further end of that curve, the entropic decline of bodily functions, and to have registered that this too is equally as disruptive of whatever social fabric may exist:

> POZZO (*Suddenly furious*): Have you not done tormenting me with your accursed time! It's abominable! When! When! One day, is that not enough for you, one day like any other day, one day he went dumb, one day I went blind, one day we'll go deaf, one day we were born, one day we shall die, the same day, the same second, is that not enough for you? (*Calmer.*) They give birth astride of a grave, the light gleams an instant, then it's night once more.
>
> (*Waiting for Godot*, p. 89)

In my comments on *Godot*, I have been trying to depict it as belonging to a unique category (though being by no means the only work to be so categorised) in that it not only uses discourse but is about discourse, not only deals with power but demonstrates it in an experimental setting from which other factors have been removed. It explores a paradox at the heart of language: that this is something which generates meaning only through its abstract systematicity, but achieves thematic relevance through the strictly material means of printing or of acoustic events. *Waiting for Godot* is, nominally, all to do with an abstract, absent figure and his authority; in practice, it is peopled with very concrete figures attempting to cope with the *hic et nunc* of existence. With the social structures that sustain domination attenuated or removed, it enables us to focus on the exercise of power and its capacity for creativity.

It is a simple matter to demonstrate the resemblances between *Waiting for Godot* and *The Caretaker*: the absence of a stable social milieu; the characters' heavy reliance upon the exercise of memory, coupled with considerable problems in achieving this feat; the absence of women; even, at a perhaps more trivial level, the recurrent difficulty in matching feet to appropriate footwear. But even to list these similarities is, by implication, already to indicate the differences.

Let us take memory as an example of these differences. As an audience, we may be intended never to know for sure whether the monk just the other side of Luton really did tell Davies to piss off. We are not, however, confronted with the same order of problems regarding his possible existence as we are with the assailants who attack Estragon between Acts I and II. It is not that Davies is a reliable informant – he clearly is not – but any untruths in the story are generated by his cunning or paranoia rather than by the impossibility of recapturing past events in all their self-authenticating fullness. In this play, at least, an external reality exists; the problem is rather to connect with it. The obscenity may or may not have been uttered, but the ontology of the obscene (i.e. off-stage) poses a different order of difficulty. Davies's papers may be a fiction, but Sidcup is factual enough; the shocked reaction generated in the film version by Mick's sudden offer to run Davies down there came from a puzzlement amongst the audience as to what the pair would *do*, rather than from any concern as to where the location shooting might take place.

Memory relies on the constancy of time for its proper functioning. Both in its text and in its stage directions and programme notes, *The Caretaker* takes care to ensure that its audience has a sure grasp of the passage of time, even whilst it plays tricks with the conventions of its presentation: blackouts within acts can last for several hours, whilst the interval between Acts I and II is only a few seconds. Time is a constant only to the audience, however, and is excluded from the characters on the stage; there are no clocks on the set, just as there are no mirrors, and Davies cannot long carry in his head an idea of what that external time is. Time is like the gas supply; there is no doubt of its existence, it is just that the cooker is not connected.

As a result of the constancy of time, it becomes possible to project lines of action outside the confines of the play itself. Davies is still on-stage at the end of Act III, but it would be perverse to doubt that his marching orders will soon take effect. *Godot* ends on a note of more radical doubt.

VLADIMIR: Well, shall we go?
ESTRAGON: Yes, let's go.
      (*They do not move.*)

                                        (*Waiting for Godot.* p. 94)

Just as there is a real time out there in *The Caretaker*, so there is a real society. At a trivial level, this can be demonstrated by listing the number of 'period' props required for the stage (the 1960 vintage Electrolux vacuum cleaner and so on) in contrast to the literally timeless *Waiting for Godot*. More centrally, there is an economy which depends on casual labour in cafés and on 'them Blacks coming up from next door' for the execution of its more menial tasks, just as it affords opportunities to the kind of speculator and entrepreneur that Mick aspires to be. There is also a welfare state which stamps cards, pays pensions, prosecutes defaulters, and, at its least benign, performs terrible therapies upon the brains of unwilling patients such as Aston. It is a poor production which does not induce a frisson in its audience during Aston's long speech at the end of Act II, but this effect is at least partly dependent upon a knowledge of the freedom with which ECT was used during the 1950s.

Given these differences in context, it is not surprising that there should be differences also in the way in which dialogue functions in the two plays.

DAVIES: . . . How many more Blacks you got around here then?
ASTON: What?
DAVIES: You got any more Blacks around here?
ASTON (*Holding out the shoes*): See if these are any good.
DAVIES: You know what that bastard monk said to me? (*He looks over to the shoes.*) I think those'd be a bit small.

(*The Caretaker*, p. 23)

As conversation this is recognisably 'odd', but only because it is in partial breach of the normal convention that questions generate either answers or embedded questions-and-answers. Moreover, it is possible to make motivational sense of some of the oddity: Aston seems unwilling to respond to Davies's racism, for instance. The oddity of the dialogue in *Godot* is more radical than this. When Pozzo in Act I says his adieux to Vladimir and Estragon, and then finds that he is unable to depart without literally taking a run at it, he is providing a parody of all the closing sequences in all conversations. The following passage has some superficial similarities to the one quoted above, but there are more important differences.

VLADIMIR (*Alarmed*): Mr. Pozzo! Come back! We won't hurt you! (*Silence.*)

ESTRAGON: We might try him with other names.
VLADIMIR: I'm afraid he's dying.
ESTRAGON: It'd be amusing.
VLADIMIR: What'd be amusing?
ESTRAGON: To try him with other names, one after the other.

(*Waiting for Godot*, p. 83)

In this sequence, questions can in fact be matched up with answers, but, hearing the play for the first time, an audience is likely to conclude that Estragon would be amused to see Pozzo dying. It is only two lines later that it is prompted to perceive that Estragon is responding to his own suggestion and ignoring Vladimir's contribution. This inability to get conversational structures off the ground is the verbal equivalent of the protagonists' inability to pick themselves up once they have fallen, or to coordinate their efforts in attempting to do so. It is a further stress upon the separation between the physical nature of utterance and the idealist, if necessary, fiction of its capacity to achieve consistency of reference.

Since I have been stressing differences between *Waiting for Godot* and *The Caretaker*, it is probably important to conclude by stressing that the latter is as concerned with issues of power and domination as the former. In *The Caretaker*, though, this concern is mediated by the control of space. This is not immediately apparent, since the set is designed to generate an impression of undifferentiated chaos. Nevertheless, the disposition of bodies enacts a social order. During his work at the café, Davies attempted to secure his status by saying it was not his place to take the bucket out to the back; so far as we can see, he lost his job for attempting to sit down amongst the customers. His misplaced concern to exclude the 'Blacks' from using the toilet is his way of asserting his superiority over them, just as Aston's ability, amidst all the clutter of the room, to prescribe where Davies shall sleep, and with what orientation, is one of the ways in which his control over his visitor is established. When Davies makes his bid, in Act III, to reverse this relationship, it is the disposition of the sleeping arrangements that he selects as the *causus belli*. Mick's frenetic and pyrotechnic bursts of planning involve the transformation and manipulation of space; more labouriously, Aston ponders whether a room requires a partition or an oriental screen.

In *Discipline and Punish*, Foucault explores the ways in which the control of space entails the control of society, with rank as a key term which encompasses both a physical and a moral ordering of individuals as elements in a society.

> In discipline, the elements are interchangeable, since each is defined by the place it occupies in a series, and by the gap that separates it from the others. The unit is, therefore, neither the territory (unit of domination), nor the place (unit of residence), but the *rank:* the place one occupies in a classification, the point at which a line and a column intersect, the interval in a series of intervals that one may traverse one after the other. Discipline is an art of rank, a technique for the transformation of arrangements. It individualises bodies by a location that does not give them a fixed position, but distributes them and circulates them in a network of relations.[10]

The 'network of relations' that we see on stage is a small enough one, and the one attempt to change the serial ordering collapses in the third act. What is significant in this play, however, is the way in which this ordering articulates with the larger one sustained by the outside world; the solicitors and insurance agents of Mick's rodomontades, the bureaucrats that Davies fears, the men with electric pincers of Aston's terrible recollection – and the mother who signed the papers that permitted the deed. This woman is perceived as the betrayer of her son to a wider social ordering, and she reappears as the occupant of the spare bed in Mick's aggressive fantasising, the putative bed-partner of the 'caretaker' who embodies all that can be seen as revolting in fleshly contact. She is the ultimate disposer of moral space in a society where the family is the key unit, and the ranking of siblings the type of all relationships.

Notes

1. M. M. Bakhtin (writing as V. N. Volosinov), *Marxism and the Philosophy of Language*, second edition (Cambridge, Mass.: Harvard University Press, 1986), p. 39. First published in Russian, 1929; first English translation 1973.
2. M. A. Bernstein, 'When the Carnival Turns Bitter: preliminary reflections upon the abject hero', in G. S. Morson (ed.), *Bakhtin: essays and dialogues on his work* (Chicago: University of Chicago Press, 1986), p. 104.
3. Ibid., pp. 111–12.
4. V. Mercier, 'The Uneventful Event', in *Irish Times*, 18 February 1956, p. 6.

5.   J. L. Austin (ed. J. O. Urmson), *How To Do Things With Words* (London: Oxford University Press, 1962).

6.   M. Foucault (ed. C. Gordon), *Power/Knowledge: selected interviews and other writings 1972–77* (New York: Pantheon Books), p. 139. First collected and published in translation 1980 (Brighton: Harvester).

7.   Ibid., p. 59.

8.   Ibid., p. 142.

9.   Ibid., p. 56.

10.   M. Foucault, *Discipline and Punish: the birth of the prison* (Harmondsworth: Penguin, 1977), pp. 145–6. First published as *Surveiller et Punir: naissance de la prison* (Paris: Gallimard, 1975).

Page references to *Waiting for Godot* relate to the second edition (London: Faber & Faber, 1965), and those to *The Caretaker* to the volume of Pinter's works entitled *Plays: Two* (London: Methuen, 1977).

7

Forms of Dissent in Contemporary Drama and Contemporary Theory
RICK RYLANCE

This chapter will examine some features of contemporary dramatic practice in the light of developments in contemporary literary theory. I do not, however, intend to examine the former from the standpoint of the interpretative practices of the latter. I am, instead, interested in the two as related phenomena. My particular field of interest is dissent, and specifically the question of how dissident theorists and dramatists conceive of the relationship between text and audience. I wish to develop this in relation to, on the one hand, radical post-structuralist theory (which I take to be the major expression of recent critical dissent), and, on the other, work by three socialist dramatists Howard Barker, Howard Brenton and John McGrath. But I will begin by setting out my sense of the dominant direction of relevant theoretical arguments on the problem of how readers make meanings. I will then look at the dramatic practice of Barker and Brenton before, in the third section, turning to that of John McGrath.

THE READER'S ROLE IN THEORY

From the start, the theoretical criticism which has flourished since the mid-1970s opposed 'liberal humanism'. By liberal humanism was meant, in the first instance, the literary criticism then dominant for three decades whose guiding theorists were the *Scrutiny* circle in Britain and 'New Criticism' in America. But, the particular revision of this work was backed by a larger engagement with the consensual outlook for which they spoke. Humanistic liberalism, of course, sharply distinguished itself from the 'free market' economic liberal-ism of Gladstone or Margaret Thatcher. Its hallmarks were a concern

for 'culture', quality of life, and sensitivity to language and, therefore, to certain spiritual values. Quality works of literature enabled
profound living at the spiritual peaks, and were thus intrinsically
opposed to the 'Benthamite-technocratic' industrial world.

By the mid-seventies, however, liberal humanism appeared to
many to have fallen into a rather complacent disengagement from
the social and literary interests of a new generation. By the late
seventies, its language seemed thin and awkward, its techniques of
analysis had lost purchase on new problems, and its values no
longer commanded ready assent in literary studies or the intellectual
and political culture at large. At the same time, the means of transmission for its ideas also came under attack, and the present admin-
istration has asked threatening questions of the public education
system and 'liberal education', the principle of state funding for the
arts (especially the oppositional arts), the maintenance of 'quality'
public broadcasting independent of the market, and the consensual,
if ill-defined, sense that limitations should be placed on the 'free
market' media if quality broadcasting and journalism was to encourage a civically-minded culture. During the eighties, therefore, the
attack on humanist literary criticism coincided with broader structural and ideological shifts.

The response of radical theory to this has been contradictory. On
the one hand, most new theoretical developments have been produced by thinkers who are opposed to the ideologies and practices
of Margaret Thatcher and Ronald Reagan. On the other hand, there
are certain disturbing resemblances between these theories and their
ostensible opponents. Both desire to end consensual thinking and
emphasise conflict, and both have encouraged the use of the language of specialised sub-group technocracies. Indeed, Edward Said
argued as early as 1982 that the growth of a complex and arcane
specialist language in literary theory unsettlingly parallels broader
developments in the Reagan era. Advanced literary theory, in his
account, is another rather mystificatory development of the 'information age', and theorists are of a kind with other information
mandarins: the media personnel, 'experts', 'advisers', policy 'scien-
tists', and 'intelligence' analysts who populate our highly-managed
cultural discourse. Self-consciously modern, tooled-up theory,
therefore, is a defensive response by a threatened discipline and
profession, designed to preserve an 'information' fiefdom in a competing world.[1]

I have some sympathy with Said's case, for it is undeniable that structuralist and post-structuralist thinking has pressed on towards a high-tech refurbishment of critical language which – in its high theoretical abstraction – has enacted the attack on humanism which its arguments proposed. While maintaining a leftist political posture, it has spoken the language of a technocratic elite in a way many have found politically compromising, rebarbative and unnecessary. Particular resentment has been caused by the attack on the communicative, emotional and representational functions of literature supposedly over-valued in 'untheorised' humanism.

The attack was mounted on two main grounds: that humanist ideas rest on a naive belief in personal communication between reader and author, and that both these subjectivities are functions of a psycho-sexual and ideological conditioning which determines their natures. The first argument reduces and trivialises the question of the human and experiential dimensions of literature, and anyway is contradicted by the distinctive writing practices of the new theory's best stylists. The second (essentialist) argument seems to me only partially true, and needs much more careful inspection of evidence than I am aware it has received in theory circles. Nonetheless, as a result, there has been an odd alignment between post-structuralist theory and old New Criticism, for both emphasise the verbal form of a literary work rather than its content or context. For recent criticism, the author is dead, and so, to all intents and purposes, is the immediately human situation which provides the occasion and content of works of literature. The nouveau specialisms, therefore, have tended to confine their attention to verbal 'text' and its tropes, and have largely failed to address the inter-subjective, communicative and historically differential features of literature, as Jerome McGann, amongst others, has argued.[2]

Nouveau Text is therefore like the old New Critical 'poem itself' in its radical separation from the experiential dimensions of works of literature. Nouveau Text is also like the old New Critical poem in that it seems to be composed of variations on a limited number of themes and formulas. Humanist formalism preferred its best works to re-enact honoured traditions; nouveau formalism – especially in its deconstructive guise – prefers Text to enact the paradoxes of sceptical rationalism, and has tended to focus on the epistemology of self-consciousness, identity and reference in language. Much of this criticism has, therefore, somewhat monotonously re-enacted its own philosophical dilemmas, as Frank Kermode has remarked.[3]

But there are of course substantial differences between these two formalisms also. Old formalism was, indisputably, conservative, whereas recent theory challenges the status quo in its interpretative model, its institutional relationships (what is 'literature' after all?), its sense of relevant intellectual affiliation (broadly 'continental' rather than Anglo-American), and its refreshing concept of the desirable good in the human person (who is to be open, indefinite, less-masculine and subvertable). Its strong argument with old human-ism, therefore, has been its challenge to humanism's conception of social role and duty, and ethical and spiritual dogmatism.[4] Whereas old poems embodied human situations ('life') in themselves and realised them through the morally-efficacious protocols of irony, 'organic form' and so on, post-structuralism has celebrated variety, dispersal and the lapse out of order and coherence. Thus *nouveau* Text is adventurously 'open', whereas old works (in Roland Barthes's famous binary distinction) are timidly 'closed'.

Similarly, whereas old formalism (in the doctrine of the affective fallacy) excluded the reader, an influential strand of post-structural-ism has included the reader as a necessary part of its relativised hermeneutics. If there are no reliable epistemological grounds for positing stable interpretative norms, the argument runs, then of necessity the individual experience is paramount. This is particu-larly the case because post-structuralism sees most of us as deluded consumers of interpretative conventions which we use with the same confidence we give to standard weights and measures. In this view, because instability is assumed to be good in itself, desirable interpretation is always fugitive. It is made on the run from standard formats in a cat-and-mouse interaction with convention. The best reading is thus a kind of desirably unsteady, permanent interpreta-tive revolution made with some resistance to the pressures of mean-ing exerted by the text being read, and with substantial scepticism towards the interpretative conventions of the epoch – or so the theory goes. For it is then an important question how far the prac-tices of deconstruction have themselves become dull routine. In addition, one might wonder how it is that these interpreters escape the deadening inauthenticity which awaits most of us. And we might further wonder what this view implies about communal language, for there is a real theoretical difficulty here. In the theoretical basis of much of this work, language is social; the best interpretation, how-ever, is only individual. The difficulty arises because this theory cannot conceive of any collective language which is other than imprisoning (a significantly common metaphor in much of this thinking).

Roland Barthes, in his later work, has been an influential theorist of the reader's activity in this mode. The essay 'From Work to Text' (1971), for example, celebrates the 'free play' of meaning realised by the 'passably empty' subject-critic as he 'strolls' through the Text's imaginary landscape. Here 'what he perceives is multiple, irreducible, coming from a disconnected, heterogeneous variety of substances and perspectives'. The Text therefore 'defers' the signified, and revels in the signifying plurality thus released against orthodoxy.[5] These theories of textual free play have much in common with the libertarian invitations of the late sixties to get rid of 'the policeman in the head'. (This ultra-populist invitation being rendered of course in the language of an excitingly accomplished intellectual mandarin.) The reader of Text, in this account, becomes a wandering Rousseauist free spirit, or a proxy Parisian street activist hurling signifiers at internal policemen.

Barthes's libertarian pluralism is not the only post-structuralist theory of active readership. If Barthes's view is that of a transposed leftist ultra, the influential American critic Stanley Fish has offered another libertarian version of this activity developed from his work on Renaissance literature begun in the mid-sixties. Fish's theory, however, has more in common with Wall Street than insurrectionary Paris, and his idea of 'interpretive communities' appears perfectly homologous with the theories of the free market which have prospered during the eighties. In Fish's view a reader's interpretation is theoretically unconstrained because literary text – like the free market – contains myriad opportunities. Textual meaning depends largely on the critic's interpretative enterprise and is limited only marginally by the availability of verbal raw materials. If you can persuade others to buy your reading then you are in the game. What checks interpretative anarchy is less the pressure towards meaning exerted by the text, than the free market in readings and the 'authority' of the prevailing 'interpretive community'. This authority is formed by, and exerted through, the senior levels of the profession whose members have risen to be such because they have sold their readings most widely. This, it seems to me, is Reaganomics in literary criticism, and the model proposed for literary activity is that provided by the activities of international corporate capitalism. If my reading of Fish is correct (and you know it makes sense), then the fears expressed by Edward Said carry additional weight, and what seems an attractively open theory dissentingly at odds with dogmatism might be understood as merely collusive with things as they are. Interestingly, Fish has recently taken issue with Said on the question-begging grounds of professional morale and good practice.[6]

It will be clear that I am unhappy with the model of readerly activity offered by both Barthes's radical libertarianism, and Fish's transposition of free-market economics. Both these theories, despite their apparent openness, seem severely reduced accounts of this general human activity. In fact, far from acknowledging the reader's importance, they reduce that person to a solipsistic spectre, I think this for a number of reasons.

First, the interpretative encounter envisioned by post-structuralist theory is one in which the text becomes a mere reflection of the interests of the critic. It has ceased to be an activity which might challenge, or unsettle assumptions. This is the paradox of the theory. Though it is ostensibly 'open', in fact it numbingly repeats its own premises and obsessions. Second, though, again, ostensibly an 'open' situation, in fact this democracy of reading conceals a hard-headed professionalism which in reality controls the dispersal of meaning quite severely. The language so often deployed to suport libertarian ideas in actuality confines discussion to insider professionals. Third, the hostility to ideas of collective language results in a false and exclusive choice between a free 'I' and a malign 'we' which is too close for comfort to present ideologies of the efficacy of self-interest. Fourth, these theories, because limited in language and human scope, curtail both the range of material to be examined and the human situations to be considered. Post-structuralism has offered to challenge 'the canon'; but in fact it has merely 're-read' the same old texts. There has been a dreadful lack of effort – except by feminists and occasionally critics interested in 'working-class' writing – to look for new kinds or dimensions of literature. As a result the 'canon' or 'tradition' has been little disturbed by theoretical trumpets. (And I repeat the feminist exception to this.) Finally, because of its lack of interest in human occasions, the experiences and interests addressed by most post-structuralist discourse merely reflect its personnel; that is, information professionals and the cosmopolitan *avant-garde* – a powerful sub-group within bourgeois culture which is as exclusive as its language is difficult to understand.[7]

With these remarks in mind, I will now turn to the dissident drama of the same period.

THEORY INTO PRACTICE

The relationship between literary theory and practice is closer than we sometimes imagine. In 1978, when F. R. Leavis died, Peter Hall wrote in his diaries of the 'inspiration' that Leavis's moral imperatives offered: 'he somehow inculcated a feeling that art was to do with better standards of life and better behaviour'. Leavis thus provided a humanistic rationale for Hall's kind of theatre which was backed by a widespread textual practice ('practical criticism'): 'All the textual seriousness at the basis of Trevor [Nunn]'s work and of mine comes from Leavis, and there is a vast band of us. Comical to think that Leavis hated the theatre and never went to it. He has had more influence on the contemporary theatre than any other critic.'[8] Others have different perspectives. In an interview in 1982, Trevor Griffiths accepted that 'I think my practice is probably Lukacsian ... the whole idea of a character working as a confluence of important social and political and moral forces within society, in real historical time.' Though he added the necessary caution: 'I didn't read Lukacs and say "Oh I want to write that way." But reading Lukacs offers some insight into the way one works.'[9] One way of understanding the relationship of theory to practice, then, is not to see it as the relationship between a produced object and its interpretative metalanguage, but as two different sectors of a complex literary culture responding to related problems. This, in fact, was the drift of early poststructuralist argument, though I doubt it has been its subsequent practice. I want, therefore, to look at the work of two recent dramatists – Howard Barker and Howard Brenton – in the light of the theoretical developments sketched in the first part of this essay. In particular I want to examine both sets of material as responses to the dissent of the 1960s.

Howard Barker's work has never quite been comfortably assimilated to that of the generation of socialist dramatists (Brenton, Hare, Edgar, Griffiths and McGrath are the usual names) with whom he has been regularly classed.[10] He has never had a high activist profile through the touring or fringe groups, for instance. Though he calls himself a socialist, his politics (like those of Roland Barthes, incidentally) are difficult to determine with much precision. Also his work has never had much of an airing on television; nor has he had the use of the mainstream national stages. While its tone and manner has consistently alienated, he has not enjoyed the celebrity of scandal. Recently, however, he has sought to define his considerable output theoretically. This definition strikingly resembles the ethos and direction of radical post-structuralism.

Barker, too, was an early enemy of humanism. In an interview in 1980 he attacks the liberal humanist consensus: 'I certainly don't intend to aim for more "maturity", "fair-mindedness" or any other of the weary baggage of critical humanism. . . . It's death in drama.' And he attacks the 'wicked, paralyzing posture' of humanistic guilt. He describes his political stance as uncertain: 'It is easy to say you are a revolutionary socialist, but it is stale with cliché and a certain vanity. I knew that then, as now, I believed revolution necessary but unlikely. That tension is at the hub of my work.'[11] Since then he has attempted to come to terms with the 'extinction of official socialism' and has concluded that 'when the opposition loses its politics, it must root in art'.[12] This rejection of party socialism for the freedoms represented by art, was, of course, a feature of much sixties theory on the left from Marcuse to Danny-the-Red.[13] In a sequence of manifestos, Barker has described his new theatre as 'tragic theatre' ('49 Asides for a Tragic Theatre', 1986), 'catastrophism' ('The Triumph in Defeat', 1988), and the theatre of loss ('Understanding Exits as Complexity Takes a Bow', 1990).[14] It has been most fully expressed in several recent plays, principally *The Possibilities* (1988), *The Last Supper* (1988) and *Seven Lears* (1989). It is a bleak, difficult practice.

Barker's argument assumes collapse and disintegration. This is both a condition and a desideratum. The condition is provided by the deterioration of the ethical and social policy consensus of the 1960s and with it the general moral community. While it lasted (Barker argues) this enabled a range of theatrical practices which could be taken as a 'common ethical ground among artist, actor and audience'. These, he says in 'The Triumph of Defeat', include 'the two sacred groves of contemporary theatre – clarity and realism', to which he adds populism. Their collapse means a new theatre is needed and enabled, but this new practice cannot repair a damaged culture with new maxims and rallying points. Rather, theatre should reflect its ruin. Most of his plays, therefore, create smashed and savage mental and physical landscapes. The acceptance of disintegration, he argues, shifts the ground of ethical argument.

Barker's 'new kind of theatre must locate its creative tension not between characters and arguments on the stage but between the audience and the stage itself' ('The Triumph in Defeat'). If there is no moral language worth having, obviously there is no moral language worth speaking. The new ethical practice, therefore, needs to be trans-actional and not expressive. However, because, by declaration, there is no public language available, this action must be private, disruptive and essentially internal. The theatre of tragic catastrophism revels in the destruction of the consensual grounds of debate. This is why collapse is a desideratum. Ethical action, for Barker, can only base itself on 'disruption', 'instability' and 'loss', and the kind of experience which tragedy used to make available. This loss and letting go, he argues in 'Understanding Exits', is in turn a release of the imaginative, the unconscious, and therefore the freshly possible, from the shackles presently imprisoning them. These shackles include orthodox narrative, naturalistic, everyday language (which, 'thin on metaphor, annihilates ambiguity'), and the oppressive presence of the need for tidy, assignable meaning. Thus the new theatre, through transgression, liberates the members of its audience from the tyranny of 'understanding', and opens the possibilities and truths of the perverse and the contradictory. In the name of a democratic plurality of meaning, it creates a 'radical elitism of the imagination'.[15]

Barker's conception of his new theatre mirrors the radical cognitive scepticism and suspicion of communal discourses to be found in much post-structuralism. It is also reminiscent of the jubilant celebration of the release from 'the meaning' found in Roland Barthes. Indeed Barker is prone, like Barthes, to speak in the language of ecstatic sexuality to convey the process of creative tension and loss. It is a freeing from shame and guilt as well as from an imprisoning rationality. Thus both post-structuralism and catastrophe theatre celebrate the literary as disruptive plurality and 'chaos', and emphasise the individual reader or spectator's experience at the expense of the collective.

Barker's aesthetics are, like Barthes's, anti-referential. In the programme-text to *The Last Supper* he writes:

> I gnawed at English socialism for ten years, from *Claw*, through *A Passion in Six Days*, to *Downchild*, coming at last to History, which is where I had begun [Barker studied History at university], neither official history nor documentary history, whose truth I deny, but the history of emotion, looking for a politics of the emotions. I discovered that the only things worth describing now are things that do not happen, just as the only history plays worth writing concern themselves with what did not happen. New writing began at the Royal Court with the description of things that were not

seen (i.e. real life). Writing now has to engage with what is not seen (i.e. the imagination) because real life is annexed, reproduced, soporific.[16]

Like many of his contemporaries, Barker rejects the Royal Court naturalism of the late fifties. As in much post-structuralism, there is a delight in paradox (the history of what has not happened) and the collapse of referential history into discourse. Relatedly, everyday life is thought to be routinised and damaging, and this comes strongly from the same late-sixties ideas which sponsored Barthes's libertarian textual hedonism and related phenomena.

Like Barthes in 'From Work to Text' Barker is out for a stroll. In 'Understanding Exits' he invites the audience to 'wander freely in the wastes of the imagination' and the metaphor draws on common ideas. (Barker insists on the European dimensions of his concerns, and is published by John Calder, traditionally Britain's leading publisher of the European and transAtlantic *avant-garde*.) But the metaphor has other sources and resonances – for instance in Romantic poetry, and Barker's wanderings in the imagination resume some powerful Romantic topics and themes.

Like the great Romantic poets, Barker develops his argument through the manipulation of mythic and literary materials. The literary bearings of *Seven Lears* are obvious, and clearly *The Last Supper* (subtitle 'A New Testament') draws on Christian myth, painterly and literary conceptions of this subject, and classical notions of the writer's role (the hapless poet is called Apollo). This is interleaved with the recent history of Eastern Europe and a sardonic glancing account of postwar British Labourism (the soldiery are called McAttlee, McStain and McNoy). Barker, therefore, is a vigorously deconstructive and intertextual writer in a manner both thoroughly modern and thoroughly Romantic. Barker's characters, and their spectators, wander – though without heroism – like Romantic protagonists among war, empire and ruin. Dislocated from orthodoxy, betrayed by institutions and politically baffled by the collapse of opposition, they seek solace in the imagination and in the force of human desire. Wandering in the wastes of the imagination, however, they are denied the consolations of nature in our dirty twentieth-century greenhouse. So the characters in *The Last Supper* stare yearningly from a window like their intertextual fellows in *Endgame*, while the imaginations of Barker's audience stroll across stages peopled by victims of catastrophes, political and ecological, happened, happening or to come.

This bleakness, of course, sets Barker apart from Barthes – though not entirely. For if Barker is Byronic or unredemptively Blakean in his catastrophe scenarios, Barthes's hedonistic utopianism is a pastoral in a still distinctively Romantic manner. (And I think it is no accident that many leading American post-structuralists have been Romantic specialists.) In 'From Work to Text' – with a theoretically startling glance towards the authenticity of personal experience – 'the author of these lines' strolls 'on the side of a valley, a *oued* flowing down below . . . ; lights, colours, vegetation, heat, air, slender explosions of noises, scant cries of birds, children's voices from over on the other side, passages, gestures, clothes of inhabitants near or far away'.[17] Barthes, here – though in the age of the family outing – could be Wordsworth before the solitary reaper, or Shelley before the skylark. That is to say, with more generic propriety, that Barthes's are a form of the occasional essay – like those of the English Romantics Lamb or Hazlitt, for instance. As such they make contradictory theory. For what we are most conscious of, in reading them, is not the author's death, but his engaging, sophisticated, always interesting and provoking personality, and the distinctive, 'authored', fineness and delicacy of his wording. What is on display in an essay like 'From Work to Text' is a sensibility, and range of human engagements, rather than a theoretical position.

This contradiction in Barthes engages a similar one in Barker's much darker pieces. Both seek to deny the specificity of context and sensibility. But Text or catastrophic theatre does not in reality come from verbal outer-space, or an Alaska of the imagination. It is part of a human practice with human dimensions, contexts, responsibilities and settings. And it really is poor argument by Barker in 'Understanding Exits' (and New Critical and post-structural formalism) to trivialise the issue merely to one of 'single' meaning or authorial intention. For few writers ever realise only one intention, few texts ever have just one meaning, few in the audience are content with one disposable authorial purpose. Attending theatre is a social event, and discussion and questioning usually follow. To say that clarity produces servile conformity, or that understanding implies a squalor of the imagination, seems to me to be (at least) reductive. The engagement with the present crisis in values, the effort towards newer, better forms of living, are made, like theatre itself, in public. Yet in Barker's version it is a private affair. In his impatience with the failures of collectivism, in his antagonism to the 'banality' and 'triviality' of mass culture, and hostility to the reductions of rationalistic englightenment, Barker individualises the soul and makes the imagination's moral good frustratingly obscure. It forces him, indeed, to pretend that his often-exhilarating imaginative voyages are suspended in the social nowhere between stage and auditorium. Like readers in post-structuralist theory, Barker's audience, though stimulated and provoked, are privatised into solipsism, seeking, like psychoanalytic patients, consolation in the pleasures of loss. At this point I am troubled by the connotations of his elitism of the imagination.

Barker's work seems to me unique in British theatre at present. However, the general shape and tendency of his arguments are not; they are part of a general trend in the way we think about responses to art in a period which belligerently undervalues them and in which art has ceased to have much to say to a social world and common, ordinary experience. This world (it is one which features so movingly and necessarily in Raymond Williams's thought) is too often contemptuously dismissed in much recent theory and dramatic practice, and the result is stalemate, political despair and the aggressive hostility of defeat. Howard Barker's fiery gifts for language and theatrical metaphor are strikingly original, but his pessimism is not, and it is indicative of a general style of dissent within the culture at large. Dissent has ceased to have faith in common purposes, has ceased to think about shared discourse as anything other than mendacious ideological imposition, and has hastily opted for the privacies of the Text in the mind. This revealing pessimism is further reflected in the directly agitatory drama of the period written by men.

If Barker's elitism revolts against the banalities of populism, then for the 'other Howard', Howard Brenton, the libertarian, activist populism of the late sixties was ideologically, imaginatively and dramatically crucial, as he recalled in an interview in 1974.

> May 1968 disinherited my generation in two ways. First, it destroyed any remaining affection for the official culture. The situationists showed how all of them, the dead greats, are corpses on our backs – Goethe, Beethoven – how gigantic the fraud is. But it also, secondly, destroyed the notions of personal freedom. Freaking out and drug culture, anarchist notions of spontaneous freedom, anarchist political action: it all failed. It was defeated. A generation dreaming of a beautiful utopia was kicked – kicked awake and not dead. I've got to believe not kicked dead. May 1968

gave me a desperation I still have.[18]

This is quite a different politics, but it implies a similar attitude to audiences.

Brenton's combative theatre hitches an aggressive populism (no more Goethe or Beethoven) to an agitatory critique of the ways in which the cultural nightmare of the past lies on the young limbs of the living. Many of his best theatrical metaphors come from this idea: the ravaged ghost of Churchill rising again in *The Churchill Play* (1974), or the layering of different times and experiences in cycles of repeated atrocity in *The Romans in Britain* (1980). The political and dramatic theory behind this comes from sixties Situationism, as he says in the interview. Last year Brenton reviewed the Situationist International exhibition in Paris, and, re-reading Guy Debord (the leading theorist of Situationism), concluded that 'I still find its powerful vision of the way the century works rings true', though he deplored its 'dark side': the Angry Brigade and the Red Army Faction.[19]

Situationism evolved from surrealism and was developed during the sixties as a political critique of modern capitalist culture.[20] The fullest statement of its politics is Debord's *La Société du Spectacle* of 1967, which follows from some features of Marxist-existential critiques of the inauthenticity of 'everyday life' in modern culture by Sartre and Henri Lefebvre. It is thus part of the mainstream of oppositional theory of the period and overlaps with the rather ambiguous critique of the duplicities of popular culture and everyday life contained in Barthes's *Mythologies* of 1957. (I say ambiguous because Barthes seems to rather enjoy the popular duplicities he reveals.)

Debord's book pictures a world where authenticity is no longer possible. We exist speciously through the fetishised, alienating categories of the 'spectacle' of consumer representations. In this world Being degrades into Having, which degrades in turn into mere Appearing. To combat this Debord looks to the revolutionary action of the working class now politicised as the 'class of [authentic] consciousness'.[21] How the theory becomes practice in this way is unclear, largely because this (now rather dated) collectivist gloss is a simple generalisation of an individual, artistically-driven, anarchist-inclined rebellion. The connection between it and the general events of 1968 is easily grasped, though, as are the reasons for its appeal to dramatists like Brenton and other counter-culture activists in Britain.[22]

Like the milder, though more sophisticated, post-structuralism which came in its wake, Situationism attempted to combat the accumulated tyranny of the past by shedding individual enthralments at a personal level, and by the deconstruction of public discourse at a social level, and Brenton's plays thrive on this. He is an expert diagnostician of the liberal conscience, which he reads as the acceptable face behind which the real cruelties of power and domination occur. Many of his plays, therefore, feature a central character who voices a tortured and guilty conscience – like the army doctor Thompson in *The Churchill Play*, or Chichester, the SAS man 'gone native' in Ireland, in *The Romans in Britain*, or the Makepeaces in *Weapons of Happiness* (1976). Each play is structured to invite the audience's identification with this liberal voice, only to defeat and cancel it, exposing the creed as a terrible impotent deceit. Chichester, therefore, is ruthlessly shot as he attempts reparative contact with the IRA; Thompson is sidelined in his vain effort to join the camp revolt; and Ralph Makepeace – his name the ironic quintessence of liberal humanism – ends his play commenting on the young workers who occupy his factory: 'God, the little shits! Children of the Revolution? I want them to . . . To bleed like pigs in a ditch.'[23]

But alongside this exposure of the insecurities and delusions of liberalism lies also an aggressive critique of the 'spectacle' of false representations which support and nourish it. Thus the plays counter positive images of English culture in a sustained and deliberate way. Brenton's is a First World War world of blood, wire and mud in which middle-class respectables (like Caroline Thompson and Sylvia Makepeace) yearn for Surrey gardens to hide the reality of English political life. The garden thus represents both self-delusion and the camouflaging of power. It is in an expensive country garden that the Situationist assassin Jed kills the cabinet minister (and himself) in *Magnificence* (1973), and in the early play *Christie in Love* (1969), about the mass-murderer Reginald Christie, the set, the 'Garden', is a pen caged with wire and 'a filthy sight'. It stands for 'Christie's garden, his front room, a room in a police station, an executioner's shed, a lime pit' suggesting the complicity of all social structures in Christie's criminality, and the need to dig up the corpses which rot below the nation's favourite hobby.[24] In a recent piece on the revival of *The Churchill Play* by the RSC, Brenton described its origins in an unbroadcast radio play whose 'shock was its Englishness; its elegaic, Elgarian love of the Lincolnshire landscape in which the imaginary camp was erected'.[25] In plays like *The Churchill Play* and *The Romans* where national and cultural identity is a major theme, in the use of motifs like the garden, and in the assault on liberalism, Brenton attempts to 'disrupt the spectacle' of Englishness and its images.

Brenton's violent exposure of the hidden and the mendacious in English life is notorious, for he aims to offend. His dramatic practice is thus theoretically coherent as long as the audience he so offends can be thought to be complicit with the spectacle to be disrupted. The question of the venues in which his work is performed is therefore relevant, for the argument about audiences and venues in political theatre over the past decade or so has been severe. Should dissenting writers go for the big stages, with the political and perhaps artistic compromises this entails, or should they look for independent, smaller venues and organisations giving greater autonomy of political and artistic expression? Howard Brenton has tried both, though arguably his best work has appeared on the big stages – perhaps because his imagination reaches for big themes, large audacious metaphors and a big, generalising language. *The Romans in Britain* is a case in point. The play aimed to explore the limits of liberal tolerance in a quite calculated way and took on sexual crime, homosexuality, Ireland, imperial history, and the English racial self-image. In the resulting fuss this liberalism in fact held. Both conservatives and liberals claimed vindication, but both were chastened.[26]

So what did *The Romans in Britain* reveal about the spectacle of liberalism and its opponents? In the end it revealed a complicity between them. Brenton's dissidence needs a tolerant screen of liberalism for its dramatic practice, and liberalism needs *The Romans* to validate its tolerance. For instance, the play was about imperialism, but on the third page of the programme was an advert for Barclays Bank International then up to its ears in South African investment. The advert features a line drawing of a cheery businessman and a Japanese Geisha. It is a thoughtless, perhaps offensive, stereotype. The compromises of this liberalism cut both ways therefore: we tolerate your metaphorical buggery, you tolerate the selling of imperialist investments. If Brenton's target, and his subject, and his audience (in the prestige institutions of liberal culture, the National Theatre, the RSC, and the BBC) is English liberalism, then this is also the condition and ground of his work too. This dependency on the liberalism it assaults perhaps explains the flip-side of Brenton's theme, which is not the joys of a better world realised alternatively. It is a Hobbesian vision of man's degradation, cruelty and malice.

In a programme piece for *The Churchill Play* Brenton meditates upon the state, and the illustration which Hobbes provided for it in *Leviathan*. In this familiar metaphor the big body of the state is made from the tiny bodies of the citizens who compose it, and Brenton wonders what it would be like to be in the armpit, or between the toes. Hobbes's big body has become, for England, the corpse of Churchill, rotting on the culture's back. But Brenton's conclusion seems to be not that this is the result of a deformed society in a particular history, but that it is human nature. Though the plays enact their assaults on liberalism, and gesture towards revolution, their analyses seem more powerfully to address metaphysical questions like Mike's at the close of *The Churchill Play*: 'What's human?' The regular answer, in Brenton, seems to be cruelty, death and rot, and this pessimism is vitiated only by the relish of its retelling, as though the only joy is the confrontation with Thersites.

Brenton, then, like Barker, turns in disgust from humanism. He explores the outer edges of liberal culture, playing cat-and-mouse with its tolerance and conventions, in much the same way – though far more interestingly, I think – that post-structuralists 'play' with Text. The reasons for this are complex, but they seem to concern the ways in which dissent has come to terms with the legacy of the sixties. That uneasy negotiation is far from concluded, as the unwillingness of both Barker and Brenton to relinquish their interest in the ideas of the period testifies. Even in the announcement of defeat and failure its hold is maintained, which is why, perhaps, the characters in their plays wander their ruins haunted by so many ghosts.

THE AUDIENCES OF JOHN MCGRATH

In this final section I want to offer a more positive argument in relation to the work of John McGrath. It centres on the relationship between text and audience – both in the theatre and the study of literature – and it thus implies a theory of meaning which is based on the human occasion or context in which literature is produced and consumed. I wish to suggest that our usual procedures for analysing literature tend to be exclusive, and this reflects the social basis of the profession. Some elements of recent literary theory have emphasised this *in theory*, but the dominant trend in recent work has been to lose sight of the social features of this process in the information ghetto of the *avant-garde*. The apparently liberationist politics of this late version of disappointed romanticism are thus compromised by its neglect of communication (for theories of Text), of agency (for theories of determined subjectivity), of communal discourse (for the solitary reader), and of common experience (for the mysticism of radical incomprehension).

These features are, in turn, related to the difficult legacy of the sixties. In dramatists like Barker and Brenton, the aggressive frustration and disenchanted withdrawal has been not just from the mainstream political process (which is conceived largely as a fraud), but also from the patterns of activity, and the discourses and languages, of everyday life. For it has been a major feature of this legacy (as for instance in Situationist theory) that 'everyday life' is a mere expression of the ideological forces that shape it, and that people 'caught' (like prisoners) within it are mere victims of ideological entrapment. The apogee of this theory was the strongly determinist and structuralist-derived version of Marxism challenged by E. P. Thompson, Raymond Williams and others in the late seventies.[27] These writers noted the easy way in which, once the social process had been conceived as inevitably and flatteningly powerful, it could be then so easily forgotten as attention was turned to the desocialised formalities of Text, or a new version of epochal history, or abstract theorising about 'Power', or the tricky contortions of the subject under analysis. In his influential 'The Mirror Stage' (1949), for instance, Jacques Lacan, for understandable historical reasons, conceived of the world as a concentration camp. Our efforts to think of ourselves otherwise were stated to be merely imaginary. Though more hopeful avant-gardists planned the Great Escape through the fissures and lacunae and tunnels of Text, it was not at all clear towards which Switzerland of the unconscious they were running.

But the world is only metaphorically like a concentration camp despite Howard Brenton's images and Lacan's puzzles, and Thompson and Williams noted that to think so, to live theoretically in such a world, is to turn one's back on the diversity of human activity, and to trouble oneself only with talking to fellow prisoners. It is the great advantage of John McGrath's work that he looks beyond the theatrical and theoretical gates, and that his practice is based on contact and mutuality. If the dramas of Brenton and Barker enact division, defeat and the spoiling effects of the way things are, McGrath's work, whilst recognising these, still celebrates communication and the possibilities of sharing.

McGrath's case is best argued in *A Good Night Out – Popular Theatre: Audience, Class and Form* (1981). At the centre of it is the observation that a theatrical event is not merely textual. The language of theatre is composed of other elements by virtue of the fact that the experience it offers is social. These elements include not only the words and other features of what happens on stage (music, sets, lighting, movement, and so on), but also

> the nature of the audience, the nature, social, geographical and physical, of the venue, the price of tickets, the availability of tickets, the nature and placing of the pre-publicity, where the nearest pub is, and relationship between all these considerations themselves and of each with what is happening on stage. For when we discuss theatre, we are discussing a social event, and a very complex social event, with a long history and many elements, each element also having a long and independent history.[28]

Several arguments follow from this kind of analysis. First, a too-exclusive emphasis on the text pulls theatrical activity out of its social context (this is a problem for critics, of course, not usually for writers). Second, a disregard for the other, non-staged elements elides theatre's social context and forms the *practical* assumption that theatre is a middle-class activity with only middle-class concerns. Third, if you want to attract non-traditional theatregoers you have to attend carefully to the changed artistic as well as social dynamics because both form and content reflect and create audiences. None are timeless or universal. Fourth, there are artistic possibilities available from traditions outside those of mainstream ('highbrow' and middle-class) theatre and these have a rich, varied and interesting history. Much of this is plain good sense, but let us examine some of these ideas further.

Like many primarily socially-based interpretative models, McGrath's can be thought reductive. For instance, he condemns Harold Pinter (a writer I admire) for an indulgence in absurdity, mystery and enigma – the significant failure to say anything significant, as McGrath puts it (p. 84). This is a crude response, but in a real sense Pinter's work *is* obfuscatory about social contexts and relations, and it is possible to see a correlation betwen this and the kind of West End or South Bank venues within which he usually works. For it follows that lack of attention to social context diminishes its importance and therefore generalises into timelessness the experiences of the essentially middle-class clientele that attend performances of his plays, and Pinter's dramas have shifted progressively upwards in class-location. At the same time they have remained within the same naturalist–expressionist, single-room format. The corresponding elision of social experience, of a world outside the tormented sensibilities of the inhabitants of these rooms, is an important omission.

But McGrath's critique of contemporary theatrical practice is aimed also, and perhaps primarily, at oppositional or dissident theatre which he sees as compromised by the contradiction between its message and its venues. The Royal Court naturalism of the late 1950s, for instance, McGrath notes, was largely played before traditional theatre audiences. Like nineteenth-century 'industrial' fiction it put the working class onstage, but the important questions are, for whom, and for what ends? McGrath has similar doubts, too, about Brecht, and about much contemporary

'political' theatre which is on the side of the workers but expresses itself in the language of high cultural theatre – important and excellent though that may be. The work of Brecht and Piscator in the 20s is the best example of this genre; they have had many followers from the American Guild Theatre in the 30s down to Brenton and Hare today. (pp. 61–2)

Similarly, the attempt to localise the significant action in the solitary imaginative world of the spectator (as Howard Barker does) would find no favour with McGrath. Theatre is a communal event, it 'is not about the reaction of *one sensibility* to events external to itself, as poetry tends to be; or to the *private* consumption of fantasy or a mediated slice of social reality, as most novels tend to be. It is a public event, and it is about matters of public concern' (p. 83). Again, one can think of all kinds of objections to these definitions of poetry and fiction, but you see the point he is aiming at. To make art a private affair is to fall victim to the

sentimental, nostalgic image of the romantic poet [which, McGrath points out, is historically quite inaccurate], a truly dreadful concept of the artistic vision piercing through the gloom of contemporary reality, seizing upon and encapsulating in a few pithy phrases the spirit of our time, all done by 'instinct' or 'inspiration' with no effort of the mind, and all packaged for the convenience of posterity. (p. 84)

This critique of contemporary theatrical dissidence is related to McGrath's understanding of the political legacy of the sixties also. McGrath was in Paris in 1968 and his reaction, as recorded in an interview in 1985, has little of the acrimonious bitterness of some of his contemporaries.[29] There is a frank acceptance of pastness in his tone, and a sense, too, that the significant action lies elsewhere. This view is supported in *Radical People's Theatre*, an interesting recent book by Eugéne Van Erven. Van Erven examines a range of post-1968 oppositional drama from Europe and the United States, and finds that the majority dissident tradition does not lie in confrontational pessimism, but in 'decentralised, anti-establishment theatre in alternative spaces for popular audiences'.[30] Though these developments, twenty years on, are, for diverse reasons, on the decline, the search for non-traditional theatre audiences, the willingness to move out to non-traditional theatre venues and into the habitats of these audiences, the eagerness to explore collaborative writing or audience involvements in educational or skills programmes, the use of popular forms or conventions, and the willingness to form alliances with non-arts, non-theatre organisations like trade unions or political parties, suggest a direction and ethos of operation which is strikingly different from the theoretical or theatre programmes described earlier. Van Erven's example from Britain is McGrath's 7:84 company, and his book very helpfully shifts the perspective on McGrath's work from Scottish isolation, to a kind of international centrality.

What are the advantages of non-mainstream, working-class venues and forms? The first advantage is of course political. If you wish to change the minds of the working class and increase their consciousness of their times and history then there is no point looking to do so on the South Bank. Similarly, there is no point going to working-men's clubs or Highland village halls – as 7:84 do – and performing a sensitive, expressionist piece about metropolitan *angst*. Not only will the subject matter be inappropriate, so too will the form. For it is unlikely that the audiences will be able to appreciate the formal conventions within which such a play is made, enjoyed or understood. One needs, therefore, to use more appropriate forms, and, once one looks, the range of forms available from working-class traditions of performance is really quite large. What is more, they are well-suited to telling stories which range over long time-periods, or which require vivid metaphors to explain complex facts or processes, or satirical political points, or which need to be flexible enough to involve local audiences. Thus *The Cheviot, The Stag and the Black,*

Black Oil (1973) uses the free-wheeling form of the Highland *ceilidh* to tell 200 years of Highland history, and *The Game's a Bogey* (1974), an urban play about the socialist economist and educationist John MacLean, uses the variety turn, Punch-and-Judy, and parodies of the TV game-show to represent processes of economic exploitation.[31]

So there is a utility in using these forms. But in emphasising working-class audiences and working-class forms in this way, McGrath is also working against the habitual ways of understanding working-class life and working-class experience which have been dominant in the modern world. These theories – which are a cornerstone of much liberal humanism in the Leavisite or New Critical tradition – have judged working-class culture a write-off. Working-class culture, and majority habits, threaten 'real' culture (as in Leavis's juxtaposition of 'Mass Civilisation and Minority Culture'). Real culture is about 'fine' living, fine cultural products, and a robust sensitivity (it was characteristic of the language of this group that it went in for oxymorons). It represents values which could never quite be formulated, but could be intriguingly sensed by the cultural peer-group and enacted through the group enjoyment of quality literature. Mass civilisation, on the other hand, was dead wood, or more accurately a kind of disease inflicted on, through or by the masturbatory herd (this is the language of Q. D. Leavis's *Fiction and the Reading Public* of 1932). Popular life and culture was thoughtless, routinised, degenerate and unsophisticated, and this view persisted and became commonplace in for instance (with different emphases and inflections) the language theories of Basil Bernstein, the educational outlook of the Black Papers, the entry policies and syllabuses of British educational institutions, the writings of disgruntled 'Movement' men, and the wan jeremiads on popular culture by Richard Hoggart and Kenneth Baker.[32]

This liberal-humanistic prejudice was, ironically, reinforced in subtle ways by the more theoretically rigorous ideas (usually from the left) which offered to replace liberal humanism in the later sixties and seventies. The practical effect of the critiques of ideologically-saturated everyday life mounted by, say, Guy Debord or Louis Althusser was to reinforce these disabling and narrow stereotypes. In this light McGrath's work with 7:84, and his willingness to look straightforwardly and seriously at working-class culture, has, along with that of other individuals and groups (like the novelist James Kelman or Ken Worpole and the Federation of Worker Writers and

Community Publishers), helped to extend the imaginative range of our present literary culture by acknowledging a body of work or experience normally excluded from our cultural perceptions.

Now this argument is *not* that if only we opened our eyes we would find a pastorally-desirable working-class world beneath our feet in social terms. Of course lives led within the working class can be narrow, dishevelled, hating, violent and resentful (many middle-class lives are similarly damaged). That is not the argument, and to hold to it would be absurd romance. The argument is that narrowness of outlook, and the restrictions of our habitual perception, distorts our imaginative sympathies and our sense of the possible and the various. At the same time this way of seeing encourages a deep-seated pessimism and hostility, and a retreat – angry or conforming – into little orbits of language and thinking which become ever narrower as evermore pervasive and into which, I think, contemporary dissent has wandered. In *A Good Night Out* John McGrath's enlarged sense of the possibilities, and determinants, of theatrical form comes from looking carefully at working-class theatre and realising its possibilities for narrative, entertainment, pace and 'breaking the illusion'. The purposes for this, indeed, might include working *against* the less-desirable attitudes of the working-class audience one wishes to reach through the forms most familiar to them. McGrath's theatrical practice, therefore, comes from a versatile and skilful tradition of performance in variety and vaudeville aimed principally at the working class, and which theatrical dissidents have in fact used regularly since the thirties. In the sixties Ken Loach and Tony Garnett used semi-professional, club-land entertainers as actors in their social-issue films like *Cathy Come Home*. This world was itself the subject of an interesting television documentary. *The Entertainers*, made by John McGrath for Granada in 1964, and the whole tradition was used by Trevor Griffiths in *Comedians* (1976) as a metaphor to explore the two versions – social democratic and revolutionary – of British leftist thought: the conflict between the two, of course, being also a generational conflict typical of the late sixties and early seventies.[33] Therefore when McGrath discusses the theatrical possibilities made available by, say, a night-out in an inner-city working-men's club, or Ken Dodd's skills as a comedian, he is alert not just to a range of practical techniques, but also to an important working-class theatrical history which has only recently begun to be researched and documented.[34]

One of the disappointing things about recent (non-feminist) theory is that its worthy challenge to the principles on which the literary canon has been chosen has only questioned the principles and rarely brought new work into view. But recent studies of working-class theatre have substantiated McGrath's argument in *A Good Night Out* that his practice with 7:84 stems from a long history.[35] The company themselves have revived important Scottish plays from the thirties and forties, brought to their attention by older members of their audience. As McGrath wrote in the programme for their revival of Ena Lamont Stewart's *Men Should Weep*, 'their existence pointed to our own work as a continuation of a very strong tradition of popular theatre in Scotland, rather than a fad from the 1970s'.[36] This theatre adapted mainstream naturalism, and had a sophisticated acquaintance with European developments in both drama and film, as recent studies have demonstrated. But it also found its sources, as autobiographical memoirs – especially those of Ewan MacColl – make clear, in music-hall, the Worker's Arts Clubs, and the highly theatrical debates among working-class autodidacts and study groups (a culture which E. M. Forster and his liberal-humanist successors have only managed to patronise).[37]

The existence of this material sets interesting questions for our sense of our appropriate activities as literary critics. The liberal-humanist tradition which formed literary studies believed that the reading and study of literature put us importantly in touch with central human values. But its emphasis on restrictive definitions of quality, its pessimistically fearful account of the decline of the modern world, and its intolerant and rejecting attitude towards the experiences of most living human beings, meant that it could assume that the analysis and appreciation of the formal qualities of a limited range of great works was identical with the most significant moral and social experience.

This elision of formalism with more generally discursive and social questions has continued in recent theory, which, in the name of a radical politics of interpretation, has rediscovered a relish for the ornate description of the twists and turns of language tropes. Both formations have needed to legitimate themselves by reference to the social world, but the emphasis on textual formalism has in practice meant the evaporation of any sustained attention to it. As a result works that nakedly display their convictions or affiliations, or membership of other cultural traditions, have tended to vanish from view. What then does one do with work by John McGrath and 7:84, or the worker's theatre texts which have been recently published?

This work does not lend itself to the kinds of formal analysis usually practised on canonical texts. It is low in ambiguity, irony, and ambition to turn metaphysical. Its language is demotic, its imagery often sparse and unoriginal, its forms come from a history barely visible from our usual studies. But to say, therefore, that these texts are negligible is unacceptable on grounds that are as intellectually convincing as they are morally and politically so. The study of the human and social contexts of making meaning, and finding and developing expression, seems to me as valid as the study of Text in its New or Nouveau versions. The emphasis this work places on the use of communal, shared languages and forms, and on the human, emotional and social contexts and relationships of the business of making meanings, provides a model of communication which – to make the very minimal case – is closer to that envisaged by both the best education and the best democratic practice, than that envisaged by the theoretical *avant-garde*. I am not worried by the argument that this throws away our 'best texts'. I like those too. But in a time when our society, our culture, our literature, and our education is so based on exclusion, it's perhaps best not to want just 'the best' or 'the Text' on those terms in theory or drama.

Notes

1. Edward Said, 'Opponents, Audiences, Constituencies, and Community', *Critical Inquiry*, 9 (1982), 1–26.
2. See, for instance, the essays collected in Jerome J. McGann, *The Beauty of Inflections: Literary Investigations in Historical Method and Theory* (Oxford: Clarendon Press, 1985).
3. Frank Kermode, *Essays on Fiction 1971–82* (London: Routledge & Kegan Paul, 1983), pp. 5–8.
4. For a succinct account see Martin Jay, 'The Morals of Genealogy: Or is there a Post-Structuralist Ethics?', *Cambridge Review*, 110 (1989), 70–74.
5. Roland Barthes, 'From Work to Text', trans. Stephen Heath, reprinted in *Debating Texts: A Reader in Twentieth-Century Literary Theory and Method*, ed. Rick Rylance (Milton Keynes: Open University Press, 1987), p. 119.
6. See Stanley Fish, *Is There A Text In This Class? The Authority of Interpretive Communities* (London: Harvard University Press, 1982). For the argument against Said see Fish, *Doing What Comes Naturally: Change, Rhetoric, and the Practice of Theory in Literary and Legal Studies* (Oxford: Clarendon Press, 1989), p. 212.
7. For a relevant analysis of cultural formations see Raymond Williams,

Culture (London: Fontana, 1981), esp. Ch. 3.

8. *Peter Hall's Diaries: The Story of a Theatrical Battle*, ed. John Goodwin (London: Hamish Hamilton, 1983), p. 347. Entry for 18 April 1978.

9. Trevor Griffiths, 'Countering Consent: An Interview with John Wyver' in *Ah! Mischief: The Writer and Television*, ed. Frank Pike (London: Faber & Faber, 1982), p. 39.

10. John Bull, *New British Political Dramatists* (London: Methuen, 1984) is probably the standard work, though it interestingly pushes both Barker and John McGrath rather to the edges of its account. For a more diverse, if less analytical, coverage see Catherine Itzin, *Stages in the Revolution: Political Theatre in Britain Since 1968* (London: Methuen, 1980).

11. Howard Barker, 'The Small Discovery of Dignity', in *New Theatre Voices of the Seventies*, ed. Simon Trussler (London: Methuen, 1981), pp. 195, 193 and 187.

12. Howard Barker, '49 Asides for a Tragic Theatre', *Guardian* 10 February 1986, p. 11.

13. For example, Herbert Marcuse, *An Essay on Liberation* (Harmondsworth: Penguin, 1969), and Gabriel Cohn-Bendit and Daniel Cohn-Bendit, *Obsolete Communism: The Left-Wing Alternative*, trans. Arnold Pomerans (Harmondsworth: Penguin, 1969).

14. Howard Barker, '49 Asides' (see note 12 above); 'The Triumph in Defeat', *Guardian*, 22 August 1988, p. 34; 'Understanding Exits as Complexity Takes a Bow', *The Times Higher Education Supplement*, 5 January 1990, p. 16.

15. Barker's own phrase in a recent television discussion with Michael Ignatieff, *The Late Show*, BBC2, 23 January 1990, '49 Asides' also argues for the necessary elitism of tragedy to combat banality and triviality.

16. Howard Barker, *The Last Supper: A New Testament* (London: John Calder, 1988). The programme-text contained interleaved, unnumbered pages from which this quotation is taken.

17. Barthes, 'From Work to Text' (see note 5 above), p. 119.

18. Howard Brenton, 'Petrol Bombs Through the Proscenium Arch', in *New Theatre Voices of the Seventies* (see note 11 above), p. 97.

19. Howard Brenton, 'Showcase Spectacles', *20/20*, 20 May 1989, p. 26.

20. Peter Wollen, 'Bitter Victory: The Situationist International' in *An Endless Passion . . . An Endless Banquet: The Situationist International – Selected Documents from 1957 to 1962 and Documents Tracing the Impact on British Culture from the 1960s to the 1980s*, ed. Iwona Blazwick (London: ICA/Verso, 1989), pp. 9–16. See also Stewart Home, *The Assault on Culture: Utopian Currents from Lettrism to Class War* (London: Aporia Press, 1988) and Griel Marcus, *Lipstick Traces: A Secret History of the Twentieth Century* (London: Secker & Warburg, 1989).

21. Guy Debord, *Society of the Spectacle*, translator not named and no copyright claimed (no place: Rebel Press/Aim Publications, 1987), pp. 88–9.

22. For general accounts see Robert Hewison, *Too Much: Art and Society in the Sixties 1960–75* (London: Methuen, 1986), and Jonathan Green,

Days in the Life: Voices from the English Underground 1961–1971 (London: William Heinemann, 1988). For drama see Peter Ansorge, *Disrupting the Spectacle: Five Years of Experimental Fringe Theatre in Britain* (London: Pitman, 1975).

23. Howard Brenton, *Weapons of Happiness* (London: Methuen, 1976), p. 76.

24. Howard Brenton, 'Author's Production Note', *Christie in Love and Other Plays* (London: Methuen, 1970), p. 4.

25. Howard Brenton, 'Taking Liberties', *Marxism Today*, December 1988, p. 35.

26. John Sutherland, *Offensive Literature: Decensorship in Britain 1960–1982* (London: Junction Books, 1982), pp. 180–90, is a useful account.

27. E. P. Thompson, *The Poverty of Theory* (London: Merlin, 1978); Raymond Williams, *Marxism and Literature* (Oxford: Oxford University Press, 1977) and several essays in *Problems in Materialism and Culture* (London: Verso, 1980) and *Writing in Society* (London, Verso, n.d.); Raphael Samuel (ed.), *People's History and Socialist Theory* (London: Routledge, 1981).

28. John McGrath, *A Good Night Out – Popular Theatre: Audience, Class and Form* (London: Methuen, 1981), p. 5. Subsequent references to this work will be found in brackets following quotation.

29. John McGrath, interviewed by Tony Mitchell, 'Popular Theatre and the Changing Perspective of the Eighties', *New Theatre Quarterly*, 1 (1985), 396.

30. Eugène Van Erven, *Radical People's Theatre* (Bloomington: Indiana University Press, 1988), p. 1.

31. John McGrath, *The Cheviot, The Stag and the Black, Black Oil* (London: Methuen, 1981); *The Game's A Bogey: 7:84's John MacLean Show* (Edinburgh: EUSPB, 1975).

32. For a stimulating recent account see Alan Sinfield, *Literature, Politics and Culture in Postwar Britain* (Oxford: Blackwell, 1989), esp. Chs 4 and 12.

33. See Trevor Griffiths, 'Transforming the Hush of Capitalism', in *New Theatre Voices of the Seventies* (see note 11 above), p. 132.

34. For inner-city Manchester see *A Good Night Out*, Ch. 2; for Ken Dodd see 'Popular Theatre' (note 29 above), 392.

35. André van Gyseghem, 'British Theatre in the Thirties: An Autobiographical Record' and Jon Clark, 'Agitprop and Unity Theatre: Socialist Theatre in the Thirties', both in *Culture and Crisis in Britain in the Thirties*, ed. Jon Clark, Margot Heinemann, David Marolies and Carole Snee (London: Lawrence & Wishart, 1979); Bert Hogenkamp, 'The Worker's Film Movement in Britain, 1929–39' in *Propaganda, Politics and Film 1918–45*, ed. Nicholas Pronay and D. W. Spring (London: Methuen, 1982); Raphael Samuel, Ewan MacColl and Stuart Cosgrove, *Theatres of the Left 1880–1935: Worker's Theatre Movements in Britain and America* (London: Routledge, 1985); *Agit-Prop To Theatre Workshop: Political Playscripts 1930–50*, ed. Howard Goorney and Ewan MacColl (Manchester: Manchester University Press, 1986); Richard Stourac and Kathleen McCreery, *Theatre as a Weapon: Worker's Theatre in the*

Soviet Union, Germany and Britain 1917–1934 (London: Routledge & Kegan Paul, 1986); Colin Chambers, *The Story of Unity Theatre* (London: Lawrence & Wishart, 1989).

36. See also Linda MacKenney, 'The Strife of the Miner Genius', *Guardian*, 18 June 1985, p. 9 on 7:84's revival of the Scots miner-playwright Joe Corrie, and McGrath, 'Popular Theatre' (note 29 above), 390–91 on McGrath's adaptation for the 1984–85 miner's strike of Miles Malleson's thirties play *Six Men of Dorset*.

37. See MacColl's essays in Samuel, MacColl and Cosgrave, *Theatres of the Left* and *Agit-Prop to Theatre Workshop*, ed. Goorney and MacColl (note 35 above).

8

An Age of Surfaces: Joe Orton's Drama and Postmodernism

ADRIAN PAGE

Orton once wrote, 'Unlike Wilde I think you should put your genius into your work, not your life.'[1] It is a sad reflection on this ambition, therefore, that Orton's drama is so often judged in the context of his dramatic life and death. Martin Esslin begins a study of his plays with an account of the playwright's imprisonment for defacing library books.[2] His conviction that the plays are no more than an extension of a puerile desire to 'shock at all costs' leads him to diminish their importance. Esslin seems to allow his distaste for the antics of Orton to colour his evaluation of the work.

The characteristic which Esslin finds particularly disturbing is that the plays appear to lack any morally righteous metalanguage which offers a positive criticism of contemporary society. In addition the characters lack substance; behind them there is 'literally nothing' according to Esslin. All this adds up to an impotent rage against society which was expressed in purely negative terms.

This very same characteristic, the absence of any positive values, is precisely the basis of C.W.E. Bigsby's praise of Orton's drama.[3] For Bigsby Orton has obvious affinities with postmodernist novelists such as Pynchon and the 'death of character' is merely a symptom of the postmodern condition in which Orton wrote. This divergence of opinion illustrates the way in which personal values are the foundation of critical opinion in modern drama. Like Leavis, Esslin demands a view of life which is morally acceptable and inspires us towards virtue if he is to praise a play. Bigsby, on the other hand, applauds the plays' negativity.

If there is a direct parallel between the playwright and his work it is perhaps in the Ortonesque notion of character that it emerges most clearly. Bigsby writes that 'In his plays, role playing is not a series of

142

false surfaces concealing a real self.'[4] The 'self' in Orton *is* the totality of appearances; there is only a series of outward appearances which succeed each other.

Orton the man also appears to have existed in order to create an impression. In the persona of Edna Welthorpe, for example, he managed to conduct a correspondence with another character of his own creation in the national press vilifying his own plays. In one much-cited incident he offered to lend an actor his own late mother's false teeth to use on stage in a production of *Loot*. Rather than explaining his plays, Orton's biography poses further questions about his motives which remain unanswered. Terry Eagleton has pointed out that 'the biography of the author is, after all, merely another text',[5] and in Orton's case the fictionalisation of his life in, for example, John Lahr's screenplay, *Prick Up Your Ears*, has only added to the complexity of the task of understanding Orton.

Despite the growing recognition that Orton belongs to the postmodernist scene, few readings of the plays have so far attempted to develop the perspective which Bigsby adopts. The three best-known plays, however, *Entertaining Mr Sloane, Loot*, and *What the Butler Saw*, can all, in their various ways, be read within a postmodernist problematic which literary theory brings to light.

Sloane provoked a bitterly hostile reaction when it was first staged, particularly because of its treatment of sexuality, yet the odd thing was, as Bigsby observes, that the play made no attempt to present itself as realism. The answer to the question of why the play should arouse such anger lies partly in its intertextuality. The ideological presentation of love and sexuality in contemporary popular culture was diammetrically opposed to Orton's cynical vision. In Hitchcock's film *Shadow of a Doubt*, first shown in 1943, for example, a murderer flees to the west of America to avoid detection. He stays with his sister and strikes up a close friendship with his niece which is only disrupted when she discovers his guilty secret. The murderer attempts to kill her but dies in the attempt and the niece is consoled by the detective who has tracked the murderer down.

The differences between this narrative and *Sloane* illustrate the degree to which *Sloane* was a radical departure from contemporary ideology. Hitchcock's film plays on the sexual tension between the murderer and the niece with its faintly incestuous overtones. The relationship poses the question of whether goodness can resist evil and whether sexual temptation can overcome the instincts of a good person. It is, of course, reassuring to see that the recognition of evil is sufficient to dispel any relationship between the man and the woman. As in the myth that the Devil cannot disguise himself completely, but must bear some trace of his true nature such as a cloven hoof, the evil murderer is unable to conceal his true self for long. The murderer's character is also rigidly Aristotelian, in that it is the very substance of the plot. Having once committed an evil act he is bound to continue to murder until he is stopped for good. In this sense character determines the plot of the film, which shows that a man who is essentially evil necessarily embarks on a course of action which leads to self-destruction.

In *Sloane*, a similar situation occurs with a murderer seeking shelter. In this case, however, the murderer is not rejected once his guilt is discovered. Despite the fact that he kills their father, Ed and Kath collude in covering up his crimes in order to satisfy their own desires. In place of an individual whose moral essence governs his actions, *Sloane* shows us a guilty party who is deliberately exploited once he is compromised by his crimes. In place of the dialectic of good and evil, Orton's text offers 'the demeaning reality of biology which constitutes the only metaphysics',[6] as Bigsby puts it.

Nietzsche wrote that, 'Given that nothing is "given" except our world of desires and passions . . . is it not permitted to ask whether that which is given does not suffice for an understanding of the world?'[7] *Sloane* can be read as dramatising this hypothesis. The fundamental principle of desire is what ultimately determines the course of events, and not the main character's commitment to evil. Sloane himself finds that he becomes more the subject of desire rather than the author of malevolence. The source of Sloane's actions is not an essentially evil self, but the social order which others impose upon him. The play's radically cynical presentation of morality may therefore explain its hostile reception.

Foucault distinguishes two types of subject: 'subject to someone else by control and dependence, and tied to his own identity by conscience and self-knowledge'.[8] Sloane finds himself making a gradual transition from subjection in the former sense to subjection in the latter. At first he is burdened by the knowledge of who he is and what he has done. When Kemp recognises him as a murderer, this is made more acute. It is Kath who offers the opportunity to conceal his identity by her eagerness to satisfy his every whim. By the Second Act it appears that Sloane has learnt how to exploit her eagerness, but the final outcome shows that he is not the master of his own subjectivity. In his progress towards his sexual enslavement

Sloane gradually has to acknowledge that, 'Being vouchsafed to us is changing, not identical with itself, it is involved in relationships',[9] in Nietzsche's words. He is finally obliged to submit to the authority of the social formation in his new household.

Initially, however, Sloane is unaware of his lack of personal autonomy. Like the child as described by Lacan, Sloane first enjoys the mirror-phase in which he perceives himself as a unified free agent who is loved by the mother because he supplies a lack. Kath, a much older woman, offers just such an uncomplicated reflection of Sloane's vanity. Later, however, he is forced to acknowledge the existence of the symbolic order, 'a wider familial and social network',[10] as Eagleton calls it, with an emphasis on law and morality.

The symbolic order which Sloane encounters is quite unlike the classical situation in which the Father prohibits the male child's desire for the Mother in order to assert his own rights to her. The father-figure in Kemp who reminds Sloane of the existence of the legal system is killed, leaving only a woman and a gay man to constitute the social network into which he must now accommodate himself. In this situation the absolute authority of the Father is absent. In its place there is only a triangular relationship in which each character has desires which are incompatible with those of the other two. Sloane appears to like young girls, which both Kath and Ed find distasteful; Kath's desire for Sloane is repugnant to Ed and Sloane, and Ed's feelings for Sloane clash with both Sloane himself and his sister. Here the overthrow of the Oedipal situation is, however, not a *liberation* of schizophrenic desire, as Deleuze and Guattari suggest in *Anti-Oedipus*.

The traditional systems of law and morality are displaced and what remains is a Nietzschean microcosm in which 'There are no moral phenomena, only moral interpretations of phenomena.'[11] In the absence of any absolute moral imperative, the characters can only assert that their own form of sexuality is the right one. When everyone speaks on behalf of their own interests it is power which determines who will satisfy their desires. Ed and Kath form a parody of the traditional parental relationship in which Sloane's sexuality is produced. His 'polymorphous perversity' is not purely an outcome of his own lax morality.

Some commentators regard Orton as encouraging the liberation of libidinous energy as a celebration of carnivalesque anarchy, but in this text the absence of the usual social constraints leads only to a more concerted struggle to manipulate others. The six-monthly sharing of Sloane is an intertextual reference to the myth of Persephone who was obliged to spend half of every year underground for having strayed into the subterranean kingdom of Pluto. As Ed remarks to Kath: 'You showed him the gates of Hell. He abandoned hope every night when he entered there' (p. 143).

Morality ceases to be a metalanguage in this situation, since moral relativism has taken over, yet the characters do not abandon their attempts to defend themselves. In the Third Act Ed and Kath exchange bitter recriminations:

> KATH: I gave him three meals a day . . .
> . . . What more could he want?
> ED: Freedom.
> KATH: He's free with me.
> ED: You're immoral.
> KATH: It's natural. (p. 141)

The concept of what is 'natural' in sexual affairs has become entirely relative for each of the characters. As a term its meaning becomes an example of pure Derridean *différance*, since Ed, for example, as a gay man finds Kath's heterosexual desire disgusting.

Although the play's 'morality' has degenerated into a straightforward competition for self-gratification, Ed and Kath cling to a pseudoplatonic explanation of their desires. As Foucault writes, 'In the Platonic reflection on love, the inquiry concerns the desire that must be led to its true object (which is truth) by recognising it for what it truly is.'[12] Ed, for example, warns his sister against Sloane since young men 'take advantage', yet when they are introduced and Sloane has encouraged his gay fantasies of leather-clad eroticism, his tone changes: 'You picked a nice lad there. Very nice. Clean. No doubt upright.' (p. 89). Orton's characters effectively deconstruct the Platonic ideal by what Jonathan Culler calls 'working within the terms of the system to breach it.'[13] Culler gives the example of the concept of a cause, and argues that when we infer a cause such as heat from an effect such as pain, we also have to propose the existence of a further cause which prompts us to seek an explanation of our pain. In the case of *Sloane*, the characters attribute their desire to Sloane's morality, yet clearly recognise him as moral only because they first desire him. The concept of Platonic love therefore fails to explain their behaviour as they seem to suggest.

Kath's world seems to be about to collapse when Sloane is

compelled eventually to confess that he has never found her attractive, yet she concedes that she might have deceived herself. Her response to this revelation is to demand that Sloane kisses her hand, 'in the manner of the theatre'. Ed derides her 'cruel performance' and compares it to that of a prostitute faking an orgasm. Kath's acting, which reflects the metadramatic note in the play's title is, perhaps, a rational response to the postmodern world in which she finds herself.

Postmodernist society's divorce of the signifier from the signified is represented here. Although Sloane has made love to Kath, the behaviour which signifies love need not be related to any such emotion. Once the social determination of subjectivity is apparent to Sloane, he acts only in order to conform to social expectations. The lack of any genuine passion, however, does not daunt Kath, who settles for the signifiers of emotion and continues to want Sloane.

Like the theatre audience, Kath has willingly suspended her disbelief in the reality of what she sees because the appearance is gratifying in itself. The theatre is in this sense an analogy of the postmodern society where all claims to truth are, in fact, false. In the theatre we know that a piece of painted wood only signifies a window, yet we allow ourselves to be entertained by the play of signifiers. As an audience we know that the actors' behaviour is only an attempt to produce the signifiers of emotion, yet in the absence of reality, the appearances are a satisfying substitute.

There is no sense, then, in Kath expecting Sloane, the decentred subject whose bisexual gender is forced upon him, to exhibit 'true' feelings. Acting, or 'entertaining' is the only rational response for the postmodern subject who appreciates the fact that his behaviour is produced rather than inspired from within an autonomous self.

Loot is usually read as a play which shows the pervasiveness of corruption. Maurice Charney is one among many critics who insists that 'McLeavy is the only honest solid citizen in the play',[14] yet this seems to reduce the potential meaning to a simple moral lesson in the impotence of ordinary citizens when confronted with the criminal fraternity. It is tempting to assimilate Orton's text into the Jacobean tradition with sinister Machiavellians and their ineffectual dupes, yet the example of *Sloane* indicates that innocence is an absolute quality we should not expect to find in Orton.

McLeavy is not strictly innocent in either the legal sense or in terms of his awareness. When McLeavy opens his wife's coffin and discovers the loot, he is guilty of complicity in the crime by not denouncing his son. He appears to heed Fay's warning that to reveal the crime would 'Kill Father Jellicoe', and McLeavy is a man who cares more for his reputation than for the letter of the law. Early on in the play, however, he professes complete faith in the upholders of law and order, and is even prepared to overlook their indiscretions. When Fay alerts him to the fact that Truscott has no credentials to pose as a Water Board official, he replies, 'As a good citizen I ignore stories which bring officialdom into disrepute' (p. 217).

McLeavy's confidence in the authorities is in fact a cynical disregard for civil liberties rather than a blind faith in all authority. It is McLeavy who describes the prevailing mentality, 'whose respect for the law is proverbial: who'd give the power of arrest to the traffic lights if three woman magistrates and a Liberal MP would only suggest it' (p. 248). Despite his own willingness to allow the authorities *carte blanche*, McLeavy is also able to deride the attitude which he himself holds. When the crime is eventually discovered, his belated offer to give evidence on behalf of the prosecution is further evidence of this split in his awareness; he cannot see that he is guilty of the same failing as everyone else. As Macherey puts it, 'Ideology's essential weakness is that it can never recognise for itself its own real limits: at best it can learn of these limits from elsewhere'.[15] The play shows McLeavy's ideological contradictions for what they are by dramatising their consequences.

It would be wrong on this reading to play the role of McLeavy as a completely naive character, since he condones duplicity when he believes it to be in his best interests. His great failing in the play is his inability to grasp the nature of the postmodern legal system and the contribution of his own ideology to it. Lyotard's assessment of the legal system in postmodernism is that the law *is* what the law *does*. Given that postmodernism has created a climate of scepticism in any ultimate truths beyond human institutions there is nothing to corroborate legal judgements. Legality is defined institutionally as what an expert consensus agrees upon. Lyotard argues that

> It is assumed that the laws it makes for itself are just, not because they conform to some outside nature, but because the legislators are constitutionally the very citizens who are subject to the laws. As a result the legislator's will – the desire that the laws be just – will always coincide with the will of the citizen who desires the law and will therefore obey it.[16]

McLeavy's petit-bourgeois ideology assures him that his own

will and that of the law-makers will always coincide; he regards himself as one of the very citizens whose will is reflected in the legal process. For this reason he is willing to sanction whatever the legal system does, even when it is highly irregular, since he believes that the spirit of the law upholds his self-interest. What he fails to realise is that granting the legal system the power to act freely in its own preservation can bring him into conflict with it. His own authoritarianism is no guarantee of immunity when he challenges the moral autonomy of the law in the shape of Truscott.

If the legal system is independent of all other authority, then it must ensure its own survival, since to admit failure would be to undermine all law. If the law is what the legitimating institution decides it should be, then it follows that the institution cannot be wrong.

McLeavy, however, attempts to assert his own right to challenge Truscott, the law's appointed agent, on independent grounds. Christianity, for example, is shrugged off by Truscott who informs us that he is not a practising Christian. The hardened criminals in the cast may have broken the law, but they are reassuring to Truscott in that they recognise its absolute jurisdiction over their lives. McLeavy is more of a threat than the law-breakers because he denies the law's self-authenticating basis.

Lyotard describes the language of legitimating institutions such as the law in terms of Wittgenstein's language-games. The meaning of legal terms is fought out entirely within the closed legal system and they are defined in accordance with it. In order to construct a legal case, therefore, it is necessary to master legal discourse. The form which legal arguments take is that of a narrative. Truscott, for example, praises Fay's narrative confession to the murder of her husbands not for its truthfulness but for its *style*; it is the use of the appropriate language which is most important.

Farce, which Bigsby describes as 'the principal mechanism of the postmodernist impulse', is the genre which foregrounds the production of legitimating narratives. When the characters find themselves in absurd situations, they are obliged to give explanations, as when Mrs McLeavy's mummified body is passed off as a tailor's dummy. Farce therefore reveals the extent to which internally coherent narratives, however absurd, can function as explanatory narratives in a society which pays more attention to style then content. As Truscott says, 'Nothing ever convinces me. I choose the least unlikely explanation and record it in my notebook' (p. 260). Coherence within the terms of the legal system is more valid than truth.

Early on in the play, Truscott parodies Sherlock Holmes in his questioning of Fay and attributes his insights to forensic science. One reason why this scene is so amusing is that Truscott clearly fails to discover very much at all about Fay. His failure is due to the use of a detached scientific method. As Bakhtin wrote, 'In the natural sciences we seek to know an *object*, but in the human ones a subject'.[17] The characteristic of a subject, according to Bakhtin, is to produce texts, in this case explanations, and Truscott has to turn his attention to interrogation.

In his quest for the loot, Truscott is eventually successful. Despite the characters' determination to conceal their crimes, it is the series of interrogations which finally implicates them. *Loot* illustrates the process by which the characters' guilt, an apparently private mental phenomenon, is in fact discoverable in the public realm of language. As Eagleton remarks on Bakhtin's linguistic theory: 'Human consciousness was the subject's active, material semiotic intercourse with others, not some sealed interior realm'.[18] Truscott's detective work is aimed at the evaluation of the characters' linguistic texts as moves in the language-game of legal interrogation. Truscott himself, however, is a profoundly monologic thinker; as an exponent of the law, he uses the terms of the legal system strictly according to its own internal rules. In his first interrogation of Hal he finds that this prevents him from comprehending Hal's discourse:

TRUSCOTT: Why do you make such stupid remarks?
HAL: I'm a stupid person. That's what I'm trying to say.
TRUSCOTT: What proof have I that you're stupid? Give me an example of your stupidity.
HAL: I can't.
TRUSCOTT: Why not? I don't believe you're stupid at all.
HAL: I am, I had a hand in the bank job (p. 233).

Such a blatant confession without Fay's elaborate style, is beyond Truscott's experience of criminal discourse. Bakhtin describes such a situation as one that is widely used in comedy: 'a dialogue between two deaf people, where the real dialogic contact is understood, but where there is no kind of semantic contact betwen the rejoinders. Zero degree dialogic relations'.[19] Bakhtin asserts that in all dialogues the existence of a third party is presumed. This is the superaddressee whose role is often taken in comedy by the audience. We overhear this dialogue and understand what the dialogue as a whole means: that Hal and Truscott are participating in separate monologic language-games which therefore provide no basis for mutual understanding. Hal's discourse is endlessly self-referring like the self-legitimating language of the law, and probably owes something to Bertrand Russell's development of Zeno's paradoxical statement that 'All Cretans are liars'.

Orton prided himself on the logical structures of *Loot*, and when Dennis is subjected to interrogation there are again distant echoes of philosophy. Dennis's straightforward assertion that Hal is lying delights Truscott who proclaims him an 'honest lad' and offers him help. When Truscott explores the dialogic relations between the speech of Hal and Dennis he is able to infer Dennis's guilt immediately and is relieved that Dennis is resorting to a recognisable language-game. Here Truscott acts as superaddressee and assesses the contradictory statements of the two accomplices at a distance.

The scene may derive from the old logical puzzle of the two jailors, one of whom speaks the truth and the other of whom is a compulsive liar. A prisoner who wants to know which of two exits leads to freedom is free to ask either jailor one question. In this case if either jailor is asked what the other would say, each must give the *wrong* answer. The logical problem illustrates how facts which people may intend to keep secret can nonetheless be revealed when their discourse is viewed in its dialogical relations with others. When Dennis asserts that Hal is lying, Truscott's inference may not be strictly logical, yet it shows that he is attempting to probe linguistic inconsistencies which signify far more than their speakers intend. Truscott may not be able to break free from his monologic legal thinking and establish dialogic contact directly, but he is able, in his role as superaddressee, to penetrate guilty minds.

Later, when McLeavy knows the facts of the robbery he momentarily considers making a clean breast of his own attempts to cover it up. His silence, however, allows Fay to provide a convincing explanation. At this point Truscott expresses his outrage at McLeavy's behaviour and blames his son's criminal activities on the 'scandalous conduct' of his father. Although more heinous confessions have been made prior to this, Truscott is particularly offended by McLeavy's poor performance which he considers to be worse than any of the other crimes committed by the characters. When he informs Truscott that he is an honest man, the response is, 'You'll have to mend your ways then' (p. 266). Honesty confuses Truscott more than any attempt at criminal duplicity; it is, as he puts it, 'a situation for which no memo has been issued'.

Truscott's behaviour is the *reductio ad absurdum* of the postmodernist attitude towards the legal system as Lyotard describes it. If the law is governed by the necessity to preserve itself and its credibility, then the ultimate result is that a man such as Truscott can manipulate the law and cover up his own wrongdoing. The legal imperatives to obey the rules and to preserve the legal institution at all costs come into conflict and Truscott is in the situation of having to resolve this contradiction. Morality plays no part in his calculations, since as McLeavy points out, 'There are organisations devoted to doing good.'

The motto Orton chose for the play: 'Anarchy is a game at which the police can beat you', is generally read as warning that the police can overcome disorder. Read in another way, however, it implies that the police are, in fact, the supreme anarchists. Since the law has no ultimate foundations in absolute morality, it is possible to construct all manner of systems to defend the upholders of the institution.

Charney comments that this is a play in which Bakhtin's concept of the carnivalesque is evident, but the closure of the plot restores the stability of the legal system rather than actively undermining it. By locking up McLeavy who had threatened to make a full confession publicly, Truscott is ensuring that 'It's not expedient for the general public to have its confidence in the police force undermined' (p. 271). The eventual solution whereby McLeavy is locked up and his murder plotted, is a way of restoring public confidence.

McLeavy and Truscott never learn to engage in a mutually meaningful dialogue, yet the other criminals do manage to strike a chord in Truscott. One reason why they achieve this is that they have learned to appropriate the discourse of the legal system. The circular reasoning of a self-legitimating institution cannot be challenged, as McLeavy discovers, yet it can be exploited. When the criminals are anxious to persuade Truscott to leave the stage they adopt Truscott's own reasoning:

FAY: Can't he fetch the Pope's photo?
TRUSCOTT: Only if some responsible person accompanies him.
HAL: You're a responsibile person. You could accompany him.
TRUSCOTT: What proof have I that I am a responsible person?
DENNIS: If you weren't responsible you wouldn't be given the
    power to act as you do.

(*Truscott removes his pipe, considers.*)

TRUSCOTT: That is perfectly correct. (pp. 240–1)

As circular reasoning can be employed to prove any proposition, it also licenses patent absurdities. Even though such paralogisms are akin to aporia and lead towards infinite regresses, they are moments at which a rigid self-perpetuating system can be exploited for other purposes. The potential for resistance to such functionalist systems lies in speaking the same language as its agents, which can expose the system's inherent absurdities.

Farce traditionally creates a state of disorder in an otherwise stable environment which the revelation of the truth to all concerned eventually disperses. In *What the Butler Saw*, the farcical situation is not reversed by the discovery of the truth, since it is a postmodern farce where no absolute truths are accepted and chaos is an inescapable state. Orton's play parodies texts such as Wilde's *The Importance of Being Earnest*, and as Linda Hutcheon argues, in parody 'Irony makes these intertextual references into something more than simply academic play or some infinite regress into textuality: what is called to our attention is the entire representational process – and the impossibility of finding any totalising model to resolve the resulting postmodern contradictions.'[20]

In Algy and Jack, Wilde's play shows us two characters who are skilled dissemblers and manipulate the world of appearances to their own advantage. It seems at first that behind their social selves are private selves which they indulge unhindered by social obligations. Falling in love, however, creates a difficult situation for them both in that they have to live up to the false pictures which their elaborately-contrived social selves have projected to society. They are able to lie their way out of this awkward spot, however, by creating false accounts of their motives which satisfy the desires of the two women they love. Although, as Lady Bracknell comments, they live in 'an age of surfaces', outward appearances can be restored to harmony by concocting appropriate narratives. The question of whether social obligations ultimately compel the two men to act contrary to their desires is avoided when the desires of the men and women fortuitously coincide.

In *What the Butler Saw*, however, the revelation of the 'truth' fails to return the situation to stability. When Prentice finally confesses to his wife that at the outset of the play she surprised him making an ill-timed attempt to seduce his secretary Geraldine, Mrs Prentice replies, 'If we're to save our marriage, my dear, you must admit you prefer boys to women. Dr Rance has explained the reasons for your aberration.' (p. 430)

In the postmodern atmosphere of the play the institutions such as psychiatry do not recognise any confession which does not conform to the metanarratives they use to explain human behaviour. In addition the desires of the other characters are at variance, compelling Prentice to adjust his explanations to suit the person to whom he is speaking. There is no totalising model which will satisfy the various demands made on the postmodern subject.

Terry Eagleton points out that the subject of late capitalism is exposed to contradictory imperatives: as both a father and a consumer, for example, Eagleton argues that the contemporary subject is construed as someone who must obey the calls of authority, agency, duty and responsibility, yet is also a 'decentred network of desire'.[21] In postmodernism these antagonistic roles are both foisted on the subject. Prentice, for example, finds that he must explain himself to his wife who expects a sexual fantasy, and to Rance who is appointed to inspect his behaviour as a responsible psychiatrist. The parodic 'resolution' of these roles in the discovery that Geraldine is his daughter and that his wife has also committed incest with their son is an ironic reflection of the impossibility of truly reconciling these opposites. The additional irony that Rance's lurid explanation of the behaviour in the surgery corresponds to the goings-on, also shows that totalising models become absurdities.

Readings of the play, however, have tended to attempt to discover a *modus vivendi* for the postmodern subject who lives in this condition. For Maurice Charney, the play is 'a model for how the rational man can conduct himself in an irrational world'.[22] Bigsby maintains that Orton was attracted to Wilde's poem to liberty celebrating the 'great Anarchies which mirrored his wildest passions and gave "my rage a brother".'[23] Sexuality is therefore a form of aggression in Orton according to Bigsby, a calculated affront to the complacent moralising of the middle class. Both interpretations see Orton as preferring either Apollonian strategies or Dionysian energy rather than vacillating between these two poles. Orton certainly saw the theatre as a locale to unleash Dionysian excess, yet he also noted that the process of writing was a continual combination of Apollonian and Dionysian principles.[24] It is perhaps more productive to see this play as a deconstruction of the binary opposition between chaos and order whereby neither exists entirely independently of the other.

Rance tells Prentice when he comes to inspect his psychiatric establishment, 'I am a representative of order, you of chaos' (p. 417), yet this simple opposition is contradicted by the action. Rance states propositions which appear, on the surface, to draw a moral from the hectic events around him: as he says, 'You can't be a rationalist in an irrational world. It isn't rational.' (p. 428) The irony is, of course, as Derrida observes, 'we can pronounce not a single destructive proposition which has not already had to slip into the form, the logic and the implicit postulations of precisely what it seeks to contest'.[25] Thus Rance expresses his lack of faith in rationality in rational terms; it does not follow from his ability to offer apparently good advice, that he is a consistently stable character.

The fact is that Rance's apophthegms ring true, yet his behaviour is conducive only to creating yet more madness. Ironically his attempts to impose order only succeed in promoting chaos. He tells Prentice that 'Ruin follows the accusation, not the vice. Had you committed the act, you wouldn't now be facing the charge' (p. 411). This is particularly evident in the case of Geraldine who, although guiltless, is accused of madness and therefore suffers the indignity of being restrained and shorn of her hair. In the world of postmodern self-legitimating institutions such as psychiatry, people are mad if the profession describes them as such.

Once Geraldine is declared mad, she can say nothing which appears rational to Rance. 'Why have you been certified if you're sane?' he asks her (p. 379). The only way in which Geraldine can redeem herself is to accept the legitimacy of the psychiatric profession and admit her madness. As Rance says, 'No madman ever accepts madness. Only the sane do that.' (p. 415) Foucault discovered the same procedure at work in psychiatry, and in *The Birth of the Asylum* he describes the mystifications by which eighteenth-century therapeutics 'tried to persuade the madman of his madness in order to liberate him from it'.[26] The attempt to produce reason produces madness instead, as in the case of Geraldine who eventually begs to be undressed, ironically succumbing to hysterical behaviour which Rance used as a pretext to certify her. The postmodern institutions which recognise no external justifications for their practices eventually resort to the simple exercise of power, since ultimately there are no grounds for their actions.

Given this fundamental principle, Rance advocates indulgence in anarchic pleasures, since as he asserts, 'When the punishment for guilt or innocence is the same it becomes an act of logic to commit the crime.' (p. 432) The logic of the representative of order leads to chaos. When Rance attempts to put his own maxim into practice by seducing Geraldine himself, he finds, however, that he too is compromised and has to lie to Mrs Prentice that 'It's a new and hitherto untried type of therapy' (p. 439). Indulgence may be the only gratification to be had, but it does not necessarily go unpunished.

Prentice, on the other hand, is primarily devoted, as his wife says, to 'the liberation and exploitation of madness' rather than curing patients, but again, in a contradictory move, he makes efforts to extricate himself from the farcical situation by restoring *order*. As he produces more and more bizarre explanations of the strange happenings, however, he only succeeds in producing a string of excuses which it becomes increasingly difficult to weave into an overarching metanarrative to satisfy all parties. Rance's 'documentary novelette' which gathers together all Prentice's fantastic explanations, reminds us of this.

In desperation at his failure to recover stability, Prentice eventually decides to put Rance's maxim into practice, saying, 'I'm suspected of the offence I may as well commit it' (p. 251). The results of undressing Sergeant Match are, nonetheless, worse than he expected and Prentice vows never to engage in sexual intercourse again. Neither reason nor anarchy is a principle of action which leads out of the tangled web which has been created.

The process which is at work is one which closely parallels the postmodernist theory of performance which divorces the stage event from the written text. Gerald Graff identifies Artaud and such of his followers as the sixties group, The Living Theatre of Julian Beck, as artists who have produced an appropriate response to the loss of meaning in postmodernism.[27] Since there is no universal meaning, all we can do is return to expressions of the primal drives, such as eroticism, which exist outside systems of representation. Graff suggests, therefore, that postmodernist theatre is Dionysian, but Artaud's Dionysian ambitions were, as he accepted, unrealisable. Derrida comments that 'There is no theater in the world today which fulfils Artaud's desire.'[28]

The ultimate failure of Artaud's style lies in the inevitable paradoxes of postmodernism. Italo Calvino, for example, in *If on a Winter's Night a Traveller* explores the paradox that the writer who accepts that the reader is free to interpret his or her text is then faced with a dilemma: how is it possible to write without steering the reader towards their own freedom and thereby depriving them of it? Similarly Artaud's theatre calls for the spontaneous production of emotions, yet by formulating a system, spontaneity is automatically impossible. Artaud recognised this in that he knew that as soon as his performers began to create forms of expression they would become repeatable; people would recall performances as having certain meanings and the once-and-for-all uniqueness of the event would be lost. Eventually even representing the unrepresentable becomes an acknowledged form of representation, a lifeless style among all the others.

Derrida therefore comments that the murder of the 'father' of representation, the Author, takes place not once, but is continually re-enacted: 'this murder is endless and is repeated indefinitely. It begins by penetrating its own commentary and is accompanied by its own representation, in which it erases itself and confirms the transgressed law. To do so, it suffices that there be a sign, that is to say, a repetition'.[29] Derrida here is talking about the inevitability of non-representational theatre becoming, in some sense, representational, but his remarks apply equally well to *What the Butler Saw*. The 'law' that rationality is strictly impossible in this world is confirmed as it is transgressed. When Prentice attempts to espouse anarchy as a system to regain some semblance of order, he precipitates more anarchy. The way to prove that it is impossible to be rational in this world is to attempt to be so; chaos inevitably follows. The way in which the text proceeds is to suggest principles which can be abstracted from what happens, yet which are then refuted by events. It is the belief in the possibility of a universal harmony returning to the scene that motivates the characters to continually search for order, a pursuit of the 'metaphysics of presence', since each injection of Apollonian thinking only gives rise to yet more anarchy.

Orton's play therefore depicts not a *state* of anarchy but the continual generation of anarchy and remains open at the end rather than closing this possibility. Another text to which this is intertextually related is Euripides' *The Bacchae*.[30] Mrs Prentice, for example, 'fires wildly at Nick' injuring her own son as Agave attacks Pentheus in *The Bacchae*. The moral of Euripides' play seems to be that neither Pentheus, who from Apollonian motives despises the Dionysian rites of the Bacchae, nor Agave, who indulges in them, is adopting a safe style of life. Both principles have to coexist in a continual dialectic within us all.

Although the events of the play are brought to an end, therefore, they are not stabilised, since there is no prospect of the interaction of Apollonian and Dionysian principles ceasing. In true Carnivalesque manner the play ends with all social distinctions of rank forgotten and everyone having contributed to the spectacle by taking the position as the object of humour. Ironically, however, the cast end by climbing towards the skylight in an *orderly* group. They have adopted Rance's latest maxim, 'love must bring greater joy than violence' (p. 446) and it appears that they are about to take this message to an unsuspecting world. By now, however, we should have learned that believing in principles and establishing order are far from likely to succeed in creating a harmonious society.

The ascent towards the skylight is a move towards what Derrida calls, 'the crevice through which the yet unnameable glimmer beyond the closure can be glimpsed'.[31] The seeming closure only isolates an area of endless play which, at the end of the text is intimated by the manner of the characters' departure. What we have seen promises to be re-enacted when the cast emerge to preach a hippy doctrine of universal love. 'Closure', as Derrida remarks, 'is the circular limit within which the repetition of difference infinitely repeats itself.'[32]

Anarchy is not a state but, as *What the Butler Saw* shows, a process. As such it celebrates not a state of being but, as Derrida describes it, Nietzsche's 'joyous affirmation of the play of the world and the innocence of becoming'.[33] A quality for which all Orton's work is justly admired.

Notes

1. John Lahr, *Prick Up Your Ears: the Biography of Joe Orton* (Harmondsworth: Penguin, 1980), p. 334.
2. See Martin Esslin, Joe Orton: 'The Comedy of (ILL) Manners' in C.W.E. Bigsby (ed.), Stratford-Upon-Avon Studies, Vol. 19, *Contemporary English Drama* (London: Edward Arnold, 1981), pp. 95–107.
3. C.W.E. Bigsby, *Joe Orton* (London: Methuen, 1982).
4. Ibid., p. 17.
5. Terry Eagleton, *Literary Theory* (Oxford: Blackwell, 1983), p. 138.
6. Bigsby, op. cit., p. 30.
7. Friedrich Nietzsche, *Beyond Good and Evil* (1886), p. 36.
8. Michel Foucault 'The Subject and Power' in *Michel Foucault: Beyond Structuralism and Hermeneutics* by Hubert Dreyfus and Paul Rabinow (Chicago: University of Chicago Press, 1982), p. 212.
9. Quoted in J.P. Stern, *Nietzsche* (London: Fontana, 1978), p. 146.

10. Eagleton, op. cit., p. 167.
11. *Beyond Good and Evil*, p. 108.
12. Michel Foucault, *The History of Sexuality*, Vol. 2 *The Use of Pleasure* (London: Penguin, 1987), p. 244.
13. Jonathan Culler, *On Deconstruction* (London: Routledge, 1983), p. 86.
14. Maurice Charney, *Joe Orton* (London: Macmillan, 1984), p. 85.
15. Pierre Macherey, *A Theory of Literary Production* (London: Routledge, 1978), p. 131.
16. Jean-François Lyotard, *The Postmodern Condition: A Report on Knowledge* (Manchester: Manchester University Press, 1986), p. 35.
17. Mikhail Bakhtin, *Speech Genres and Other Late Essays* (Austin: University of Texas Press, 1986), p. 125.
18. *Literary Theory*, p. 109.
19. *Speech Genres*, p. 125
20. Linda Hutcheon, *The Politics of Postmodernism* (London: Routledge, 1989), p. 95.
21. See Terry Eagleton, 'Capitalism, Modernism and Post-Modernism' reprinted in *Against the Grain: Essays 1975–1985* (London: Verso, 1986), p. 145.
22. Charney, op. cit., p. 109.
23. Bigsby, op. cit., p. 64.
24. See Lahr, op. cit., p. 15.
25. Jacques Derrida, *Writing and Difference* (London: Routledge, 1981), p. 280.
26. Quoted in Paul Rabinow (ed.), *The Foucault Reader* (Harmondsworth: Penguin, 1986), p. 154.
27. Gerald Graff, *Literature Against Itself: Literary Ideas in Modern Society* (Chicago: University of Chicago Press, 1979), p. 76.
28. Derrida, op. cit., pp. 247–8.
29. *Writing and Difference*, p. 249.
30. See Niall W. Slater, 'Tragic Farce: Orton and Euripides', in *Classical and Modern Literature*, Vol. 7 (1987), pp. 87–98.
31. *Writing and Difference*, p. 249.
32. Ibid., p. 250.
33. Ibid., p. 292.

References to Orton's plays are taken from *Orton: The Complete Plays* (London: Methuen, 1976).

9

The Plays of Caryl Churchill: Essays in Refusal

JANE THOMAS

[A critique] doesn't have to be the premise of a deduction which concludes: this then is what needs to be done. It should be an instrument for those who fight, those who resist and refuse what is. Its use should be in processes of conflict and confrontation, essays in refusal. . . . It isn't a stage in a programming. It is a challenge directed to what is.[1]

Critical readings of Caryl Churchill's plays as programmes for social advancement along socialist or socialist feminist lines are often unable to account for certain gaps and contradictions in the texts other than as oversights, aberrations or, in some cases, betrayals of the political paradigm. After juggling with terms like 'bleak', 'ambiguous', 'murky', 'worrying' and 'irony' Michelene Wandor concludes that Churchill's plays display 'an equivocal attitude to change'.[2] Helene Keyssar draws attention to Churchill's 'tricky political stance' and discusses 'the absence of any positive strategy to change the dismal enslavement of women'.[3] Reservations such as these have prompted a spirited defence of Churchill's political integrity from Linda Fitzsimmons, who argues that her work advocates 'collective action in class and female solidarity'.[4] Likewise Sue-Ellen Case cites two plays by Churchill as examples of 'a happy marriage of materialism and feminism'.[5] Joseph Marohl identifies several areas of concern in Churchill's work in addition to class and gender. These include 'the proprietary family, the oppression of sexual variety through compulsory heterosexuality . . . ageism and ethnocentricism.'[6] Whilst these social antagonisms supplement the massive binary divisions of class and gender, any analysis which is confined to the level of social and economic relations, limits itself to uncovering Churchill's programme for social reform or lamenting its absence.

160

Readings such as these impose a political closure on texts which are deliberately open-ended and which seek to raise more questions than they answer.

In following up Churchill's acknowledged debt to Michel Foucault's *Discipline and Punish* in the writing of *Softcops* I hope to provide a more flexible reading of two of her best and most problematic plays *Cloud Nine* and *Top Girls* which relieves them of the necessity to provide positive stratagems for change in the fields of class and gender whilst highlighting their roles as politically provocative critiques of society.[7] However, this reading does not claim Caryl Churchill as a committed Foucauldian neither is it dependent upon her knowledge of Foucault's later work. Nevertheless, it is possible to trace in her plays a methodological approach similar to that favoured by Foucault and a corresponding concern with the operations of power and its individualising techniques.

Rather than conceptualising history as a progressive, uninterrupted process of development culminating in a culturally and morally superior Modern Age, Foucault saw it as 'episodes in a series of subjugations' or successive interpretations of a system of rules.[8] He focused on three main periods – the Renaissance, the Enlightenment and the Modern Age – in order to analyse and contrast the different manifestations of power that characterise them. Each period reveals a specific structure of thought or 'episteme' in which the production of knowledge is subject to certain formative rules and procedures which operate unconsciously in the interests of social control. In this way, what is accepted as 'normal' or 'rational' within any given episteme is revealed to be culturally constructed and determined according to its power structures.

the things which seem most evident to us are always formed in the confluence of encounters and chances during the course of a previous and fragile history. What reason perceives as *its* necessity, or rather, what different forms of rationality offer as their necessary being, can perfectly well be shown to have a history; and the network of contingencies from which it emerges can be traced. Which is not to say, however, that these forms of rationality were irrational. It means that they reside on a base of human practice and human history; and that since these things have been made they can be unmade, as long as we know how it was that they were made.[9]

The knowledge produced in a specific episteme is disseminated throughout certain disciplines and is activated in discursive practices. The forces which shape a discursive practice or 'discourse' ensure that subversive elements within a culture are silenced, contained or excluded. In this way 'truth' is seen as a conditional concept determined by the moderators of discourse. Therefore the truth of one episteme is no more accurate than the established truth of a past or the projected truth of a future era. The shaping force – or power – which constructs the archive – or unconscious terms of reference of a particular cultural epoch – permeates it so thoroughly that its operation can be traced in any of its institutions or discursive practices. Foucault concentrates on psychiatry, medicine, criminology and sexuality – the 'human sciences' – in order to reveal the ways in which the human individual is constructed as a subject and an object of knowledge.

Churchill's plays favour a transhistorical approach to their subject matter in which the truth of a previous episteme is contrasted with that of the present. *Light Shining in Buckinghamshire, Vinegar Tom* and *Serious Money* view the rationale of the twentieth century through a seventeenth-century lens. In *Top Girls* female representatives from a variety of epistemes interrogate and are interrogated by a spokeswoman for the Thatcher years while *Softcops* follows the precise epistemological configuration of Foucault's *Discipline and Punish*. In each case the temptation to pursue, establish or project a superior truth is scrupulously avoided.

At the same time her dramas focus on particular discourses: sexuality in *Cloud Nine*, gender in *Top Girls*, economics in *Serious Money* and, predictably enough, social control in *Softcops*, but at no point are the issues reduced to simple binary oppositions. Her work is not concerned with providing answers but with asking questions. It does not present a series of programmes for social reform but various analyses of power and the ways in which 'men govern (themselves and others) by the production of truth'.[10] Her plays challenge the notion of truth itself, and the power-relations which construct it in the modern age, by tracing and contrasting these formative processes as they are revealed by the study of a particular discourse in a subsequent era. They do so by privileging and articulating deviant or subversive knowledges which have been silenced or disqualified in the interests of social control and normalisation – knowledges which belong to women, children, homosexuals, racial minorities, the working class, peasants, the insane and the criminal: the outcast and the disempowered. Her investigation of the way power functions is grounded in an analysis of the forms of resistance associated with its exercise. Foucault suggests that social power disguises itself as natural law so that the historical and arbitrary appears permanent and incontrovertible. Therefore the mechanisms of power are more clearly revealed when the spotlight is turned on to what they silence, marginalise and exclude.

The characters in her plays can be seen to be constituted within a web of power-relations which they unconsciously perpetuate. Although it is clear that, at particular moments in history, individuals, groups and institutions have been able to take economic, political or sexual advantage of various manifestations of power, they are neither its inventors nor its directors. According to Foucault power relations are intentional (they work to establish social order and control) but non-subjective:

> neither the caste which governs, nor the groups which control the state apparatus, nor those who make the most important decisions direct the entire network of power that functions in a society (and makes *it* function).[11]

The network of power relations passes through apparatuses, institutions and individuals but power itself is not localised in them. Thus power cannot be seized or dismantled by appropriating the institutions or individuals in which it temporarily resides. Rather than seeking the 'headquarters that presides over its rationality' Foucault is concerned with the development of 'power techniques oriented towards individuals and intended to rule them in a continuous and permanent way'.

Michel Foucault's *Discipline and Punish* provided Churchill with a theoretical framework for her ideas on non-violent social control and, more specifically, the marginalisation, containment and silencing of subversive elements. *Softcops* was intended to show 'how hospitals, schools, crime, prisons – things whose existence in their present form one might take for granted – . . . how they're connected . . . and what effects . . . it can have on you that they are like they are. . . . Being free from that control is helped by understanding how it works.'[12]

Foucault identified a shift in attitudes during the eighteenth century as crime was regarded not as a violation of the sovereign's body or will but as a violation of the social contract. The main aim of punishment became the rehabilitation rather than the maiming or execution of the offender. This signalled a move away from corporal or capital punishment as a public spectacle and towards incarceration with its accompanying disciplinary techniques of surveillance, normalisation and examination. While the prime site for punishment was still the body, in that it was deprived of liberty and certain other benefits, its effect was directed at the mind or 'soul' of the criminal. Foucault cited Jeremy Bentham's Panopticon – a device which located individuals in separate contained spaces or cells located around a central tower or position of surveillance as the most effective and economical model of incarceration. Whilst the observed were visible at all times, the observer remained hidden from view. In this way automatic docility and discipline was ensured through the individual's consciousness of being potentially under continual surveillance. Thus the use of force to control the convict, the lunatic, the schoolchild, the worker or the patient became redundant.

> He who is subjected to a field of visibility, and who knows it, assumes responsibility for the constraints of power; he makes them play spontaneously upon himself; he inscribes in himself the power relation in which he simultaneously plays both roles; he becomes the principle of his own subjection.[13]

At the same time the Panopticon made possible the documentation and accumulation of knowledge concerning the individual. Foucault cites the production of these written reports as evidence of the birth of the human sciences and the consequent subjugation of the human subject. As Churchill says, 'you can control people without the necessity of violent means once you have a whole lot of systems to fit [them] into' (*FoC*, p. 73).

The central character of Churchill's play *Softcops* is Pierre, an early nineteenth-century social reformer seeking a new economy of punishment aimed at increasing its effect whilst 'diminishing its economic . . . and its political cost' (*DP* p. 81). To begin with he is committed to the idea of punishment as a public spectacle displaying a perfect balance between terror and information and designed to bring home to all who see it 'the power of the law'. He is watched by a party of schoolchildren, led by their headmaster. They are there to learn from the example set by the criminals whose public maiming and execution Pierre supervises. As Foucault points out in *Discipline and Punish* these primitive methods carried with them considerable risks and frequently backfired on the agents of the law. Recognising that he had nothing to lose, the condemned man might refuse to cooperate with the authorities who would count on the salutary effect of the requisite emotions of shame, fear and repentance. Thus Churchill's Lafayette causes a riot among the crowd by substituting an incitement to anarchy in place of the speech Pierre has composed for him.

The entrance of Vidocq and Lacenaire – the archetypal cop and robber – signals a new approach to the issue of criminality and a rise in interest in the criminal as an individual and a type. Observation, documentation and analysis led to the isolation and creation of a 'criminal class' policed initially by the criminal informer and later by the criminal investigator. As Foucault suggests, crime becomes glorified as the work of exceptional natures and celebrated in the memoirs of certain criminals like Vidocq and Lacenaire themselves: 'We have moved . . . from the execution to the investigation; from the physical confrontation to the intellectual struggle between criminal and investigator' and the development of surveillance, policing and documentation as methods of social control (*DP*, p. 69). Pierre admires Vidocq for his ability to catch criminals but he is left with the problem of what to do with them once they have been caught. He poses the question, how does one encourage discipline and social control 'If you don't use their bodies to demonstrate the power of the law?'. The answer to the problem of the submission of bodies lies in the control of ideas. It is provided by the headmaster who invites Pierre to witness a 'lesson' in his school, and reinforced by Jeremy Bentham who gives him an object-lesson on the merits of the Panopticon.

In his analysis of different manifestations of the power to punish Foucault pays close attention to the growth of interest in the eighteenth century in the most economical way of rendering the body docile and productive through training and manipulation rather than simple and violent coercion. He traces the growth of disciplinary techniques of power to the Christian tradition of asceticism in its most extreme manifestation – the monastic – and its slow but steady percolation throughout all aspects of society, especially the school, the barracks, the hospital, the workshop and the prison. Based on the successful model of the monasteries these institutions slowly evolved a cellular structure accompanied by supervision and discipline. This was coupled with the imposition of the timetable, the regulation of physical activities in the interests of the efficient and economic fulfilment of a task, the introduction of a programme aimed at further improvement and development of skills, and the citing of the individual body as an indispensable component within a corporate mass which functions best when subjected to precise and economical orders. Churchill dramatises Foucault's description of La Salle's handwriting exercises and the teaching practices favoured by the Brothers of the Christian Schools, in which children are taught to respond instinctively and accurately to signals made by wooden clapper or hand claps, in order to chart the growth of automatic docility over violent coercion. In this way the potentially subversive element – the boy Luc – learns to police and control his wayward impulses. As the headmaster informs Pierre:

> I use the cane very rarely now I have perfected the timetable. I enjoy my work. I see the results of it. Their bodies can be helped by harness. And their minds are fastened every day to a fine rigid frame.[14]

The chain-gang scene which follows is a companion to the execution of Lafayette in that it points up the risks consequent upon punishment as public spectacle. However, the chain itself has a symbolic function. The constitution of the human individual as a 'criminal' and his location as a member of a 'criminal class' is both a constraining and a liberating process. While it ties the subject down to a particular identity, it frees him from the moral obligations of his complementary subject position – the 'good citizen' – so much so that he comes to personify the temptation and attractions of anarchy. Thus the boy who fought and struggled to avoid being placed in the collar suddenly and ironically rejoices at his 'liberation'. Then the offenders are riveted together by means of a chain and set free to roam the countryside as an example to others. However, their effect upon the common people is far from salutary.

> WARDER: Whole country's in an uproar, sir, when the chain gang's gone through.
> PIERRE: That's because there are no placards.
> WARDER: Lowest of the low, the chain. Don't have to behave. Not like you and me with jobs to lose. (*Sc*, p. 34)

The chain gang demonstrates that there is more pleasure in breaking the law than succumbing to it. Their song incites the children, who are meant to learn the lesson of obedience, to revolution and to the breaking of the coercive shackles of the law. Physically and intellectually battered by this confrontation with the chain gang Pierre learns that the most effective forms of restraint are not physical but mental – chains in the mind. Jeremy Bentham demonstrates this by making Pierre subject himself voluntarily to the power of the Panopticon. Isolated, illuminated and subjected to potentially continuous surveillance Pierre begins automatically to discipline himself – remaining obedient to what he believes Bentham expects of him long after his overseer has ceased to watch him. He learns the value of discipline over force as an economical manifestation of power rendered even more efficient by its invisibility, which also makes it invulnerable. Pierre becomes the principle of his own subjection whilst retaining a conception of himself as a free individual. The disciplinary apparatus of power is transformed from the spectacle where 'thousands of people [watch] over one prisoner' to the machine whose moving parts are individual subjects and whose source of energy is power. As Bentham indicates, the machine requires no operator – it is totally self-perpetuating.

Pierre applies the power of the panoptic machine to the inmates of a House of Young Prisoners and in particular to one boy – an adolescent version of the recalcitrant Luc of an earlier scene. Churchill quotes almost verbatim from the extracts of rules governing such institutions cited by Foucault to demonstrate the transformation in attitudes to crime and punishment during the eighteenth century. In addition to its observatory functions the Panopticon facilitated the production of knowledge concerning those fixed in its all-seeing gaze. Deviant elements within society were isolated and analysed in such a way that common attributes and specific differences could be noted and categorised. Thus individuals became constituted as types or 'cases'. The enigmatic and anarchic threat to order and control is named – subjugated at the level of language – and therefore apprehended. Once 'known' the individual becomes a site for training and normalisation. Subjected to Bentham's panoptic method Churchill's deviant adolescent accepts a function (a role or identity) and a place in the social machine.

Foucault claims that the disciplinary mechanisms of power – which include hierarchical observation, normalising judgement and that subtle combination of both the exam or normalising gaze through which individuals are judged and classified – gradually permeated the social fabric during the course of the eighteenth century. They effected startling transformations in a number of institutions including prisons, workshops, hospitals and schools and led to the appearance and growth of the human sciences. Intimate knowledge of their subjects qualified teachers, doctors, social workers and psychiatrists as articulators of 'truth'. Foucault refers to the institutions and organisations which effect normalisation through the use of disciplinary techniques of power as the 'carceral network'.

By the end of the play Pierre is transformed from an agent of the sovereign's pursuit of revenge to an agent of normalisation. It opens as he supervises a public execution. It closes with him supervising an isolated and self-contained group of individuals on a beach possessing no apparent identity other than that of 'MEN'. We know that they must be dissidents for they are relatively silent, under surveillance and subjects of investigation (Pierre is consulting their files). A holidaymaker quizzes him about the group fixing a succession of labels on its members – 'workers', 'convicts', 'patients', 'loonies' – which Pierre fails to acknowledge. The point is that membership of one dissident group implies membership of them all. The knowledge that Pierre has produced concerning one individual (a would-be trade unionist) constitutes him as a member of the working class, a criminal, mentally unstable, a sexual deviant and a sick man.

As in previous scenes one member of the group – Legrand – (possibly the adult Luc) reveals himself to be resistant to the disciplinary techniques of power. In the past he learned to 'contain' himself, now he breaks out with a vengeance and is shot dead in the process of attacking Pierre. In the opening scenes of the play Pierre exhorted his audience of children to look and learn from the spectacle of power manifested in Lafayette's execution. Now he apologises for having been forced to reveal the power lurking behind the apparently benevolent face of modern forms of social control. Legrand has failed the system by adapting imperfectly to his appointed role. At the same time the system has failed him by resorting to forms of violence when its bluff is called. However, the moral is clear. Power will seek to contain and normalise any dissident individual or activity by the most economic and effective means in the interest of social order. In the end the type of dissidence is immaterial, as is the disciplinary mechanism employed, so long as the end is achieved. Pierre, befuddled by alcohol, unwittingly reveals all whilst rehearsing the speech he will make before the minister who is to lay the foundation stone of our modern disciplinary society:

I shall just explain quite simply how the criminals are punished, the sick are cured, the workers are supervised, the ignorant are educated, the unemployed are registered, the insane are normalised, the criminals – No, wait a minute. The criminals are supervised. The insane are cured. The sick are normalised. The workers are registered. The unemployed are educated. The ignorant are punished. No. I'll need to rehearse this a little. The ignorant are normalised. Right. The sick are punished. The insane are educated. The workers are cured. The criminals are cured. The unemployed are punished. The criminals are normalised. Something along those lines. (*Sc*, p. 49)

The ending of *Softcops* is characteristically unresolved. Although order and calm appear to have been restored after the shooting incident, the malfunction of one component caused a temporary hiatus in the smooth operation of the disciplinary apparatus. This is reflected in the suspension of activity on the stage as the 'MEN' stop 'enjoying themselves' and turn to look at Pierre. This can be interpreted as a moment of realisation, insecurity or possibly even revolt as the cover is temporarily removed to reveal the workings of power. In any case it is meant to have a salutary effect upon the audience whose gaze is now also focused on Pierre. The startling effect of the gunshot discomposes the audience, immediately forming a link between us and the anonymous group of revellers on the beach. Like them we momentarily glimpse the way the system operates and must interrogate our conception of ourselves as autonomous and free individuals. The ending does not advocate a revolution against the agents of normalisation in that even if Legrand and his companions had managed to overthrow Pierre and his hidden guards they would not have been able to liberate themselves from the effects of power. Pierre is neither its source nor its inventor, he is merely its agent. At the same time the apparent humaneness of the modern carceral society is revealed to be no more progressive than the old inquisitorial system. Individuals are merely reconstituted as subjects of power and objects of its necessary correlative knowledge.

Softcops was originally written in 1978 and first produced in 1984 – a year in which, as Churchill reminds us, audiences were peculiarly sensitive to the presence of Orwell's 'Big Brother', the intangible but all-seeing eye of the Panopticon.[15] At the same time, Churchill's anonymous group of males is presumably representative of all deviations from the bourgeois norm including non-whites and women. By her own admission gender did not constitute a focus for her ideas until the late seventies when a number of events helped to consolidate the discourse on gender and sexuality. These included the publication in Britain of seminal texts on feminism such as Kate Millet's *Sexual Politics* (1977), the rise of socialist feminist theatre groups such as Monstrous Regiment and the first English translation of Volume 1 of Michel Foucault's *The History of Sexuality* (1978). Churchill's play *Cloud Nine* (1978/79) examines the ways in which human beings, and in particular women, children and homosexuals, have been constituted as subjects and objects of knowledge through the relatively modern discourse of sexuality.

The spread of the carceral network as dramatised in *Softcops* facilitated and encouraged the dissemination of what Foucault refers to as a 'normalising power' throughout the emergent bourgeois capitalist society of the nineteenth century. Sexuality formed the specific focus point for this power as it provided a means of access to both the individual and the species body or population. In addition Foucault isolated the study of sexuality as the most valid approach to the question of how the individual subject is constituted. Foucault's analysis of sexuality strikes directly at the association of sexual with political liberation characteristic of certain aspects of left-wing thought which he labels '*Freudo-Marxisme*'.

The 'repressive hypothesis' is founded on the notion that the freewheeling sexual attitudes of the seventeenth century gave way to 'the monotonous nights of the Victorian bourgeoisie' when

> Sexuality was carefully confined; it moved into the home. The conjugal family took custody of it and absorbed it into the serious function of reproduction. On the subject of sex, silence became the rule. The legitimate and procreative couple laid down the law. The couple imposed itself as model, enforced the norm, safeguarded the truth, and reserved the right to speak while retaining the principle of secrecy. A single locus of sexuality was acknowledged in social space as well as at the heart of every household, but it was a utilitarian, and fertile one; the parents' bedroom. The rest had only to remain vague; proper demeanour avoided contact with other bodies, and verbal decency sanitised one's speech. (*HoS*, p. 3)

It is intimately linked to the consolidation of the middle class and the rise of capitalism and describes the systematic channelling of energy into forms of sexual activity calculated to ensure a vital population, the reproduction of a labour force and the continuation of dominant forms of social relations. Thus any attempt to liberate or articulate hitherto repressed and silenced sexual pleasures became associated with personal freedom and resistance to power.

Foucault argues that sexuality is a product neither of nature nor of biology. It is an historical construct whose development may be traced to the 'polymorphous techniques of power'. It is evidence of the ways in which power seeks out individuals, penetrating and controlling even their most intimate and idiosyncratic pleasures through 'refusal, blockage, and invalidation, but also incitement and intensification' (HoS, p. 11). It does so through the channels established by discourse. The liberation of truths concerning the sexual identity of the self was not so much repressed in the nineteenth century as constituted within language, 'driven out of hiding and constrained to lead a discursive existence' (HoS, p. 33). The gradual extension of power over the individual and the population was manifest in a 'whole grid of observations regarding sex'. The establishment of the legitimate, fertile heterosexual couple as the sexual norm led to the identification of all other peripheral sexualities as deviations and perversions. The discretion and privacy accorded to the norm was accompanied by the will to establish the truth of unorthodox sexual activity through scientific investigation and the incitement of the hitherto unnoticed perverse subject to produce the truth about his or her own sexuality through the technique of the confession. Foucault argues that 'the interplay of sex and truth' bequeathed to us by the nineteenth century continues to dominate us in the twentieth century albeit in a modified form:

> We must not think that by saying yes to sex, one says no to power; on the contrary, one tracks along the course laid out by the general deployment of sexuality.

The irony of this deployment is that we believe it to hold the key to our 'liberation' (HoS, pp. 157–9). For Foucault the movement for sexual freedom is part of the same historical network as the repressive machinery of power it seeks to challenge.

Churchill's Cloud Nine can be seen to identify sexuality not as a focus of oppression but as a site for struggle. The title refers to the sensation of orgasm as experienced by one of the older female contributors to the workshop sessions which prefaced the writing of the piece, but the play itself is more concerned with analysing the way power can be seen to constitute rather than repress desire. As such it is not a celebration of the role that forms of sexual pleasure – heterosexual or otherwise – play in the liberation of the individual. Rather it can be seen as a direct attack on 'Freudo-Marxism' and the idea that the primary locus of power lies in sexual repression and that consequently sexual liberation deals a body blow, in every sense of the word, to power. Churchill has been criticised for 'reducing Victorianism and Imperialism to sexual totalitarianism' and applauded for asserting that 'sexual liberation is political freedom, sexual repression leads to violence and a negation of oneself'.[16] A Foucauldian perspective on *Cloud Nine* reveals that neither is the case. The play mirrors *The History of Sexuality* in its acknowledgement that the roots of contemporary sexual identities lie in the nineteenth century's obsession with discipline and normalisation in which subjects were incited to produce the 'truth' about themselves by constituting their sexual desires in discourse. By the same token it demonstrates that while individuals in the twentieth century may be interrogating or celebrating their sexual identities, the network of power relations in which they are caught – economic, parental, personal and domestic – remains fundamentally unchallenged.

Act I of *Cloud Nine* takes place in colonial Africa in 1879, shortly after the date Foucault claims for the entry of homosexuality into sexual discourse. Act II is set in London exactly one hundred years later, in the year of the play's first production, although the characters are only a quarter of a century older. As in *Softcops* the audience is invited to identify with the characters onstage although the specificity of the stage directions suggests that the play's observations are especially relevant to a 1979 audience. However, Churchill's chronological game-playing implies that power relations have changed little since Victorian times. The second act is fragmented, in contrast to the first, which is structured as a traditional dramatic narrative, echoing Foucault's theory that while we can read the archive of an earlier era, our own remains inaccessible because we are unconscious of the rules and procedures which govern us.

Seen from a Foucauldian point of view, Act I becomes a series of confessions couched in both monologic and duologic form which interweave to form the network of power relations which constitute Victorian colonial society. Foucault cites the confession as one of the main rituals relied upon by Western societies to produce 'truth'. In the act of confessing, the characters constitute themselves as sexual beings producing truths about themselves which support the power structures in which they are situated. The character who receives, validates and judges the confessions of the others is Clive, who functions as the agent of domination and normalisation and the master of truth. In the field or discourse of sexuality the panoptic gaze is bourgeois, white, male, heterosexual and monogamous. In the opening scenes of the play Clive constructs himself according to the norm. He also constructs (or introduces) the other characters in relation to it. Thus his wife Betty is identified with all the acceptable womanly traits of modesty, naivety, sensitivity, delicacy and sexual ignorance. Mrs Saunders is the spirited widow and guarantor of Clive's virility, Harry Bagley the macho hero, loyal friend and bearer of the British Standard into the darkest heart of Africa, and Edward the manly young heir. As the play progresses, the characters are incited or forced to make the difficult confession of the 'truth' about themselves which is verified and judged by Clive. Betty's adulterous fancy for Harry is construed as a product of 'dark, female lust' which is normally neutralised by the domestic responsibilities of the wife and mother: a verdict dutifully echoed by Harry in his standard-bearing role. Harry's furtive but compulsive homosexuality is classi-fied as 'the most revolting perversion . . . a disease more dangerous than diphtheria'. Clive's use of religious terminology such as 're-pent' and 'sin' pleasingly emphasises the origins of the confessional technique. Edward's effeminacy and budding homosexuality are dismissed as an example of childish disobedience and a temporary aberration brought on by too-close and lengthy contact with women. As each articulates their desires in language their subjectivity or truth is constituted in ways which are culturally specific. Once clas-sified as deviant they become immediate targets for normalisation. Betty embraces her domestic role, Edward temporarily adopts the trappings of masculinity and Harry the outward semblance of het-erosexuality through his marriage to Ellen. Interesting variations on this theme are Clive himself and Mrs Saunders. Clive rationalises his own adulterous deviation from the norm as the result of Mrs Saunders's primitive power over him. In the act of disproving his hypothesis and thereby rejecting the only identity available to her she dooms herself to anonymity and dislocation:

MRS SAUNDERS: I was leaving anyway. There's no place for me here. I have made arrangements to leave tomorrow, and tomor-row is when I will leave. I wish you joy Mr Bagley.

(*Mrs Saunders goes.*)
CLIVE: No place for her anywhere I should think. Shocking
behaviour.[17]

Distressing though the process of normalisation is, it is presented
as preferable to the constraints placed on those whose desires cannot
be articulated in language and who are therefore doomed to silence
or a shadowy, peripheral existence. The independent single woman,
Mrs Saunders; the elderly woman, Maud; and the lesbian, Ellen have
conspicuously small speaking parts. Ellen's lesbianism is ignored by
her confessor, who also happens to be the object of her affections and
later, when it is haltingly articulated by Joshua, it is condemned as a
falsehood by Clive.

The disciplinary techniques of individualisation examined in Act
I of *Cloud Nine* are highlighted further by Churchill's celebrated
technique of cross-casting. Actors cast against their gender, age and
sexual orientation draw attention to the fact that the characters they
portray are cultural fictions even after their 'true confessions'. They
also point up the complex power relations at work in the process of
self-identification. The fact that Betty is played by a male actor
suggests that, as a result of the domination of discourse by men,
women have constituted themselves in relation to a male truth.
Similar interpretations apply to the character of Edward who is
played by an adult, and the black servant Joshua who is played by a
white. At the same time the portrayal of Edward by a woman raises
provocative questions concerning the 'true' identity of any man in
reaction against conventional masculine norms. These issues are
examined in more detail in Act II.

Despite the centrality of sexuality in Act I it is clearly not the sole
determinant of identity. Other discourses, which include economics,
class, race and the family, tie individuals to their identity and situate
them in a complex and mobile hierarchy of power relations such as
those between Clive and Betty, Edward and Joshua. Though whites
have power over blacks masculinity still prevails over femininity.
While children are subject to adults they share the racial privileges of
their fathers. The economic determinant is demonstrated by Ellen,
one of the Victorian period's 'Odd Women'; and Maud, the wid-
owed mother. Lacking male economic providers of their own they
are forced to depend on another woman's – in this case Clive.

While certain individuals' races and classes may benefit from the
rules and procedures which govern particular discourses they do

not originate them. Thus liberation from one form of subjection will not guarantee total freedom for any individual. Act I closes with the symbolic shooting of Clive by Joshua. Act II examines the effects of the displacement of the white male arbiter of heterosexual truth.

On the surface Act II appears to subscribe to the Repressive Hypothesis so persuasively interrogated by Foucault. In contrast to their Victorian counterparts the twentieth-century characters enjoy a more positive and open sexuality. The patriarch Clive is confined to the ghostly margins of memory and the past, and free sexual activity has led to the collapse of that bastion of the capitalist state – the patriarchal family. 'The message' declares Elizabeth Russell, 'is Wilhelm Reich's' (p. 159). Normalisation has given way to self-realisation through the free enjoyment of masturbation, homosexuality (male and female), promiscuity, bisexuality and possibly even incest but the furtive paedophilia of Act I is conspicuously absent from this proliferation of polymorphous sexualities. However, in dramatising the process of 'self-realisation' undertaken by Victoria, Edward, Gerry and Betty *Cloud Nine* not only interrogates Reichian sexual essentialism, but raises disturbing and to some extent unanswerable questions concerning the role of power in the constitution of the individual subject and the nature and possibility of resistance. As Act II unfolds, the search for an identity – the articulation of truth about the self – gives way to the struggle against identity.

The discourse on modern sexual repression is represented by the universal theorising left-wing intellectuals Martin and Vicky whose doctrine is 'You can't separate fucking and economics' (*CN*, p. 309). Martin identifies himself as a 'liberated man' – liberated that is from the conventional masculine role based on sexual and domestic domination: 'not the sort of man who makes women cry'. He sees his role as helping Victoria to free herself from gender repression through sexual pleasure. His analysis is that the road to independence lies in sexual experimentation and the achievement of multiple orgasms. At the same time he is unwilling and unable to refrain from the use of domination and coercion in the imposition of his own 'truth' on Victoria. Sexual essentialism becomes male liberationalism and therefore supports rather than challenges the existing gender hierarchy, allowing men even greater access to women's bodies. The same is true of certain forms of feminism, including liberal left-wing and biological feminism in that both refuse to acknowledge the role of power in the construction of the self. Martin's desire to understand women can be seen as another version of the 'power-knowledge' process: an example of power subjugating and containing what is alien to it at the level of language (Martin is 'writing a novel about women from the woman's point of view'). When Victoria, Edward and Lin attempt to summon the eternal feminine principle or goddess it is Martin who appears and takes advantage of the orgy that ensues. In his desire to subjugate women to his own rationality Martin is revealed to be operating by the same rules as Clive.

Victoria is also unable to conceptualise the necessary redefinition of the roles of wife and mother and the corresponding deconstruction of the traditional patriarchal family unit. Her initial response to the offer of desirable work away from London is to suggest a simple role-reversal: 'Why the hell can't [Martin] just be the wife and come with me?'

Like Martin, Edward is seeking an alternative to the available male identity but finds it in the conventional female role characterised by hysteria, emotional and sexual masochism and dependency. He enjoys cooking, knitting and being fucked. He wants to be a 'woman' and, more importantly, he wants to be a 'wife'. The absurdity and limitations of conventional forms of subjectivity are revealed when they are tried on for size. Does the effeminate Edward's dislike of men make him a lesbian? Does Vicky's lesbian relationship with Lin count as adultery against Martin? Act II of *Cloud Nine* insists on the total deconstruction of conventional gender roles like wife, and orthodox sexual truths like homosexuality. It also questions the siting of sexuality within a polemic of oppression and confirms the ubiquity of power.

The struggle against existing forms of subjection is personified by Betty, Lin, Gerry and Cathy. However, these characters do not function as manifestos for the liberation of the individual through the articulation of his or her sexual truth as much as reminders of the ubiquitous nature of power. Betty's attempt to deconstruct her wifely identity implies a deconstruction of herself – a nervous breakdown. Critics who subscribe to the Repressive Hypothesis have accepted her monologue on the new-found joys of masturbation at face value as a celebration of her liberated identity through sexual and economic independence:

> I felt myself gathering together more and more and I felt angry with Clive and angry with my mother and I went on and on defying them, and there was this vast feeling growing in me and all around me and they couldn't stop me and no one could stop

me and I was there and coming and coming. (*CN*, p. 316)

A Foucauldian reading of this monologue would see it as yet another example of the confessions which characterised Act I except that this time it is the audience rather than Clive who functions as the arbiter of truth. As in *Softcops* the boundaries of the theatrical artefact are stretched to include the audience and implicate us in the 'pleasure of analysis'. If we subscribe to the Repressive Hypothesis then we interpret Betty not as the perverse adult but as the 'liberated individual'. However, Foucault suggests that to regard power purely as an external and transgressable limit imposed on desire is to blind ourselves to its productive function. Power 'produces reality; it produces domains of objects and rituals of truth. The individual and the knowledge that may be gained of him belong to this production' (*DP*, p. 194). As if to remind us of this, the play ends with the appearance of '*Betty from Act One*' whose cultural construction was revealed through the technique of cross-casting. The mutual embrace of the two Bettys can be read as an acknowledgement of the pervasive and inescapable nature of power.

The character of Cathy lends itself to a similar reading. Cathy represents the future; she is the product of 'liberated' post-1968 parents who have dedicated themselves to the excavation and development of the essential truth of the individual. In stark constrast to her nineteenth-century counterpart – the doll Victoria – Cathy is palpably animate and articulate, especially in bodily matters. Her dress and gun suggest that she has yet to ally herself with any one gender identity and like Joshua she symbolically shoots her potential role models and oppressors. She also appears to resist guidance and interpretation in her creativity – her painting – and in her subjectivity. However, during the course of the play she is gradually and inevitably feminised by her peer-group and her elders. Betty ritually adorns her with the symbols of femininity, including the necklace that the young Edward was forced to take by stealth, and shortly after this she is violently expelled from the all-boy 'Dead Hand Gang'. At the same time the fact that she is played by a man suggests that her conscious, articulate identity is already constituted. The choice of a man to symbolise the essential natures of Betty and Cathy reveals the extent to which women are still subject to a male truth as a direct result of the domination of discourse by men.

Having analysed the past and examined the present, *Cloud Nine* is predictably enigmatic as to the future. It is possible to read the play as an analysis of the operation of a certain technique of power – sexuality – and a rejection or refusal of available forms of sexual subjection. It also functions as a critique of sexual essentialism and of the notion of individual liberation through the articulation of repressed sexual desire. However, *Cloud Nine* is non-committal when it comes to advocating new and alternative subject positions, especially within the realms of gender identity. Some interesting possibilities are suggested by the characters of Lin and Gerry: redefinitions of 'parental', 'masculine', 'feminine' and 'homosexual' roles. For Lin the construction of her sexual identity: 'I'm a lesbian' gives way to the pursuit of pleasure through new forms of relationship which involve more than one partner and, more significantly perhaps, more than one gender. At the same time she rejects the Freudo-Marxism of Victoria and Martin. Defending herself against Victoria's charge of inconsistency with regard to parenting and 'collaborating with sexist consumerism' she declares, 'I've changed who I sleep with. I can't change everything.' Although Gerry's confessional monologue constitutes him as a promiscuous homosexual (and as with Betty the audience is invited to validate his confession) it also points to the formation of new kinds of sexual relationship, the denial of sexuality as a truth-producing discourse and the rejection of certain forms of linguistic interpellation of the subject. He describes his pursuit of simple pleasure through sex during a regular train journey from Victoria to Clapham:

> by the time we sat down again the train was just slowing up. I felt wonderful. Then he started talking. It's better if nothing is said. Once you find he's a librarian in Walthamstow with a special interest in science fiction and lives with his aunt, then forget it. He said I hope you don't think I do this all the time. I said I hope you will from now on. He said he would if I was on the train, but why don't we go out for a meal? I opened the door before the train stopped. I told him I live with somebody, I don't want to know. He was jogging sideways to keep up. He said 'What's your phone number, you're my ideal physical type, what sign of the zodiac are you? Where do you live? Where are you going now?' It's not fair, I saw him at Victoria a couple of months later and I went straight down to the end of the platform and picked up somebody who never said a word, just smiled. (*CN*, pp. 297–8).

It is significant that Gerry associates monogamy and certain techniques of individualisation with *Victoria* Station – a reference perhaps to the historical context of Act I. For both Lin and Gerry sexuality is seen as a source of pleasure rather than a source of absolute truth or liberation. It takes its place alongside economics, parenting, class gender and colonial oppression as part of the network of 'micro powers' which constitute and normalise individuals. As in *Softcops, Cloud Nine* contains no comfortable resolutions to the questions it raises. It functions as a dramatisation of the way in which we must continually interrogate the particular sexual identities we assume in an attempt to alter the power-relations which militate against us. It also exposes as a fallacy the notion of liberation from power through the articulation of our repressed sexual 'truths'. The characters in *Cloud Nine* do not escape the operation of power; they merely succeed in changing the strategic situations they are in.

If sexuality is regarded as a technology of power which operates on the mind and body of the individual, then so is gender, although Foucault is surprisingly reticent on this issue. The movement that used to be known as Women's Liberation was based on a binary concept of power located in relationships between the sexes. The 'liberation' of women from male dominance was seen as the key to the overthrow of power and this analysis prevails in certain sections of the radical feminist movement. Likewise essentialist feminism is characterised by the desire to discover and privilege the inviolate femininity which patriarchy seeks to repress or deny. A Foucauldian perspective on feminism reveals it as a specific and localised power-struggle which seeks to challenge the ways in which the individual woman is constituted as a subject. Those involved in this particular 'immediate' struggle

> criticise instances of power which are the closest to them, those which exercise their action on individuals. They do not look for the 'chief enemy', but for the immediate enemy. Nor do they expect to find a solution to their problem at a future date (that is, liberations, revolutions, end of class struggle). . . . They are struggles which question the status of the individual: on the one hand they assert the right to be different and they underline everything which makes individuals truly individual.
>
> On the other hand they attack everything which separates the individual, breaks his links with others, splits up community life, forces the individual back on himself and ties him to his own identity in a constraining way.[18]

Churchill's *Top Girls* can be seen as a manifestation of this struggle and a critique of any form of feminism based on a simple binary opposition of gender.[19]

In Act I, scene I of *Top Girls* five women from different historical periods are invited to a celebratory meal hosted by Marlene: a female representative of the 1980s. During the meal Marlene proposes a toast 'To our courage and the way we've changed our lives and our extraordinary achievements' (*TG*, p. 13). Up to this point only three of the women have told their story – Isabella Bird, Lady Nijo and Pope Joan. Of the remaining two Dull Gret is yet to speak (other than in monosyllables) and Patient Griselda is yet to arrive. Isabella, Nijo and Joan appear united by the fact that their stories have some basis in reality whereas Griselda and Gret are obvious fictions invented by a male imagination. Thus the latter can be read as feminine archetypes: products of the truth-producing discourse of patriarchy which has constituted individuals as 'women' and labelled them as deviant, disruptive, enigmatic and therefore targets for the will to knowledge. Griselda represents the feminine ideal of obedience, passivity, virtue and submission. Gret is her antithesis and stands for violent rebellion, monstrosity and chaos. Isabella, Nijo and Joan chart courses between these two poles of womanhood, moving from conformity through breakdown to rebellion and as such their struggles mirror Betty's from Act II of *Cloud Nine*. Throughout this first scene complex and complementary relationships are set up between Marlene and her guests which transcend time, age and class and which imply that she is also involved in an attempt to emancipate herself from a conventional feminine role.

If *Top Girls* is read as a critique of forms of resistance which conceptualise power as repression in the form of male law and taboo then Gret and Griselda can be seen respectively as extreme manifestations of a radical and essentialist feminist stance. Both positively endorse certain gender specific attributes while Gret concerns herself with locating the source of power (or evil) in order to 'pay the bastards out' (*TG*, p. 28). As was the case with sexuality both feminine norm and deviation are revealed as social constructs produced at the level of discourse and thus imply subjection to the prevailing strategies of patriarchy.

Isabella Bird, nineteenth-century Scottish traveller, negotiates a position between 'making scones' and 'lassoing cattle'. She begins by trying to conform to the role of clergyman's daughter and dutiful wife and ends by declaring, 'I cannot and will not live the life of a lady' (*TG*, p. 20). Isabella's identities were created and dictated by her father and her husband, so that on the death of her father she felt 'half [herself] gone'. This process of self-annihilation is completed with the death of her husband: 'and he faded away and left me. There was nothing in my life' (*TG*, p. 11). The new role she creates for herself involves an appropriation of what were defined by her culture as wholly masculine pursuits: travelling alone and placing herself in danger and discomfort in order to seek adventure. She ends Act I, Scene I with a description of herself in the company of Berber Sheiks, in male attire ('full blue trousers and great brass spurs') and enjoying the uniquely masculine privilege of conversing as an equal with the Emperor of Morocco.

Lady Nijo loses her *raison d'être* when she loses her position as Emperor's concubine: 'There was nothing in my life, nothing without the Emperor's favour' (*TG*, p. 12). She dedicates what is left of herself to religion because it is 'a kind of nothing', and spends the rest of her life emulating vagrant Buddhist priests secure in the conviction that she is fulfilling her father's wishes.

Joan identifies herself with a conventionally masculine role right from the very beginning, dressing as a boy in order to gain access to intellectual establishments: 'There was nothing in my life except my studies. I was obsessed with the pursuit of truth' (*TG*, p. 12). The truth that Joan pursues corresponds with the meaning to their existence sought by Isabella and Nijo after the deaths of their male facilitators. At the same time, as a universal intellectual in the Foucauldian sense Joan pursues the particular regime of truth favoured by her society for, as Foucault indicates, truth is merely an interpretation of reality rather than its essence.

The inviolable essence of reality is symbolised by God and Joan believes that by becoming Pope she will know God. However, as she is to discover, it is impossible to separate power from the production of truth through knowledge. Power uses knowledge to justify and support the institutions and regimes that discipline and control society. One of the truths of a patriarchal Catholic society is that 'women, children and lunatics' cannot be Pope – they cannot be arbiters of a male truth. While her gender remains a secret she can erect her own interpretation of reality: 'I realised I did know the truth because whatever the Pope says is true.' However, as soon as her disqualification is discovered she loses her power and her life. Femaleness, as it is constituted within a patriarchal discourse, disqualifies a subject from full participation in the production of meaning. It renders her silent and excluded.

Patriarchy has isolated maternity, or the potential for maternity, as the essence or badge of femaleness and it is the incontrovertible fact of Joan's parturition that is her downfall. Denial of or indifference to their maternal capacity characterises all of Marlene's dinner guests – even Patient Griselda who defends Walter's apparent infanticide with the words 'It was [his] child to do what he liked with.' Nijo gives up her children in order to avoid 'embarrassment' and Isabella prefers horses. Gret is the only one who expresses anger at the deaths of her children, which she seeks to avenge through an attack on the agents of evil – the devils – or, in radical feminist terms, the agents of patriarchy – men.

Although Marlene has much in common with all of her guests, she is identified most closely with Joan in her succession to a position of dominance. Joan's papacy: 'I never obeyed anyone – they all obeyed me', is contrasted with Marlene's Managing Directorship, 'over all the women you work with. And all the men'. Joyce's attack on her successful sister could well have been directed at the erudite Joan: 'You was the most stupid/for someone so clever you was the most stupid, get yourself pregnant. Not go to the doctor, not tell' (*TG*, p. 80). Marlene's refusal to 'turn into the little woman' to gratify her would-be sexual partners echoes Joan's helpless transformation from Pope to woman in the act of childbirth. At the same time Marlene's interrogation of Joan and sympathy for her situation is the result of experience. Pregnancy threatened *her* success but, unlike Joan, she was able to 'get rid of it somehow'. Joan's fundamental ignorance of the implications of having a woman's body and living a 'woman's life' is echoed in Marlene's ignorance of the conditions of existence for most of her sex: 'anyone can do anything if they've got what it takes' (*TG*, p. 86). Likewise Joan's inability to recognise the reality of pregnancy mirrors Marlene's refusal to acknowledge that the 'truth' of her womanhood cannot be articulated within a male-produced discourse.

Marlene, Win and Nell are 'Top Girls' in that they have climbed as high as possible in a male-dominated field but the ironic implication is that they have achieved this liberation by embracing a subjectivity that has been validated by patriarchal power or, to put it another way, they have forsaken a phallocratic female identity in order to embrace an equally phallocratic male one characterised by the dismissal of and disdain for all things female including their clients and the unfortunate Mrs Kidd.

If Marlene is a twentieth-century version of Joan then Win and Nell mirror Nijo and Isabella respectively. Like Nijo, Win's life is made up of a series of unsatisfactory or illicit affairs with men, whereas Nell shares Isabella's wanderlust. Through their close identification with Joan, Nijo and Isabella, the subjectivities of Marlene, Win and Nell are revealed to be constituted by a gendered patriarchal discourse – figments of a male imagination just like Griselda and Gret.

The critique of radical and essentialist feminism as a liberation from power is continued in the characters of Joyce and Angie who can be read as modern equivalents of Griselda and Gret. Joyce endures, whereas Angie rebels against the agent of repression: 'I'm going to kill my mother, and you're going to watch.' *Top Girls* also dismisses socialism as yet another misguided version of revolutionary politics – one which has little or no validity for women. Joyce locates the source of 'evil' in the class system, venting her wrath on 'the cows I work for' and their status symbols. Angie's positive endorsement of her own essentially negative characteristics is indicated by her secret club with its limited membership which Marlene patronisingly dismisses as 'a plot to take over the world'. At the same time the apparently incongruous menstrual blood-tasting episode involving Angie and Kit can be read as a reference to a radical feminist celebratory rite. The implications are clear. Theories of liberation which conceive of power as essentially repressive and external are simplistic, deluded and doomed to failure.

Churchill's methodology as demonstrated in *Softcops*, *Cloud Nine*, and *Top Girls* reveals an antipathy to any notion of historical progress. In *Top Girls* Marlene has freed herself from the constrictions imposed on Nijo, Joan and Isabella. She does not depend on relationships with men to give meaning to her existence; she travels alone with confidence and in comfort; and she has achieved and retained a position of supreme authority within her organisation. However, her solution to their dilemmas is presented as equally compromising and negative. Hers is simply a different version of the truth and the consequences are, as Angie's final scream reminds us, equally 'Frightening'.

Top Girls has been criticised for failing to provide a transcendent female figure and 'the positive inspiration that many spectators crave'.[20] Churchill claimed that she 'quite deliberately left a hole in the play rather than giving people a model of what they could be like'. Like *Softcops* and *Cloud Nine*, *Top Girls* is not concerned with the illusory search for the origins of power and the elaboration of strategies aimed at its overthrow. It functions as an analysis of the operation of power through the techniques of individualisation. Foucault claimed that resistance to these techniques should take the form of struggles against modes of subjection, not in order to discover our essential identity but to refuse it and create alternative and resistant roles for ourselves within the necessary confines of power.[21] *Top Girls* engages in such a struggle in order to interrogate the meaning assigned to femaleness within patriarchal discourse. As women, our very use of language irrevocably situates us within a power-struggle – a struggle for meaning and truth. We achieve consciousness of ourselves and others through the assumption of patriarchal definitions of what it means to be a 'woman'. At the same time we assume a more or less powerful position in the hierarchy of norm and progressive deviation from the norm. In *Top Girls* the hierarchy is headed by the successful male with women and girls marking its lowest position. If normalisation guarantees access to truth and the production of meaning, then women must deny and conceal their maternal function in order to participate fully in a patriarchal society. Although it is clear that motherhood is a subject position produced by power rather than existing outside it, it is important to recognise it as deviant and therefore potentially subversive. The consistent negation of motherhood practised by the characters in *Top Girls* draws attention to its importance as a possible antithetical or resistant stance available to those who seek to alter the strategic situations between men and women. As Churchill indicates: 'I meant the thing that is absent to have a presence in the play. . . . I thought, what the hell; if people can't see the values, I don't want to spell them out' (*FoC*, p. 61). What is 'frightening' is the single-minded abandonment of the future generation by 'Top Girls' throughout history.

Notes

1.   Michel Foucault, 'Questions of Method', *Ideology and Consciousness*, 8, Spring, 1981, p. 6.
2.   Michelene Wandor, *Carry On Understudies: Theatre and Sexual Politics* (London: Methuen, 1986), pp. 167–74.
3.   Helene Keyssar, *Feminist Theatre*, (London: Macmillan, 1984) pp. 77–101.

4. Linda Fitzsimmons, '"I won't turn back for you or anyone": Caryl Churchill's Socialist-Feminist Theatre', *Essays in Theatre*, 6 (Nov. 1987), (19–27), p. 19.
5. Sue Ellen Case, *Feminism and Theatre* (London: Macmillan 1988), p. 85.
6. Joseph Marohl, 'De-realised Women: Performance and Identity in *Top Girls*', *Modern Drama*, 30 (1987), (376–88), p. 376.
7. See Author's Note to *Softcops*, Caryl Churchill, *Softcops and Fen* (London: Methuen, 1986), p. 3.
8. See D. F. Bouchard (ed.), *Language, Counter-Memory, Practice: Selected Essays by Michel Foucault* (Oxford: Blackwell, 1977), pp. 147–51.
9. 'Structuralism and Post-Structuralism: An Interview with Michel Foucault' by Gerard Raulet, *Telos*, 55 (Spring, 1983), pp. 195–211, p. 202.
10. 'Questions of Method', p. 6.
11. Michel Foucault, *The History of Sexuality Vol. I: An Introduction* (London: Allen Lane, 1978), p. 95 (henceforth referred to as *HoS*).
12. Caryl Churchill interviewed by Lynne Truss in *Plays and Players* (Jan. 1984), p. 10 in *File on Churchill* compiled by Linda Fitzsimmons (henceforth referred to as *FoC*).
13. Michel Foucault, *Discipline and Punish: The Birth of the Prison* (London: Allen Lane, 1977), pp. 202–3 (henceforth referred to as *DP*).
14. Caryl Churchill, *Softcops*, p. 33.
15. See Author's Further Note to *Softcops*, p. 3.
16. Christian W. Thomsen, 'Three Socialist Playwrights: John McGrath, Caryl Churchill, Trevor Griffiths', *Stratford-upon-Avon Studies*, 19 (1981), pp. 157–75 (169); Elizabeth Russell, 'Caryl Churchill: Sexual Politics and *Cloud Nine*', *Revista Canaria De Studios Ingleses*, 12 (April 1986) pp. 153–60, p. 159 respectively.
17. Caryl Churchill, *Cloud Nine* (wr. 1978, perf. 1979) in *Churchill Plays: One* (London: Methuen), pp. 243–320, p. 287 (henceforth referred to as *CN*).
18. Michel Foucault, 'The Subject and Power: an Afterword' in H. L. Dreyfus and P. Rabinow, *Michel Foucault: Beyond Structuralism and Hermeneutics* (Chicago: University of Chicago Press, 1982), pp. 211–12.
19. Caryl Churchill, *Top Girls* (London: Methuen, 1982) (henceforth referred to as *TG*)
20. Case, p. 67; Keyssar, *Feminist Theatre*, p.98
21. See 'Afterword: the Subject and Power', an afterword by Michel Foucault in H. L. Dreyfus and P. Rabinow, *Michel Foucault: Beyond Structuralism and Hermeneutics* (Chicago: University of Chicago Press, 1982).

10

Staging 'The Other Scene': A Psychoanalytic Approach to Contemporary British Political Drama

WENDY J. WHEELER and TREVOR R. GRIFFITHS

In this essay we argue for a privileged relationship between the imaginary structure of the theatrical event and the imaginary structure of human subjectivity. We will examine in detail three examples of the considerable body of recent British drama which has been expressly concerned with political issues, in the light of Laplanche and Pontalis's work in refining Freud's ideas about Fantasy.[1] As well as David Hare's *Plenty* (staged 1978), Trevor Griffiths's *Occupations* (staged 1970), and Howard Brenton's *Greenland* (staged 1988), which all explore the relationship between what have been traditionally conceived of as discrete areas of human activity (the personal and the political), we will also refer briefly to a number of other works both by these writers and also by others such as Howard Barker, Caryl Churchill and David Edgar which address similar issues.[2] Drawing on Laplanche and Pontalis we will read contemporary political theatre in the light of two linked themes: firstly, that all fantasies (those of the artist as much as those of the dreamer) are structurally dependent upon the organisation of fantasy described by Freud as the primal fantasies, and, secondly, that these fantasies are erotic and are organised through sexuality and sexual difference. In applying psychoanalytic thought to the question of theatrical representation we will offer an account of that 'other' scene which both lies behind and also organises the theatrical representation itself.

Throughout Laplanche and Pontalis's essay, as throughout Freud's own work, there is a persistent metaphor of the theatrical: the 'patient's inner world of imagination' is her '"private theatre"', and the unconscious is repeatedly described as both a stage-setting and a scenario. The structure which the primal fantasies retrospectively construct is offered to us as a 'theatre' which . . . 'assign[s] limits to the "imaginary" which cannot contain its own principle of organisation' and through which, as in the theatre, 'There is convergence of theme, of structure, and no doubt also of function.' Freud regards the child, endlessly curious and excluded from the secret sexual heart of the family, as pre-eminently, we might say, an *audience*; watching and listening to the sights and sounds of the family: its sayings, its history, its articulated relationships, its obscure and obscured noises, its visible, invisible and half-glimpsed and half-heard secrets and signs.[3] Within and from this web of what will *come* to be perceived as signifiers the child must find or, more accurately, *fantasise* its own identity, its own place.

For Freud, the three primal fantasies of origin are the fantasy of parental coitus (the 'primal scene', which 'accounts' for the child's origins), the fantasy of seduction (which 'accounts' for the afflux of sexuality), and the fantasy of castration (which 'accounts' for the recognition of sexual difference). These fantasies, which are retrospectively engendered at puberty through Nachträglichkeit, emerge from an earlier economy of hearing and seeing which makes it possible for the child to organise a relatively coherent identity in relation to the profound questions it asks about its own origins. Significantly for our analysis of theatrical dynamics, Laplanche and Pontalis stress the importance of Freud's recognition of 'the unconscious as a structural field, which can be reconstructed, since it handles, decomposes and recomposes its elements according to certain laws'. This means that the subject, although always present in the fantasy, may be so in a desubjectivised form:

> Fantasy, however, is not the object of desire, but its setting. In fantasy the subject does not pursue the object or its sign: he appears caught up himself in the sequence of images. He forms no representation of the desired object, but is himself represented as participating in the scene. . . . As a result, the subject, although always present in the fantasy, may be so in a desubjectivised form, that is to say, in the very syntax of the sequence in question.[4]

Within a representation, then, the psychical 'pay-off' (wish-fulfilment) for the watcher and listener takes the form of a 'putting into the scene' of desire and is not necessarily to be found in a simple identification with a character but in the general syntax of the representation. The different 'roles' which the subject is capable of taking up may change across the syntax of a play, or indeed may be satisfyingly represented by a complex configuration – a scene or a part of a scene. This intricate interrelationship makes it possible to argue for the existence of a structure which crosses the representation of the theatrical event from 'author' to audience and which offers multiple points of entry for both.[5]

Most of the work which has used this theoretical approach has been concentrated in the area of film studies. Here, however, we want to develop the theory in relation to the specificity of the theatrical apparatus. In the theatre, and unlike film, the economy of seeing and hearing we are offered is just as immediate and as *vital* as the drama of the family from and through which we negotiate our precarious subjectivity. The *danger* of theatre, the possibility of *failing to maintain the illusion*, of extraneous noises which *should not be heard*, of the collapse of the role and of the fiction of assumed identities, of fluffed or forgotten lines, of props which make noises which they shouldn't, all combine to reproduce precisely the erotic, libidinal, *danger* of the Oedipal family which the primal fantasies emerge to structure and contain. Thus we are arguing that the theatrical event, or rather its 'other scene' (i.e. of the primal fantasies), repeats and re-enacts the structural conditions which enable subjectivity to emerge, by representing, with the same effect of *danger*, precisely the imaginary conditions of their emergence. The success of the lure of the theatrical *mise-en-scène* may then depend partly upon the extent to which it puts into play in structured form the three primal fantasies of origin in which the audience invest, and from which they gain satisfaction in the form of the representation of the boundaries of identity in the context of the story which the play then unfolds. The pleasures of these texts in performance depends, then, on them addressing questions, in however refractory a way, which are fundamental to existence within the symbolic order. The potential applications of such ideas in the political area are obvious. The dramatists under review have been eager to intervene in cultural and political debate in interviews, media appearances, newspaper articles and letters and membership of human rights organisations.[6] They have specific points of view which they have expressed clearly in non-theatrical as well as theatrical interventions: they *want* to say something about contemporary British political life; they *want* to have a political effect. Our prime concern is with this question of *want* (desire) as it arises within a psychoanalytic register and its encoding in the dramatic event. Within the psychoanalytic register *want*, implying both need and lack, is always problematic. Want is always inscribed as a desire which is formulated in terms of the 'stage setting' of fantasy, as the *mise-en-scène* of desire.[7] If the imaginary representation is always structured around and through the primal fantasies, and the final 'lure' of the representation lies in its transformations of the structuring material of subjectivity itself, then the question arises of the extent to which a self-consciously political theatre is possible. We shall utilise the insights variously provided by the psychoanalytic account of fantasy to examine such transformations as they occur within and across a number of contemporary political plays. We will consider *Plenty* mainly in terms of the fantasy of parental coitus, *Occupations* mainly in terms of seduction, and *Greenland* mainly in terms of castration. The retrospective engendering of these fantasies through the *Nachträglich*, which is a significant structuring element in all three plays, is fundamental to our discussion. We are not, of course, suggesting that all plays will manifest all the primal fantasies to the same extent. Nor will they necessarily always manifest themselves in an obvious form, although they are engrained in contemporary political theatre in very many ways, from the story of the self-castrating badger in *Occupations* (p. 31) through Beaty's 'My balls are in your gift' (*Thirteenth Night*, p. 15) to Liz in *Destiny* ('I want a reason to have children' p. 375) or Skinner's last question in *The Castle* ('does anyone remember' p. 43).

It has been a major insight of the feminist movement that sexuality is political. With notable exceptions, an early contemporary feminist flight from Freud, however, has meant that a concomitant insight has often been missed. Politics and political discourse may run on an engine that is sexualised.[8] The difficulties inherent in dealing with such an insight are well exemplified in *Plenty* where political project and sexual strategy co-exist in an unstable relationship. This is particularly clear in the transformation of the play into the film where the political is subordinated to the sexual. *Plenty* deals with events between 1943 and 1962, focusing on Susan, an Englishwoman active with the Resistance in Occupied France and her growing postwar discontents (and ultimate mental illness) which are used to reflect on the postwar situation. Both versions end with a flashback to wartime but the film is otherwise purely chronological, whereas the play begins in 1962 before returning to 1943. In both versions the roots of

Susan's increasingly aberrant behaviour are located in the events in France. In the film, however, her relationship with the agent Lazar is given greater prominence and made explicitly sexual: they are shown making love early in the film. This offers a quasi-romantic peg on which a whole interpretation of the film can be built, in which Susan eventually finds her lost lover again, and her dissent and restlessness are seen as basically personal and sexual. This is symptomatic of what happens in the film generally: sexual discourses displace political ones. What the play opens up fantasmatically is a movement of passion across three registers, from the political to the sexual to the sacrificial. Susan, the character who bears the burden of Hare's account of the socialist vision ('I intend to show the struggle of a heroine against a deceitful and emotionally stultified class'), is also shown as 'mad', powerless and marginalised, one of what Michelene Wandor terms 'ciphers (as romantic victims) of a view of male despair'.[9] As Hare puts it: 'In England the opposition to *Plenty* forms around the feeling that from the start Susan Traherne contains the seeds of her own destruction, and that the texture of the society in which she happens to live is nearly irrelevant, for she is bent on objecting to it, whatever its qualities.'[10] The *woman* here, as a signifier upon the stage, is made to bear the weight of the political project but, as Hare's remarks suggest, audience responses to Susan have generally been unsympathetic. In the play's sexualised political discourse, which is both acknowledged and *un*acknowledged, it is the woman who bears the burden of socialism, of wanting but not bringing forth what she wants. Here the old, unanswered, Freudian question, 'What do women want?' finds an easy transition into a political discourse. Susan stands for the failure of socialism to say *clearly* what it wants, and, most pertinently perhaps, to say what its pleasures really are. The fantasy structure of the play allows a too-easy movement which equates the patriarchal account of femininity with the capitalist account of socialism. Both are as 'impossible' and as 'frustrating' as the failed primal scenes which the play offers. The sexualised semantics feminise this failure because then its contaminated condition can be dealt with. It is the contamination of the other, of femininity, of madness, from which the project must be, and is, ritually cleansed.

How is this cleansing, this textual sacrifice of Susan accomplished in terms of the psychodynamics of the theatrical event? Clearly, the simple theatrical event of hearing and watching (in 'secret' and in the dark) contains elements of the primal-scene fantasy, but in the play the fantasy and the pleasure it affords are disrupted. In Scene 6 Susan and her friend Alice are joined by Mick, by whom Susan has attempted to get herself pregnant. Alice offers a fantasmatic point of entry for the audience 'on stage' or 'in the scene' as the child who sees and hears the story of the parental coitus. What the 'child' hears, however, is that the coitus has failed – which must be profoundly disturbing of the pleasure which the fantasy might be expected to yield. Further this representation of the fantasy *inverts* the primal scene inasmuch as we are told that Mick and Susan's copulation some-times took place with Mick's mother listening downstairs. So a failed and inverted primal scene may in part account for the play's failure. Moreover it is this scene which gives us some clue as to the struc-tural role of the apparently anachronistic Alice.[11] She is a highly multivalent signifier who offers several possible subject-positions for the audience: most immediately, she offers an onstage locus for the audience, always watching and listening; by inference in terms of behaviour (drugs and sexual activity) she is the love-child of the sixties whose birth is roughy contemporaneous with the political audience Hare addresses; and, again by inference, as the fantasy child of the 'parents' whose coitus in 1951 she sees and hears. Her adolescence and sexual and political awakening are again contem-poraneous with that of that same supposed audience. So, the play's apparently rather arbitrary end in 1962 coincides with the point at which the fantasy child Alice might be supposed to be leaving the phase of sexual latency and entering the phase of genital sexuality and repression which results in the formation of primal fantasies. The audience is thus at this point offered the possibility of beginning to fantasise an identity in which the wish crosses over from a sexual to a political identity, the origins of which Hare (born 1947) here offers to account for.[12] The primal scene which Alice witnesses ends with a failed castration (i.e. a failed articulation of sexual difference) as Susan shoots at Mick. In psychoanalytic terms this implies that Susan, and everything she stands for, is hysterical, i.e. she doesn't know what her gender is, she doesn't know how to mark out the boundaries of the identity which will allow her to reproduce herself. Hence, presumably, her failure to conceive.

In the play, although not in the film, Alice appears before the primal scene which should, structurally, account for her. The film actually produces an alternative primal scene, in which Susan and Lazar make love, but this is barely inferred from the play. That the film actually inserts this psychological corrective may, of course, say something for the commercial canniness of film producers. When the seduction scene, between Susan and Mick, does occur in the play, it precedes the account of a primal scene in Scene 6 and follows the castration scene which opens the play (but not the film) where Susan's husband Brock appears as a naked drunken bloody apparent corpse and Alice 'takes his penis between her thumb and forefinger' (p. 11). The play actually reverses *in toto* the coherent order of the primal fantasies, thus subverting the sexual investment in the political message. The film, more confident, in its displacement of the political in favour of the sexual, 'corrects' the psychosexual syntax so that a primal scene is followed by a seduction scene which is followed by a reworking of the primal scene which is followed by a castration. The insertion of the second primal scene is not particularly disturbing because the syntax is merely interrupted rather than, as in the play, actually reversed. The play's unsatisfying inverted fantasy scenario is, thus, simply handed back to the audience at the end of the play for the audience to rework or to begin work upon. The play, it turns out, is not about a simple vision, but about a vision of a future which demands a ritual sacrifice. That sacrifice of a feminised socialism having been completed as Susan sinks into a drug-induced *false* fantasy of a past signified by Lazar's seduction, the cleansed audience is sent forth to begin the fantasy again, to reinvest a new symbolic order and to jolly well get it right this time.[13] The film, in fact, corrects almost everything that is 'wrong' with the play, but it does this by articulating the text in a quite different direction, towards the film melodrama in which the *main* problem is feminine sexuality. As a result of this the text is denuded of its political content. If the film Susan is more sympathetic, this depends to a great extent on the connotations that Meryl Streep brings with her. Hare is thus given the sympathetic Susan he thinks the play needs, but the 'price' is a reduction in specific political content. The transference from one medium to another thus brings along with it a transference of focus and of material demands in which Hare is denied the final *coup de grâce* to the project which he might have hoped for.

Plenty anchors itself most firmly in the idea of resistance, the subversion of the French Resistance and of Susan's continual resistance to class incorporation. But resistance also has a meaning within the psychoanalytic register where it means the resistance which founds repression and upon which the entire economy of fantasy is based. Here, however, the fantasy which resistance produces is inverted; that is, it fails to account for the political identity which *Plenty* demands, or it produces that post-1962 political identity as a failure. *Plenty*'s final resistance, however, is in the sphere of sexual politics, for the failed identity which it produces, in Susan and in Alice, is female. Finally, like psychoanalysis itself, in order to account for its own theoretical position, *Plenty* must commit an act of double violence in which identity depends on an idea of socialism as feminised and femininity as sacrificial.[14] Hare's project in *Plenty* replicates this double violence in what it does to socialism. By feminising socialism, *Plenty* makes it, like femininity, the locus of the impossible and fantastic demand that socialism's identity be affirmed in a movement of continual sacrifice on identity in which identity is always defined by what it is opposed to, by what it lacks, by what it isn't. Resistance then becomes pathological and tips over into the psychotic's wholesale foreclosure upon the possibility of entry into the social order at all. The inverted and incomplete primal fantasies which *Plenty* plays out are fantasies of a psychotic failure to achieve identity. That it does so via a fantasy of the problematic which patriarchy makes of feminine sexuality makes it simply a restatement of the old formulation that the woman who fails to accept that power (and sexual difference) is defined by the phallus is mad. In encoding this politically, *Plenty* suggests, at the level of its fantasy production, that the alternative vision which socialism offers is mad because it only has a theory of the power of the other, and that its practice resides only in opposition and resistance itself and not in the taking-up of power. The woman is sacrificed, perhaps, because the woman with real power is no longer a 'real' woman (implying that socialism with real power is no longer real socialism). Power means the negotiation of reality in which the purity of the fantasy is lost. To have power is to lose the pure and idealised vision, is to be contaminated with the grime of the quotidian. Perhaps, for the old puritan idealism of a pre-Gramscian Left, the sacrifice in the theatrical ritual of purification is the cleaner option. That this cleanliness may take the extreme form of *sterility* is a problem which *Plenty* only very indirectly addresses.

Trevor Griffiths made a more direct assault on the problem from another direction in *Occupations*, where Gramsci himself figures as a leading character.[15] The fantasy structure of *Occupations* exposes the unconsciously *compelling* nature of what Marx described as the terrific dynamism of capitalism. It does so by retrospectively articulating the fantasy of seduction within a structure of fantasy scenarios in which what is at stake is the failure of socialist ideas to seduce or *occupy* their audience. The movement of fantasmatic desire within the play offers a number of possible positions for the audience, from that of the direct political subject of the address (the potential revolutionary and 'occupier' of the means of production), through various positionalities within the fantasy of seduction, to those which offer the indiscriminate desire of capital itself. Each and any of these positions may be subsumed under the general heading of seduction, from the political seduction of occupation and possession based on a utopian ideal, to that of erotic seduction and possession, and finally to that of the infinite seduction of material possessions. The particular structures of desire which the play offers are thus significantly interchangeable from the audience's possible points of view.

The objective of a seduction can generally also be described as an occupation, that is both the physical and the emotional 'taking-in', or introjection, of one person by another. In *Occupations* the erotic fantasy of seduction provides the unconscious structure upon which political questions are explored, so that in an important sense the political is itself fantasmatic, or at least profoundly dependent upon fantasmatic structuration. Here, as we consider the would-be 'seducers' in the play and the question of the psychical compulsion of the possible positions which the audience can take up in relation to them, we are concerned with both erotic seductiveness and the seduction of ideas. We will also consider the ways in which we discover retrospectively, as in the primal fantasies, that a certain structuration of desire (the capitalist structuration of desire) has been put into play. From a psychoanalytic point of view, this is a structuration of desire which, in the play's terms, offers a more seductive fantasy-scenario than that apparently offered by socialism. This desire is put into play within a set of scenarios in which the idea of the *excuse*, alibi, or displacement is central.

The importance of the idea of displacement is foregrounded in the play's two opening scenes in which a structure of desire is repeated but reversed. The first structure, revealed in the 'foreplay', is a structure of political desire; signified by the disembodied welcome to the Second Congress of the Third International, the projected political images of posters and a map of the movement of Communist forces into Poland, and the usual 4/4 march time of the Internationale. This is displaced, through a musical change to the romantic 3/4 time of the Internationale played as a waltz into an erotic, romantic desire, confirmed by the structure of the set, with its dominant bed. This scene offers itself to the audience in a way that initially allows it to be read as the aftermath of a scene of seduction. Angelica lies on the 'solid bed' (the symbolically central presence in the play's single set, which remains on stage throughout, visually underpinning the idea of seduction in both 'political' and 'personal' scenes) with her 'superb nightdress and negligee . . . rucked up about her thighs'. '[H]e had fingers like hot pincers', she says. Polya replies 'Feel sorry for his wife then' (p. 10). The audience is, however, quickly required to amend this initial reading (and the fantasies which it puts into play) and to recognise the signs of the scene as something else. The displacement here is from the supposed scene of sexual seduction to the political seduction initiated by the reference to Gramsci. The second structure of displaced desire is revealed in the fantasmatic movement from the scene of supposed seduction to the scene of political intrigue (and attempted seduction). The most obvious point at which these different seduction fantasies meet is in the scene between Kabak and Gramsci who offer us competing versions of seductiveness.

These early shifts in the audience's reading thus militate against the adoption of a settled subject position and are central to the strategy of the play. The scenarios offered to the audience may build on both the unconscious compulsion of the (fantasy) voyeur or auditor of classic scenes of seduction or they may build on the conscious compulsion of the subject of the political addresses, in which the constraints of theatrical 'realism' limit the possibilities for the audience (constructed at these points as Milanese factory workers) to those of acceptance, rejection or intellectual detachment. The structuring fantasy in the latter case is presumably that of castration, i.e. the fantasy of identification with *other* positions. Certainly the theatre audience is not expected to rush out of the theatre in a spasm of revolutionary fervour.

The structure of the play allows the audience to take up various positions in relation to the fantasy but finally offers, at the point at which fantasy is constrained by the demands of the law and hence of the symbolic, a form of closure which is an invitation to take up a certain identity which attempts, as human identity *does*, to subordinate the sexual instincts to the ego instincts. The structure through which this occurs in *political* terms is expressed in the idea of the excuse. The same excuse occurs at two different points in the play. On the first occasion Kabak excuses his forthcoming contact with the politically 'undesirable' Communist Gramsci to the anxious bour-

geois hotelier Libertini. In effect Kabak says that capitalists sometimes have to consort with communists in pursuit of the aims of
capital. At that point in the play it is apparently no more than an
excuse (and transparently untrue from the audience's point of view)
and is marginal to the bifold interplay of seductions sexual and
political which is the apparent heart of the play. The second occasion
on which the excuse is invoked is when Kabak explains to Valletta
why communism is consorting with capitalism. The excuse here is
that of pragmatism:

> KABAK: There are those inside the Soviet government who would
> argue – still, I fear – that the granting of concessions in return for
> capital, or capital equipment, credit and services, is the kiss of
> death to revolutionary socialism. Comrades who have never
> understood the first thing about capital or its uses have imag-
> ined we can, in some magical 'communist' way, run a state and
> a society without it. Fortunately, they look to have been de-
> feated. (p. 69)

We can formulate this excuse in other words: communists sometimes have to consort with capitalists in pursuit of the aims of
communism.

In this play the theme of the excuse is articulated to the idea of
seduction. Everything that happens on the stage happens within
that context so that all the interactions between the characters acquire a certain seductiveness.

In describing the structure of temporal displacement through which
primal fantasies arise, Freud insists that only the seduction fantasy,
the retrospective 'account' of the afflux of sexuality itself, is capable
of producing the shock (trauma) which founds repression and the
structure of the primal fantasies through which desire is contained
and human identity emerges.

In *Occupations* the structure which is articulated through the idea
of the excuse is the same as the structure of the primal fantasies
which is articulated through the idea of seduction. We have the same
narrative; the two events separated in the temporal sequence – the
first trivial, the second shocking – and the same temporal displacement in which the shock of the second event forces us retrospectively to construct a meaning which was not originally present. In
order to understand the interplay between the play's sexual and
political registers, however, it is necessary not only to notice the

structural similarity but to consider the content and context of the repeated excuse.

The content, which we have already discussed, is a dialectic of two terms: 'capitalists sometimes have to consort with communists in pursuit of the aims of capital' and 'communists sometimes have to consort with capitalists in pursuit of the aims of communism'. What separates the two excuses is their different contexts. The first excuse occurs in the context of attempted seductions which will fall. The second excuse occurs in the context of a successful seduction, the deal with Fiat. Whilst both terms are necessarily and dialectically *true* inasmuch as this is what happens at the end of the play, the textual implication is of the betrayal of a socialist imaginary: the communist seductions fail, the capitalist seduction succeeds.

In *Occupations* the political content and the libidinal structure of the play lean upon each other. Freud introduced this idea of leaning (*anaclisis*) to describe the antithetical, but dialectical, relationship between the sexual and the self-preservative instincts. The sexual instincts are (biologically) directed towards the preservation of the species, the self-preservative (ego) instincts towards the preservation of the individual. The articulation of the dialectic of these two instincts is expressable within a political register as the dialectic between the collective urges of communism and the individualist urges of capitalism. *Occupations* itself ends with the dominance within the dialectic of bourgeois capital. In fact, neither of these instincts is possible without the other. The political question remains that of the *form* of the synthesis, and the politico-aesthetic question that of its representation.

This is precisely the problem which *Greenland* attempts to address. In psychoanalytic terms the play attempts to represent the desire for difference through the representation of a new subjectivity and a different desire in which sexuality is not antithetical to individuation and the terms of sexual difference are less fixed. Significantly, *Greenland* sets itself, representationally, 'beyond death'. This will prove to be a central problematic within the play, as 'beyond death' may be thought to equate with an absolute end to difference rather than with its vital rearticulation.

For the critic interested in using the notion of fantasy as a way into the problems of political representation and of political identity, Laplanche and Pontalis's formulation of the ways in which desire is articulated is both central and crucial: 'Fantasy, however, is not the object of desire, but its setting. In fantasy the subject does not pursue the object or its sign: he appears caught up himself in the sequence of images. He forms no representation of the desired object, but is himself represented as participating in the secne.' [16] In *Greenland* it is precisely this question, of the possibility of the representability of the desired object (the 'end of history'), which is addressed. Within the containing structure of the 24 hours between dawn on 11 June 1987, the date of the last General Election, and dawn on 12 June 1987, *Greenland* takes us into a journey through a year 700 years in the future. It is unclear whether this fantasy of utopia is dream or death; certainly it is beyond consciousness. The play constructs its retrospective (*Nachträglich*) by positing, in Act II, a past which is the present of both the characters in Act I and the audience. The play thus constructs a fantasy of the future in which our late-twentieth-century present is a fantasy to be recovered by the archaeologists of the future, always and symptomatically, very imperfectly, as it turns out. The question of fantasy is thus central to the play's concerns.

The play is structured upon the recognition of loss, in the first place of the political loss of the General Election and everything which that loss signifies, symbolically, for the Left and for the socialist vision. It expresses, in Freudian terms, a particular account of castration; of the loss, or repression of a desire which, in at least one instance, is quite explicitly expressed. Immediately before the end of the present-day scenes Judy says: 'Come back Mummy, you bitch. I don't want you to go away. I want to hate and scream at you! (*A pause.*) I'm afraid' (p. 31), expressing the loss of the mother as the fantasy of the desired object. Castration signifies the loss, or repression, of a pre-Oedipal desire and also a symbolic exchange in which the possibility of the symbolic – of order, organisation and self-recognition (male, female, me, you, them, us) – is given in exchange. [17] With the symbolic acceptance of the castration imposed by the 'father', human subjectivity emerges as that fiction of wholeness and of identity which takes up its place in the symbolic order. In Lacan's re-reading of Freud, the father is the symbolic father whose 'law' is the law of the symbolic order. Thus the idea of the 'father' may well take on all the resonances which are so often attached to it in drama, including, specifically, the 'father' of the idea. [18] Identity is thus dependent upon the recognition of difference. The construction of subjectivity, then, is necessarily dialectical. Recognition is bought at the cost of repression; with a central splitting at the 'heart' of subjectivity in which the 'I' of the enounced is never identical with the 'I' of the enunciation. The 'I' which engages in the struggle for recognition within the symbolic is an 'I' which rests upon the shifting sands of unconscious fantasy.

If Act I of *Greenland* is articulated through the structure of difference, political and sexual, it is not without a certain anxiety about the collapse of the different into the same. The threat which is signified here is that threat of *lack* of differentiation which is posed by the unconscious.[19] Judy recognises in her mother Betty a similarity in their apparent difference:

> Why do I hate her so? Because everything I do is what she does. She is a fundamentalist, I am a fundamentalist. She to one extreme, I to another. I can only be what she is the other way round. I know the way she thinks, I feel it in my own thoughts. I hear the edge of her voice in my voice. When I am her age, I know my body will be just like hers. (p. 23)

She voices this fundamental likeness to her mother a little later in the same scene:

> You and your Christian lunatics, your anti-porners, your clean-up TV campaigners, in your gospel halls? I and my friends, street-theatre clowns, squatters, in our resource centres in shabby shops? We all want a new world. That has . . . Light. That's human, and decent, and . . . Clean? We both want . . . A new Jerusalem? (p. 24)

Loss of consciousness, whether in the dream, the fantasy, or in death, represents loss of subjectivity and the fatal repetition of the same. What we are given in Act II is precisely, inasmuch as it can be represented at all, just such a loss of fixed subjectivity (articulated here as a possible representation of death) and also, of course, a representation of a society which is living in an eternal 'now', a society at the end of history.

Judy's anger with her mother occurs immediately before the crucial 'drowning scene' which precedes Act II. Its interplay of desire and aggression prefigures not only the emergence of the ego as it is expressed within psychoanalytic theory, but also the rage of Severan-Severan, the last dialectician, for whom such loss and such rage express the engagement of the dialectic upon which and through which history is articulated:

> Damn passivity! Is the dialectic at rest forever? What is at war

with what? Peace is senility. (. . .) For a world at peace the only
authentic history is an endless 'now'. All about me see that as
liberation, freed of the past. Freed of the ravages of the old Adam!
'Liberation'! To me it is a living death. (. . .) Take me back inside!
I want to sweat in the sauna! A good birching! A good scream!
(. . .) Goodbye, citizen of the past. May misery and suffering
never entirely desert you, so that you remain human. Go! (p. 52)

Early in the play, Joan voices one of the perennial anxieties of contemporary socialism concerning the possibility of making a living
political connection between past, present and future:

JOAN: Do you have a crystal clear idea of what a just, democratic,
   socialist England would be like? A communist England? (. . .)
BILL: No. 'Course I don't.
JOAN: Nor do I.
BILL: Babbling of Utopia?
JOAN: Yes I am.
BILL: A communist society would be made by its citizens. (. . .)
JOAN: So by definition Utopia cannot be described? (. . .) People
   want to know what we want, Bill. On the doorstep. And we
   can't describe it. (pp. 28–9).

What Brenton goes on to do, a decade-old project at which he had
failed before,[20] is precisely to attempt to represent that utopia which
is the end of history, that society living at the end of time in which
past, present and future co-exist, and which *is* the unthinkable end
of the dialectic towards which, theoretically, Marxism is directed.
The result comes close to a form of mysticism and it is hard to see in
what other ways the representation of the end of difference, the end
of the dialectic, might be represented. In terms of the fantasy we are
offered, and in spite of Joan's earlier rejection of religion, perhaps the
most accurate description of the fantasy scenario of Act II is one
which would describe it as the quasi-religious *acceptance* of castration which is prefigured in the parodic passion play of Act I. There
the symbolic sacrifice which 'confines violence to a single place,
making it a signifier', concatenates a new symbolic order.[21] Thus, what
Act II can be seen as representing is not a utopia (which is sublime
and unpresentable), but the movement of a tragic desire as it is
transformed, through the various labours of the 'past', not into an
object, but into an illuminating and multi-faceted idea, Jace's jewel,

which cannot be possessed, occupied or known, but only passed on.

In this reading, socialism and a socialist society are not given to us as objects but as processes and as the movement of a desire which is, in itself, objectless. Thus, whilst the 'conscious' fantasy that *Greenland* presents to us is ostensibly a fantasy of the *rejection* of castration and of difference, what is uncovered at the level of the unconscious is the articulation of a castration fantasy which can only be an affirmation of Severan-Severan's dialectic of the misery and suffering which constitutes human subjectivity. While what is represented here is a different difference, it is nevertheless a representation which draws strongly upon precisely the kinds of tragic fantasmatic religious and mystical structures which classical Marxism sought to do away with.

The points of entry into the scenario which are open to the audience are those which are offered as Joan, Betty, Brian and Paul engage with the labour of loss, of a particular idea of subjectivity, in order that a different idea or form of difference and identity may emerge. In this Joan's labour at the lathe and the production of the jewel is central. Paradoxically, what the play labours to produce is not the end of history but the emergence of different subjectivities which constitute a new history. The end of history is the illusory object. The central fantasmatic emphasis seems rather to be upon the acceptance of castration but also upon the possibility of the production of different identities. In the fantasy one may be the labourer, the labour, the jewel (the 'crystal clear idea' of Act I) or the refracted light which splinters across stage and auditorium at the play's end.

Finally, and perhaps the most difficult question which this *political* play poses in virtue of its own, very successful, representational strategies, is the question of the extent to which any form of political philosophy which does not take proper account of the force of the imaginary and of fantasy is doomed to failure. *Greenland* does, we have argued, take such account in that it creates a fantasmatic space in which the idea of the 'goal', of the object and of the end of history and of difference, is displaced on to the idea of a movement in which desire (fantasy) is transformed by becoming its own object in the form of a play, or a putting into the scene, of desire itself. In Greenlanders' football 'your' goal and 'my' goal become the same, thus replacing the idea of an 'oppositional' difference, with one where difference is either wholly negated (the collapse of difference) or it is properly dialectical (the interpenetration of opposites). The reading of the (popular) football game in the Greenlanders' version thus becomes crucial to the reading of what is at stake in the desire through which we recognise ourselves as human. Crudely, the labour (desire) and the 'play' are an end in themselves, as Joan recognises: 'I am in a world where everything I have ever dreamed of, has happened. In here, all value is the value of labour.' (p. 46) To the extent that it is successful fantasmatically, *Greenland* both posits and also undermines the 'reality' of the political theory upon which it may be presumed to rest. What returns in the representation here is thus not unlike what returns in psychoanalysis itself, the unsettling idea that reality and fantasy are inescapably and dialectically intertwined. So a politics predicated upon the idea of a goal of indifference, rather than a process of rearticulated and renewed differentiation, is a politics which, far from being fantastic, is not, in the psychoanalytic sense of the word, fantasmatic enough. In conclusion, although these plays 'recognise' the psychosexual element of the political, the ways in which the fantasmatic structure articulates representation means that the dynamics of the ostensible project are always displaced on to another scene. In her analysis of the psychosexual fantasies which the phenomenon of Margaret Thatcher puts into play, Jacqueline Rose suggests that:

> our understanding of the libidinal undercurrents of political processes can no longer be restricted to the historically recognised moment of fascism alone – the place to which the possibility of a dialogue between psychoanalysis and politics has traditionally been consigned. . . . If we want to think about the place of fantasy in public life today, we need therefore to avoid or qualify two conceptions: the one that describes fantasy as a projection of individual self-interest . . . but equally the one that sees fantasy as an unbridled irrationalism without any logic, a conception which turns fantasy into a simple counter-image of the law.[22]

Here we have tried to address the place of fantasy as it emerges within aesthetic life today, specifically as it emerges within the work of socialist playwrights attempting to represent, in necessarily complex form, the politics of that life. The question of whether one might wish to extend the idea of representation beyond its usual meaning, and to think about the extent to which, particularly in a media-dominated age, politics is itself a matter of representation, is perhaps equally implicit in our discussion.

What we have said here has been directed towards the 'other' scene which is imbricated in the socialist imaginary, and what we think we have found there is not only the re-enactment of the fantasies which structure desire itself, which may well be true of all successful plays, but also a particular and constant reiteration of the moment of loss, failure and sacrifice – in other words of castration – which is the originary moment of a socialist political identity itself. That is to say, the moment at which that political identity recognises itself as different. These plays reformulate the problem for the self-consciously political project of answering the question of identity in the political register. How then can a socialist aesthetic take account of what psychoanalysis has to say about the centrality of the fantasmatic within all our symbolic productions?

Particularly, how can that aesthetic take account of the Freudian insight that rationality and irrationality are always articulated together, while at the same time dealing with the implications of Walter Benjamin's insight that if fascism is the aestheticisation of politics then socialism must be the politicisation of aesthetics? How can it move beyond the structural repetition of the moment of difference towards a representation of a different symbolic order?[23] How can remembering, repeating and working through, which is the project of the psychoanalytic encounter, be articulated to, and also understood as, an aesthetic practice? It is arguable that the psychoanalytic encounter has about it something of the aesthetic, not least because it was part of Freud's remarkable insight to recognise the encounter as dramatic and theatrical and also in need of the same kind of structural containment (the contract of the psychoanalytic session) which the theatre similarly provides. From a critical point of view which wishes to address the insights of psychoanalysis, the challenge is not only to read the theatre psychoanalytically, but it is also to ask in what ways particular theatrical projects (here the project of socialist theatre) can be better understood from a psychoanalytical perspective.

Notes

1. J. Laplanche and J.-B. Pontalis, 'Fantasy and the Origins of Sexuality', in V. Burgin, J. Donald & C. Kaplan (eds), *Formations of Fantasy* (London: Methuen, 1986). The essay first appeared in French in *Les Temps Modernes* in 1964.

2. The editions cited in the body of our essay are Howard Brenton, *Greenland* (London: Methuen, 1988), Trevor Griffiths, *Occupations* (London: Calder and Boyars, 1972); David Hare *Plenty* (London: Faber,

1986). We have also consulted the revised text of *Occupations* (Faber, 1980), the original edition of *Plenty* (Faber, 1978) and Hare's *The History Plays*, (Faber, 1984). Other plays quoted from are Howard Barker's *The Castle*, staged 1985 (in *'The Castle' and 'Scenes from an Execution'*, London: Calder, 1985), Howard Brenton's *Thirteenth Night*, staged 1981 (in *'Thirteenth Night' and 'A Short Sharp Shock'*, London: Methuen, 1981), and David Edgar's *Destiny*, staged 1976 (in his *Plays: One*, London: Methuen, 1987).

3. Laplanche and Pontalis, pp. 5, 17, 19 and Sigmund Freud, 'A Case of Paranoia Running Counter to the Psychoanalytic Theory of the Disease' (1915), in *On Psychopathology*, The Pelican Freud Library, Vol. 10 (Harmondsworth: Penguin, 1979).

4. Laplanche and Pontalis, pp. 16, 26.

5. In dramatic modes which follow linear time schemes, address the audience indirectly through an invisible fourth wall, and rely on identification, both of audience with action and of actor with character, there is a tendency to closure which can inhibit the taking-up of multiple positions. The variety of dramatic strategies used in contemporary British political drama implicitly recognises the importance of multiple points of entry into the fantasy for both authors and audiences. Perhaps the simplest cases are those where the audience is treated as participants in the action as with the factory workers in *Occupations* and the club audience in the second act of Griffiths's *Comedians* (staged 1975). David Edgar also asks the audience to be variously participants in a 1945 May Day rally, a 1968 student sit-in, a 1979 dinner of the Committee in the Defence of Liberty, and dazzles them with the lights of military might outside the wire at Greenham Common in *Maydays*, and, to a lesser extent, with the meeting of the Taddley Patriotic League in *Destiny*. Similarly in *Thirteenth Night* the audience is directly addressed as an audience at Central Hall, Westminister which we later learn has taken the onstage speaker's words literally enough to go and destroy the American Embassy; the expectation is clearly that we will not emulate that fictional audience. Doubling in contemporary theatre may be, in part, an economic necessity but it also serves important psychological and political purposes. In *Fanshen* (staged 1975) for example, the actors double both progressive and reactionary characters so that points about the mutability of character are actually embodied in the physical representation of individuals. In Caryl Churchill's *Cloud Nine* (staged 1979) the point is made even clearer with the cross-gender doubling and one case of a white actor playing a black who has internalised white values. Other Joint Stock plays such as Sue Townsend's *Great Celestial Cow* (staged 1984) took this further with actresses of Indian origin playing white male immigration officers. This kind of doubling is matched by what happens to audiences who are asked to be other audiences: fixed subject positions are dissolved and we are offered multiple points of entry into the fantasy.

6. The most recent example, as we finished this essay, was David Hare's appearance in a list of sponsors for an African National Congress

advertisement in the *Guardian* of 6 September 1989.

7. Cultural critics, notably Stuart Hall, are now beginning to address this question of desire and fantasy within the larger political framework elsewhere; see Stuart Hall, 'Blue election, election blues', *Marxism Today*, July 1987.

8. We distinguish here between the recognition that politics is patriarchal and the, in our view, mistaken assumption, which the work of Jacqueline Rose addresses, 'that the domain of what is more easily and conventionally defined as the political can continue to be analysed as if it were free of psychic and sexual processes, as if it operated outside the range of their effects'. (Jacqueline Rose, 'Margaret Thatcher and Ruth Ellis', *New Formations* 6, Winter 1988, p. 3).

9. Hare is quoted from the Introduction to *The History Plays*, p. 15. Michelene Wandor, *Carry on Understudies* (London: Routledge & Kegan Paul, 1986), p. 156. Similar difficulties occur with other female protagonists in Hare's plays from *Dreams of Leaving* (televised 1980) to *The Secret Rapture* (staged 1988) as well as in plays by other male writers which try to take on board the insights of feminism and, particularly, the Greenham women. Hence the centrality of women such as Rebecca in Hare and Brenton's *Pravda* (staged 1985) and Amanda in Edgar's *Maydays* (staged 1983) to the political project of their plays but their absence from much of the action.

10. Introduction to *The History Plays*, p. 15.

11. In the 1978 edition of *Plenty* Hare describes her as 'intended to be a historically accurate character' (p. 88).

12. Works like *Plenty*, *Maydays*, or *Destiny* deal with the events of the last 40–50 years as part of a search for the more immediate origins of current personal and political issues; works like Churchill's *Cloud Nine*, with its Victorian First Act and characters who have only aged 25 years in a Second Act set in the present, and *Softcops* (staged 1984), heavily influenced by her reading of Foucault's *Discipline and Punish*, or Edward Bond's *Early Morning* (staged 1968), with its anachronistic presentation of the Victorian era, look at nineteenth-century origins of current personal and political attitudes to questions of identity and control. But this means that meaning is always displaced to another scene, often in a 'historical' or fictional past which in some way accounts for the present or, more rarely, in an imagined future which explains the present as a moment of origin. Hence the stress in many plays on moments of conception and birth: *Destiny*, for example, begins with the birth of independent India in 1947 (Edgar was born in 1948), and can properly be regarded as a search for origins in which the quest for a sense of belonging, of identity, is paramount in the characters' search for an endlessly deferred final cause for the machinery of capitalism and the seductions of racism.

13. For a stimulating discussion of the possible relationship between feminist political consciousness, castration, femininity and the sacrificial victim, see Julia Kristeva, 'Women's Time', in Toril Moi (ed.), *The Kristeva Reader* (Oxford: Blackwell, 1986).

14. For Freud, the attainment of femininity, of a feminine subject posi-

tion, involves a double movement of violence, in which the girl child must first be denied the desire of the mother (this is the meaning of castration for both male and female) and then must be re-identified with the mother in the recognition that she, like the mother, doesn't *have* the phallus and can only regain it by internalising it, in the form of the baby, by having it *for* the father.

15. For an interesting discussion of the relevance of the Gramscian notion of hegemony to contemporary cultural politics, see Tony Bennett, 'Introduction: Popular Culture and "the turn to Gramsci"' in T. Bennett, C. Mercer and J. Woollacott (eds), *Popular Culture and Social Relations* (Milton Keynes: Open University Press, 1986).

16. Laplanche and Pontalis, p. 26.

17. This is a difficult point, which addresses the loss of a pre-Oedipal desire (the desire of the desire of the mother) and its displacement on to an Oedipalised desire. The implication of this is that desire is only recognised as such retrospectively, from within the Oedipal configuration. For an interesting discussion of the question of the designation of pre-Oedipal desire see John Fletcher, 'Poetry, Gender and pre-Oedipal Fantasy', in *Formations of Fantasy*, particularly pp. 115/6.

18. Note the appearance of such 'fathers' as Hitler in *Destiny* and Stalin, who 'walks through the shadows' (p. 40) just before the death of Beaty, in *Thirteenth Night* and also appears in a slide at the end of *Occupations*, together with Mussolini, Hitler, and Molotov and Von Ribbentrop signing the 1939 Non-Aggression Pact, or Brenton's use of Lenin in *Magnificence* (staged 1973) as examples of allusions to origins, used non-naturalistically in contemporary political theatre. This must also implicate our own theoretical 'fathers', Freud and Lacan, here, but that is another debate.

19. 'Beyond the Pleasure Principle', explores the compulsion to repeat, i.e. repetition of the same, and is identified by Freud as the death drive in which repetition compulsion is equated with the denial of difference and a desire in which the pleasure principle is finally articulated as the desire for that state of complete non-excitation and non-differentiation which is death. Sigmund Freud, 'Beyond the Pleasure Principle' (1920), in *On Metapsychology*. The Pelican Freud Library, Vol. II (Harmondsworth: Penguin, 1984).

20. See his author's note on p. [3] of *Greenland*. Compare this with Barker's *The Castle*, ostensibly set in the Middle Ages, where there is no attempt to stage the utopian 'feminised feudal demesne' (cover) which the crusaders' return disrupts, although there is a considerable amount of reference to and description of what it was like, much of which centres on questions of intercourse and of seduction leading to pregnancy (cf. Skinner, p. 6: 'I helped your births. And your conceptions, sat by the bedroom, at the door') and Stucley's fantasy of seducing his wife on his return, a running gag in the early part of the play.

21. Julia Kristeva, *Revolution in Poetic Language* (New York: Columbia University Press, 1984), p. 75.

22. Jacqueline Rose, 'Margaret Thatcher and Ruth Ellis', p. 20.

23. Walter Benjamin, 'The Work of Art in the Age of Mechanical Repro-

duction', in *Illuminations*, trans. Harry Zohn (London: Fontana, 1973), p. 244.

Select Bibliography

Louis Althusser, 'The 'Piccolo Teatro': Bertolazzi and Brecht' in *For Marx* (London: New Left Books, 1977), pp. 129–153.

Roland Barthes, *Image-Music-Text*, trans. Stephen Heath (London: Fontana, 1977).

C.W.E. Bigsby, *Joe Orton* (London: Methuen, 1982).

_____, 'The Language of Crisis in British Theatre: the Drama of Cultural Pathology', in Stratford-Upon-Avon Studies 19, ed. Bradbury and Palmer, *Contemporary English Drama* (London: Edward Arnold, 1981), pp. 13–51.

Jacques Derrida, *Of Grammatology* (Baltimore: Johns Hopkins, 1976).

_____, *Writing and Difference* (London: Routledge, 1981).

Sue Ellen Case, *Feminism and Theatre* (London: Macmillan, 1988).

Stephen Connor, *Samuel Beckett: Repetition, Theory and Text* (Oxford: Blackwell, 1988).

John Drakakis (ed.), *Alternative Shakespeares* (London: Methuen, 1985).

Terry Eagleton, *Criticism and Ideology* (London: Verso, 1976).

_____, *Walter Benjamin or Towards a Revolutionary Criticism* (London: 1981).

Umberto Eco, 'Semiotics of Theatrical performance' in *The Drama Review* no. 21, (1977), pp. 107–117.

Keir Elam, *The Semiotics of Theatre and Drama* (London: Methuen, 1980).

Martin Esslin, *The Field of Drama: How the Signs of Drama Create Meaning on Stage and Screen* (London: Methuen, 1987).

Peter Griffith, *Literary Theory and English Teaching* (Milton Keynes: Open University Press, 1987).

Julian Hilton, *Performance* (London: Macmillan, 1988).

Helene Keyssar, *Feminist Theatre* (London: Macmillan, 1984).

Jacques Lacan, 'Desire and the Interpretation of Desire in Hamlet', in Shoshana Feldman (ed.), *Literature and Psychoanalysis: The Question of Reading Otherwise* (Baltimore: Johns Hopkins University Press, 1982).

Phillippe Lacoue-Labarthe, 'Teatrum Analyticum', in *Glyph 2* (1977), pp. 165–270.

Colin MacCabe, 'Realism and the Cinema: Notes on Some Brechtian Theses', *Screen*, Vol. 15, no. 2, 1974, pp. 7–27.

_____, 'The Revenge of the Author', *Critical Quarterly*, Vol. 31, no. 2 (1989), pp. 3–13.

John McGrath, *A Good Night Out: Popular Theatre: Audience Class and Form* (London: Methuen, 1981).

Mike Poole and John Wyver, *Powerplays: Trevor Griffiths in Television* (London: BFI 1984).

Peter Szondi, *Theory of the Modern Drama* ed. and trans. Michael Hays (Cambridge: Polity Press, 1987).

Michelene Wandor, *Carry on Understudies: Theatre and Sexual Politics* (London: Methuen, 1986).

_____, *Look Back in Gender: Sexuality and the Family in Post-war British Drama* (London: Methuen, 1987).

Elizabeth Wright, *Postmodern Brecht: a Re-Presentation* (London: Routledge, 1989).
_____, *Psychoanalytic Criticism: Theory in Practice* (London: Methuen, 1984).

Index

air